Civil Service Training in India

Civil Service Training in India

Editors
Rakesh Hooja • K.K. Parnami

Association of State Training Institutions in India, Jaipur

RAWAT PUBLICATIONS
Jaipur • New Delhi • Bangalore • Hyderabad • Guwahati

ISBN 978-81-316-0404-5

Published by
Prem Rawat for **Rawat Publications**
Satyam Apts, Sector 3, Jawahar Nagar, Jaipur 302 004 (India)
Phone: 0141 265 1748 / 7006 Fax: 0141 265 1748
E-mail: info@rawatbooks.com
Website: www.rawatbooks.com

New Delhi Office
4858/24, Ansari Road, Daryaganj, New Delhi 110 002
Phone: 011 2326 3290

Also at *Bangalore, Hyderabad* and *Guwahati*

Typeset by Rawat Computers, Jaipur
Printed at Chaman Enterprises, New Delhi

Contents

Section III

Training for Change

Section IV

Sector-Specific Training

Section V

Aspects and Components of Training

Section VI

Appendices

Introduction

Rakesh Hooja and K.K. Parnami

Quantitative and qualitative upgradation of the training function for public servants in the country is of utmost importance. What is required is a strategic, need-based, outcome-oriented, competency and capacity-building, performance enhancing, and value-inculcating approach to training that is directly related to the developmental and governance needs of the country.

Training is relevant for all members of the civil services – from the seniormost secretary to government to the juniormost clerk and peon. Nowadays, there is also much talk about the need to develop through training and related measures appropriate competencies amongst each individual working in government, whether he/she is at the level of Group A, B, C or D. Such competencies should be both generic and general which are related to the level and category of the post at which the individual is working, as also domain-specific and related to the specific schemes and programmes with whose formulation and implementation the employee is associated. We hope that the new National Training Policy, being formulated by the Government of India's Department of Personnel and Training to replace the existing National Training Policy, 1996 shall reflect the above-mentioned approach of competency building for each individual government servant as well as the government as a whole.

Accordingly, induction training and in-service training, general or foundational training and professional (domain or sector-specific) training; long courses and short courses; institutional classroom-oriented training and distance and e-learning-oriented training; training through specifically designed courses at government training institutes and the sending of government servants to attend existing courses at universities, colleges and institutes of management; training about basic principles and theories as well as practical and on-the-job training; design of courses based on training needs analysis or TNA; training of trainers or ToTs in training and teaching techniques and in both general and domain (or sector) oriented themes, and in the intricacies of implementing special schemes, programmes, or Acts; the evaluation of training initiatives; the development of adequate and appropriate training infrastructure; ensuring that all the various government training efforts are carried out in a systematic, coordinated and integrated manner; and the creation of an ethos throughout the government system which understands and appreciates the importance and value of training – are all such aspects that require detailed and careful attention.

The government has set up departments for coordinating the training function at both the central and state levels. Many central ministries have developed their own sectoral training institutes as have many state government departments in various states In addition, most state governments have created and developed State Administrative Training Institutes, or State ATIs, as the apex training institute in the state which not only conducts a large number of training courses, but also provides support to the state training departments, and also coordinates the training efforts of all governmental training institutes in the state. Some central institutes have been set up for the training of members of specific All India or Central Services. Most government departments have, based on a recommendation in the National Training Policy of 1996, designated training officers or training managers for each department to assist the head of department in all training-related matters as also to liaise with the State ATI and the department's own training centres.

Details of the system of training presently in existence at the state level and suggestions for strengthening it can also be gleaned from a perusal of Rakesh Hooja's, "Training of Public Servants at State Level" (IIPA Discussion Paper Series No.1, November 2010).

The first paper on "Multi-level Civil Service Training in India" in this volume provides an overview of the theme of the book, and touches on all the issues and facets briefly mentioned above.

In fact, the three papers that constitute the first section entitled "Training Civil Servants" provide an introduction about the governmental training system (structures and processes as well as training objectives and examples of implementation), and also briefly looks at most of the issues related to improved training for government servants.

The second section on "Training of All India and Central Services" comprises two papers on the state and district training stage of the induction training of officers of the Indian Administrative Service and one on the training of the Indian Foreign Service, which is a central service.

Thereafter, the third section with seven papers takes a look at "Training for Change". How training can help in bringing about change in behaviour (unfortunately, the author of the concerned Chapter 8, who was a nationally recognized authority on training, Dr Udai Pareek, is no more), and in organizations (Chapter 9), how training can help in ensuring the undertaking of strategic management efforts, and the possibilities of training contributing to management development are the focus of the first four papers. The next two papers concentrate on large-scale or mass "saturation training" of functionaries and officers of all departments in the case of one state, i.e., Gujarat (Chapter 11) and of one district, i.e., Kota in Rajasthan (Chapter 12) from all government departments, which were provided integrated training (separately for Class I, II, III and IV but cutting across departments for each course) through specially designed short courses conducted by a large number of specially trained trainers. The courses were designed with an aim to bringing about attitudinal change amongst the trainees and thus inducing change in the entire governmental set-up. For most trainees involved this was the first-ever experience that they had been called to attend a short training course. Similarly, large-scale training of all Drawing and Disbursing Officers (or DDOs) in various state government departments and public sector undertakings in the state of Haryana through a series of short courses is the subject of analysis of the last paper of this section. In view of the large numbers of government employees (officers and other staff), such 'saturation' or 'mass' training initiatives covering all government employees of all departments in an area may need to be made a regular feature of training for government servants.

The next six papers (five of which are authored by one of the editors Rakesh Hooja) discuss "Sector-Specific Training". The sectors covered in this section are Rural Development, Irrigation Management, District Planning, Disaster Management, and Urban City Management. Each of these activities involves government servants from a number of departments who need to work together in a coordinated manner on a number of complex issues. While discussing the sector-specific training needs and various training initiatives already tried out, or suggesting measures for the future, a number of points emerge which can also be of relevance for training in all sectors. The sector-based papers enlarge on many common issues regarding improved delivery of training and training methodologies and also on the role played by State ATIs.

The fifth section "Aspects and Components of Training" looks at aspects like identification of training needs, designing of training programmes, evaluation of training initiatives, development of trainers, use of distance education for training, e-learning, and the publication of a house journal in a training institution. This is the most theory-oriented section in the book.

The sixth and final section "Appendices" contains two documents, brought out by the HCM Rajasthan State Institute of Public Administration, Jaipur. While the first document discusses the Rajasthan State Training Policy, the second is the executive summary of the report of Impact Assessment of Trainers Development Programmes and Faculty Development Scheme of Government of India.

While putting together this collection, the editors were clearly conscious that what is required is repeated, relevant, need-based and appropriate training opportunities throughout their service career for all government servants with each government department and each government training institute developing its training strategy, training action plan and internal working procedures within the framework of the National Training Policy and the concerned State Training Policy.

Work at putting together this anthology had commenced in late 2008 when the first editor Rakesh Hooja was ex-officio Member-Secretary of the Association of State Training Institutions in India (ASTI) by virtue of his being the Director of Harish Chandra Mathur Rajasthan State Institute of Public Administration (HCM RIPA), Jaipur. His transfer put a break in the efforts. However, subsequently, Rajiv Sharma who became Director, HCM RIPA and ex-officio Member-Secretary, ASTI suggested that the editing work be completed (even though Rakesh Hooja was by then based in Ajmer as Chairman of the Board of Revenue for Rajasthan – he later shifted to Delhi and K.K. Parnami was in Jaipur at HCM RIPA) and the book published soon.

Except for one paper on "Creating City Managers", which was originally published in *Prashasnika*, all other articles included in the volume were initially published in *ASTI Journal of Training and Development*. We are grateful to the Editors of both the journals.

We are also grateful to Rawat Publications and to Pranit Rawat in particular for taking a keen interest in ensuring the quality of this publication.

Section I

Training Civil Servants

1 Multi-Level Civil Service Training in India*

Rakesh Hooja

In today's fast-changing world with increased competition at the global level, it is imperative for the civil servants to be both extremely responsible and responsive as well as competent in their working and also capable of delivering. Making the government machinery responsible and responsive for inclusive development depends to a very large extent upon the attitudes as well as the knowledge and skills of its employees at various levels.

In this background paper, it is intended to both briefly describe what is being done in the sphere of training at both central and state levels and to make a number of suggestions and recommendations in this regard. Our suggestions are being made with full consciousness that training is but one part of personnel administration and that training interventions have to go hand in hand with many non-training initiatives for improving the civil services.

Since many schemes not only of state governments but of the centre are implemented in the states and districts and it is often state government employees who constitute the actual delivery mechanism and contact points with citizens, capacity building of state government

*The author, on behalf of Centre for Management Studies at HCM RIPA Jaipur, was asked to prepare a theme paper on "Recruitment and Training of Civil Servants" by Department of Administrative Reforms and Public Grievances, Government of India, New Delhi. The theme paper was circulated at 3rd Civil Service Day on April 21, 2008, at Vigyan Bhawan, New Delhi. The author made a presentation on the occasion and the theme paper was discussed during the Civil Service Day event. Based on the discussion and comments made therein and further reflection on the topic, the author has revised the training part of the theme paper in the form of this article.

officers and staff is at least as important as that of central government employees. Accordingly, the centre needs to support training initiatives at the state and district levels. In fact, a centrally sponsored scheme should be devised for assistance to State Administrative Training Institutes (ATIs) for the training of central, state and district personnel posted within the state.

Objectives of Training

The National Training Policy of Government of India, 1996 has laid down that training in government shall strive to achieve the following objectives:

(a) Keeping up-to-date and enhancing professional knowledge and skills needed for better performance by individuals and organizations;

(b) promoting better understanding of professional requirements as well as sensitization to professional, socio-economic and political environment in which work is done; and

(c) bringing about right attitudinal orientation.

We may add the following additional objectives:

(d) inculcate values among civil servants at all levels (category A to D) as it would strengthen their sense of commitment;

(e) provide opportunities for them to prepare themselves for changing roles, duties and responsibilities;

(f) enhance job satisfaction and motivation and facilitating career progression to enable all government employees to contribute positively and to continually update their competencies;

(g) enable the civil service to become a powerful instrument for anticipating the need for, as well as facilitating the introduction of, institutional changes within the public service and public organizations;

(h) assist civil servants in developing a better understanding of the needs of the communities that they are serving, as well as enhancing capacities for responding to these needs; and

(i) increase the knowledge base of the civil services and to inculcate a professional approach in their work.

The training function should also involve assisting government departments and agencies to adopt such practices as are geared at better governance and improved public service delivery by empowering each officer to act as a catalyst for holistic and equity-based transformation of the country.

Accordingly, what is required is a strategic, need-based, outcome-based, competency-based and performance-enhancing approach to training, which is directly related to the development needs of the country. For this, the National Training Policy needs to be reviewed though not replaced by a new policy since much in the 1996 version is still equally relevant today. State governments need to be encouraged to come out with state training policies.

Institutional Pattern

As regards the training system in the Government of India, it is based upon each ministry having its own training institutions for the particular service or services attached to the ministry. For example, the Ministry of External Affairs has its Foreign Service Training Institute, the Ministry of Forests has institutes related to training in forestry, the Ministry of Home Affairs has Sardar Vallabhbhai Patel National Police Academy and the Department of Personnel has Lal Bahadur Shastri National Academy of Administration (LBSNAA), Mussoorie, which concentrates on IAS training besides a multi-service foundation course. In addition, the Department of Personnel and Training also has attached to it the Institute of Secretariat Training and Management (ISTM), which caters to training needs of Central Secretariat Services and officers posted in the Central Secretariat from various services. However, most of the institutes at the Government of India level are either focused at a single ministry or at a particular service, or like the National Institute of Rural Development, the National Institute of Disaster Management or HSMI floated by HUDCO look at individual sectors which are the concerns of only one or two ministries.

What is lacking are institutes that cut across sectors and ministries like the UK National School of Government at Sunningdale or like some of the state level Administrative Training Institutes (ATIs). The LBSNAA does cater to a number of services and a number of ministries in the Foundational Training Course for Group 'A' officers of the Government of India at induction stage. However, there is no institute offering short courses of one day, one week or up to one month's duration which cover various aspects which may be equally relevant for people from various services.

Another lacuna is that the existing training institutes cater mostly to category 'A' and 'B' officers and training of category 'C' and 'D' tends to get somewhat neglected. Not that category 'A' training does not require both qualitative and quantitative stepping up. The National Training Policy, 1996, has suggested that for the purpose of appropriate training design, the civil services could be divided into the following three levels: (a) lowest level functionaries operative at the cutting-edge that is most members of Group 'D' services and lower stages of Group 'C', (b) supervisory and middle administration levels – mostly Group 'B' but also higher stages of Group 'C' and lower stages of Group 'A', and (c) Group 'A' services.

The Training Division of Department of Personnel and Training (DoPT) is charged with matters related to the training policy. It is also the nodal agency for human resources building through the training of government functionaries. It sponsors a number of training programmes in a variety of areas for different categories of central and state government employees and provides assistance for upgradation of training equipment in government training institutes. The Training Division administers induction training to the recruits of Indian Administrative Service and the Central Secretariat Service. It also implements faculty development programme and Trainer Development Scheme by sponsoring various trainer development packages all over the country.

The National Training Policy also includes the concept of a Training Manager in each ministry/department at the central and state government levels to coordinate the training needs within the ministry/department and to interact with various training institutes and with the Training Division of DoPT. This needs to be enforced universally and is a must for all state and central government departments and agencies.

At the state government level, the state government's departments interact with the state ATI which is the apex training institute at the state level and with other training institutes of various state government departments. Some state governments have a separate training department or training cell at the State Secretariat to coordinate all training matters. Each state ATI is also in close and regular touch with the Training Division of DoPT in the Government of India.

In some states, the state ATI functions both as a government department plus one or more registered societies working in total synergy. This provides the best of both the worlds as the registered society permits much flexibility. Many of the state government ATIs also contain a number of functional/sectoral centres like Centre for Management Studies, Centre for Good Governance, Centre for Financial Administration, Centre for Disaster Management, Centre for Urban Development, Centre for Gender Studies, Centre for Natural Resource Management and Centre for Multilevel Planning, etc. Among the various departmental training institutes at the state level, the Rural Development and Panchayati Raj Department normally has under its administrative control a State Institute of Rural Development (SIRD). In some states the state ATI also performs the SIRD functions.

One aspect which is lacking in most state governments is a Secretariat Training and Management Institute on the lines of ISTM in New Delhi. Some states are considering creation of such institutes. This is one area where the Training Division of DoPT could provide financial assistance for the creation of such Secretariat Training and Management Institutes (STMIs) in each state which could either be part of the state ATI, or closely associated with it. This would enable customized and mandatory training for all state secretariat employees.

Structure of Training

The officers belonging to the Indian Administrative Service (IAS) are imparted induction training of two years which comprises a foundation course along with other services, phase I of the professional programme, state and district training and phase II of the professional course. This induction training has recently (2007) been reviewed by the Government of India Committee that looked at Induction Training of IAS Officers (the Committee to Review the Syllabus of Induction Training, Vaidyanatha Ayyar Committee, June 2007). Similarly, promotion training is provided for officers inducted to IAS through promotion from State Administrative Services or other state services. After the induction training, every IAS officer is expected to attend at least one training of a duration of one week in a block of every two years. At three important stages of their careers IAS officers are also mandatorily required to undergo mid-career training. Between the seventh and ninth year of service, IAS officers are expected to undergo phase III training for a duration of eight weeks. Between the thirteenth and fifteenth year of service they are expected to undergo phase IV of mid-career training for a duration of eight weeks, and between the twenty-fifth and twenty-eighth year of service they are expected to undergo phase V training for a duration of four weeks. Similarly, the Indira Gandhi National Forest Academy provides for mid-career training of forest service officers in the tenth, seventeenth and twenty-seventh years of service. Mid-career opportunities are also being provided in the Central Secretariat Services. Other services like IPS are building up similar systems focused on Sardar Vallabhbhai Patel National Police Academy or other service-specific institutes. Each mid-career training is expected to focus on the changed and greater responsibility for 'next level competency'. *Life-long learning is* called for and training support should be available accordingly. Along with opportunities for repeated in-service training all officers and staff should also be encouraged to improve their academic qualifications while in service. It may also be pointed out that the Vaidyanatha Ayyar Committee Report has stated that the competencies required for senior positions can only be imparted through a much longer duration programme than what phases III, IV and V for the IAS now envisage.

At the state level, the state ATIs are responsible for providing induction training to various state services comprising foundation course, the institutional/professional course, and field and district training. Similarly, compulsory promotion training is provided for all employees of subordinate services being promoted to state services. In some states, there is a provision for compulsory one-week courses on Public Policy and on Good Governance after 10 years and 15 years of service respectively.

A number of training opportunities for members of the various civil services are being provided both within India and abroad. Examples of some long-term courses available within India include Advanced Professional Programme in Public Administration (APPPA) at IIPA, New Delhi, and Postgraduate Public Policy Courses at IIM, Ahmedabad, IIM, Bangalore, Management Development Institute, Gurgaon and TERI University, New Delhi, and a nine-month course at National Defence College (where along with the uniformed services members of civil services also undergo training). In addition, opportunities are available for undergoing short courses at institutes like IIMs, Administrative Staff College of India, some state and private universities, as well as Central Training Institutes and state ATIs, etc. The Training Division at DoPT also operates a Domestic Funding Scheme for Foreign Training whereby members of civil services can apply to undergo both long and short courses at prestigious universities abroad. Thus, to some extent, what has been recommended by many, including this author, is that significant and longish training opportunities should be made available at the age of 35–40 years and also in the 50–55 age group, the need is to being meet some extent particularly for Group 'A' officers. However, with increasing globalization, the number of foreign training opportunities need to be substantially increased, while in fact such opportunities have drastically reduced compared to 15 to 20 years ago.

Need for Higher Services College

It has been felt that a Higher Civil Services College could be extremely useful in this context. It would be something like the existing National Defence College only at a higher level where officers of the level of Additional Secretary to Government of India or Principal Secretary to

State Government and the more senior of the Joint Secretaries in Government of India could be provided the opportunity for undergoing a 6 to 9 months residential course. Some areas of training, which would be covered at such a long course in the Higher Civil Services College, are being indicated in Annexure 1. Along with other training methodologies, the Higher Civil Service College should make use of small informal discussions of the trainees with eminent persons who command universal respect due to knowledge, experience, achievements and reputation. The Higher Civil Services College could also enable very senior members of the civil services to write policy papers and conduct studies about government programmes. The residential long course at the Higher Civil Services College should be one where spouses/families are encouraged to stay on campus. Often, the family can influence officers to succumb to temptations, and the stay at the Higher Civil Services College may reorient family members about what is desirable from a senior officer.

The Higher Civil Services College could also have a second unit attached to it for performing the sort of role presently being performed in the UK at its National School of Government at Sunningdale whereby a number of different types of short courses could be offered to very senior officers (say Joint Secretary, GoI) in many training areas which cut across ministries and departments. Examples of the types of courses which could be covered in this National School of Governance are in Annexure 2. The Higher Civil Services College and its second unit, the National School of Governance, could work under the supervision of the Cabinet Secretary as is the case in the UK. What is envisaged is a new two-in-one institution rather than adding the proposed training functions to an already existing institution which has its specific mandate to fulfil. This new two-in-one institute could be set up in the National Capital Region (NCR) of Delhi.

Resource Persons

For any training intervention or training policy to be successful, the quality of trainers is extremely relevant. At present, the sources of trainers in state and central ATIs are as follows:

(a) persons recruited directly to posts at the institutes;
(b) persons on deputation from various services like IAS, IPS, State Administrative Services, Accounts Service, etc.;
(c) persons on contractual appointment; and
(d) guest faculty or guest speakers invited for covering specific topics.

Some ATIs also take retired academicians or civil servants as visiting professors on the analogy of UGC's Visiting Professors Scheme to work on a full-time basis.

What could be thought of in addition is a scheme of associated experts who could be kept on a retainership basis by the training institutes to supplement the activities of the core training staff. However, the core faculty both directly recruited and on deputation is very important to building up the competency of an ATI and only limited dependence should be placed on outsourcing and on guest faculty. There needs to be a blending of the academic and the practitioner in the core faculty with reasonably long tenures at the training institute.

As regards increasing the capacity of trainers, Training of Trainers (ToT) courses are organized, particularly under DoPT's Training Division's Faculty Development Scheme and Trainer Development Programme. Some of the different types of trainings available under Trainer Development Programme are being indicated in Annexure 3. In addition, the Training Division also supports trainers undergoing a diploma course which is conducted by the Indian Society for Training and Development. Many state ATIs also conduct ToT courses for particular government programmes and schemes, or to develop sectoral training capacities in the various departmental training institutes.

A number of welcome incentives for trainers have been mentioned in the recommendations of the Sixth Pay Commission (chapter 6.4 of the report). One additional incentive could be reimbursement of a certain amount of funds each year for trainers at government institutions to purchase some books, which are directly related to their professional requirement as trainers. Some states have not provided trainers' allowances to the faculty of their ATIs or other training institutes despite recommendations by the Fourth and Fifth Pay Commissions. With the Sixth Pay Commission again recommending this, state governments need to be persuaded to implement this incentive.

The concept of *once a trainer always a trainer* needs to be followed, particularly when a trainer leaves a training institute and returns to a mainstream administrative post.

A lot of retired trainers are being used at training institutions. A possibility can be re-employing retired trainers or increasing the retirement age for trainers or encouraging the use of retired academicians or administrators as consultants to perform various training functions. Trainers should be made use of on a full-time basis at least till the age of 65 years, if not longer.

Provisions should exist for faculty from one state ATI to visit another state or central ATI to see how the faculty functions there. Similarly, heads of some state and central ATIs could be sent on study tours of public training institutions in other countries.

An issue also comes up as to what sort of a person should head a state or central ATI. Some people feel that academic experts may be suitable, however, what is required as the head of a training institute is a person with deep understanding of government and especially of government practices. Thus, people from government services are best suited to head such institutes. Heads of central/state ATIs should be selected from amongst the best, those who are much experienced in government service and who also have an aptitude for training. We have one example of West Bengal where they have employed a retired Additional Chief Secretary as head of the state ATI.

On the issue of comparison of training in government institutes vis-à-vis training in autonomous bodies like IIMs, it has been found that in many cases even the faculty of IIMs or institutions like IIPA or ASCI have little understanding of government working in particular sectors. Thus, recourse to non-governmental institutes should be taken selectively. In fact, there seems to be a misconception that a high quality educational institution would automatically be a high quality training facility. It is not necessarily true in actual practice. Faculty accustomed to teaching fresh and inexperienced students may not be suitable resource persons for the training of practitioners with several years of experience. Some reputed educational institutions often try to rely upon their name and do not take adequate interest in the quality of their training programmes, while relatively lesser known training institutions put in more effort and impart better training.

Mixed training for personnel from government and private sector should, if undertaken, be planned for meticulously by the concerned course directors and stakeholders.

Design of Courses

In fact, regardless of the type of institute or the type of training course and trainees, each training course needs to be carefully planned. Any training course needs to be based not upon easy availability of guest faculty or of already prepared training material, but should be formulated as per the objectives of the training, category of trainees, expectation from the particular course, etc. Unfortunately, in many training institutes, for several courses, a comprehensive course programme is not prepared by the core faculty/course coordinator. Involving some guest faculty is beneficial so as to supplement the basic training with practical aspects and field experiences. But, often, the guest lectures do not get arranged in sequential order as guest lecturers' availability or convenience leads to changes in course time tables. Nor is it always ensured that regular faculty and guest lectures are following a common approach during the course. Accordingly, there is much duplication and even omission of important topics as the knowledge and specialization of available guest faculty influences the coverage in the training schedule. On the other hand, in the better, more sincere, ATIs, the course coordinator prepares the course outline, detailed lesson plans and course schedule or time-table well in advance ensuring that the course is well-structured as per its objectives and that all the required topics, themes and required learnings are covered in a proper sequence. The type of pedagogy for each session, lecture, case study, panel discussion, tutorial, group exercise, etc., also needs to be planned out in advance. The course director also indicates proposed lesson plan to each guest faculty well in advance so that the guest faculty can plan his inputs and contribution accordingly. For this, the course coordinator, who should invariably be part of the regular core faculty at the ATI, needs to put in a lot of systematic labour prior to the commencement of each course.

The training capacities in a training institute need to encompass classroom training, field training, distance training, and e-learning or e-training. While for distance training, the examples of open universities and of some ATIs which are following this mode are of relevance, for e-learning or e-training, the experience of the private sector or of training institutes in other countries needs to be looked at. It should, however, be kept in mind that learning at training courses comes not only from faculty and resource persons but also from the interactions with peers who are undergoing the training.

Decentralized Institutionalization

Training not only of central government or state government employees, but also of those civil servants who work at the district level and in panchayat and municipal bodies, or work in coordination with NGOs and with community-based organizations and beneficiary or user groups need to receive equal importance. Thus, each state ATI needs to have a campus at each divisional headquarters level and eventually this may be required at each district level. Some departmental training institutes may also need to have divisional campuses.

The Government of Gujarat had a couple of years ago conducted a saturation training under the title . "V-Governance Training Programme", which comprised development training modules and conduct of short courses for officials at all levels. It was a one-size-fits, all programme. Similarly, Training Division, DoPT, with the assistance of UNDP, had sponsored intensive saturation training for functionaries at the district level through state ATIs whereby separate trainer modules for category A,B,C and D employees were developed and such training was provided to all employees (officers and staff) in a district. In some cases, the modules were prepared sector-wise, while some state ATIs felt that trainees in the district from different departments should undergo training together to ensure better understanding of each other's problems and better coordination. Encouraged by the results of the saturation training in seven states, the Training Division has jointly with DFID undertaken a Capacity Building for Poverty Reduction Programme whereby training in one or two sectors in each selected district is being provided in the saturation training mode. Such trainings are being taken up for development of replicable models and trying them out in other districts throughout the country. The Training Division could provide funds to state ATIs to take up 2 –3 districts each year in each state for saturation training of all officers and staff located in the district.

Saturation Training

This brings up the issue that if officers and staff at the district level could be provided saturation training, then can such saturation training be planned for at the state headquarters level, or at the regional and divisional level, as also for each central ministry. The concept here should be *training for all.* Till such time as the goal of saturation training on a repeated basis for each and every employee of central and state governments can be achieved, an interim goal could be at least three training opportunities for each employee during his or her service career after the initial induction training.

In this context, institutions for training of category 'C' and 'D' officers may need to be set up. Today, even induction training for these categories is virtually non-existent, while we need induction training comprising both foundational course and professional course for all Group 'B', 'C' and category 'D' personnel. For Group 'B', 'C' and 'D' functionaries opportunities for intra-country inter-state visits and study tours to places of best practices need to be created/enhanced. Particularly for Group 'B' employees opportunities should also be provided for exposure visits abroad. Similarly, part of promotion training for State Administrative/Police/Forest Service officers to All-India Services should involve their being sent to other states to see how they are administered.

Training needs assessment (TNA) is most vital for ensuring relevant and necessary training. Initially, category-wise training needs for different categories of civil servants need to be worked out and monitoring done as to see whether such training needs are actually being met. However, it has now become technologically possible to work out the training needs of each individual employee and to monitor whether that particular employee receives the required training or not. This could be linked with the performance appraisal system. This would be catering to the concept of *life-long learning* through both long and short courses.

Qualitative Upgradation

What is both qualitative and quantitative upgradation of the training function? This would require major efforts at strengthening central ATIs as well as state ATIs, strengthening of libraries, strengthening of computer learning facilities, provision of training equipment, development of classrooms, etc. Also required would be a major effort on design of new training modules, planning new courses, preparation and distribution of training material, development of case studies, of simulational exercises, use of interactive video-tapes and computers, and training games involving role play and situational replays, as well as experiential learning tools.

Today, there is a wide variation between the quality, size, constitution, etc., of various training institutions. The effort should be that each state or central ATI becomes (in its own way and depending upon its specific goals) a centre of excellence as an organization of learning for the civil services. CAPAM (Commonwealth Association for Public Administration and Management) in its report entitled *In Pursuit of Excellence: Developing and Maintaining a High Quality Public Service* indicated that the ultimate objective of a training institute is to build a high quality public service. For this, it needs to undertake the task of building capacity to enable the public service to effectively serve government and implement government's agenda, provide high quality services, implement laws, and be deserving of the trust and respect of citizens. Accordingly, each state or central ATI in the country needs to prepare or to redefine its vision and mission statements, prepare a ten-year vision document, formulate five yearly and annual action plans and programme calendars and ensure optimal implementation of the same. Training Division of the DoPT could suggest some general benchmarks of attributes for the ATIs to achieve as also an approach to preparation of vision and mission statements for ATIs which could be helped to prepare their mission statements. Training Division could start the process with its own institute, ISTM.

The Training Division has taken an initiative of developing a network of training institutions covering LBSNAA, state and central ATIs as well as institutions like IIMs. Thirty-one training institutions are initially being covered by this network. It is also expected that this will enable the development of a comprehensive training portal for sharing of training resources across the country and eventually for a comprehensive e-learning system for civil servants across the country.

Since lateral entry to the civil services is now being increasingly thought of, special training may be required for such personnel who through lateral entry join government for the first time. Such training could be in parliamentary or legislative practices, in working with the Finance Ministry or the Planning Commission, government accounting and audit, basic government procedures, etc.

Training for personnel in regulatory and other commissions as well as training for public sector undertakings will require slight change in nuance as compared to a regular training course for people in government ministries or departments.

Training institutes need to play a 'Centre for Good Governance' type of role. It should be able to suggest procedural and structural changes in government ministries, departments or agencies and then to evolve training programmes to help bring about the change. ATIs should be able to conduct capabilities reviews of various government agencies and departments. Accordingly, action research by training institutes on improving and modifying government procedures, structures, delivery systems and policy making, etc., should feed into the design of new training courses. Thus, training institutions should act as 'think tanks' for government.

There needs to be a close link between training undergone and future postings as well as promotions. Thus, career planning and training need to be closely linked. For this in-course assessment of trainees and end-of-course examinations and tests would require much more attention than at present.

Issue of Resources

As regards resources for funding of training, the question comes up as to whether training should be determined on the basis of funds which may become available for particular types of courses or whether it should be based upon an assessment of actual training needs. Merely going by a percentage of each ministry/departments establishment budget earmarked for training may not be the best method in all cases. Each ATI should have a largish flexible budget provided to it by government to plan out each year's courses along with the ministries and departments according to jointly perceived needs, plus it should be able to attract funding for specific courses from both public and private sources. The main flexible budget of the ATI should account for 65 to 70 per cent of the training courses and the balance 35 to 30 per cent courses could be dependent upon attracting of funds. Some training institutes have gone overboard in their efforts to attract funds for their activities and their programmes and their activities have become totally dependant upon the funds they attract, rather than based upon the needs of government. There needs to be a judicious mix of commercial programmes to meet part of the ATI's cost, and programmes that meet the needs of the civil services.

There are a number of large flagship programmes that are being implemented either by the central or by the state governments many of which have large provisions for training budgets. These need to be utilized optimally. The requirement for such training related to particular programmes is extremely large and, therefore, the training budget would be required not only to develop or to conduct courses and to evaluate their impact, but also to correspondingly enhance the training infrastructure, i.e., classrooms, training equipment, hostel facilities, etc. Such programmes also highlight the need for programme implementation to be intimately connected to training. Since much of the training in this regard would be at the district or state level, state ATIs could coordinate it and funding support would be required at the state level. But, the ministries concerned should centrally produce training material in various languages for use throughout the country. In fact, for some programmes, it should be made mandatory that implementation of the programme in the field should only be permitted once sufficient programme-specific training has been conducted at the local grassroots, district and state levels.

Coordination for Concerted Growth

On the subject of coordination in the training sector there is a need for coordination between the state government training departments, the state ATI as an apex training institute, and other training institutes of state government departments. Accordingly, each state ATI should be the nodal agency for all training institutions in the state and hold at least one conference of all government training institutes in the state each year. There is also a need for coordination between the Training Division of the DoPT and various central training institutes as well as Training Managers of various ministries. LBSNAA does organize an annual Heads of State Training Institutes Conference, which is limited to IAS induction training and another annual Heads of Central Training Institutes Conference dealing with the Foundation Course. Similarly, NIDM organizes annual training conferences on disaster management. The Training Division needs to organize separate annual training conferences to deal with all training policy, implementation and coordination issues.

Both the state and central ATIs need to go in for large-scale documentation so that training material can be shared among various institutes and provided liberally to trainees. Most of it should be distributed free of cost and the charges should be met from government training budgets. State and central ATIs should each bring out a journal containing information, analysis, etc. The journals could include regular type of academic articles, prescriptive articles, notes and commentaries, summary of reports, best practices, reviews, book notes, etc.

References

CAPAM. 2006. *In Pursuit of Excellence: Developing and Maintaining a High Quality Civil Service.*

Government of India. 1957. *Report of the Team for the Study of Community Projects and National Extension Services.* New Delhi.

Government of India. Training Division, Department of Personnel and Training. 1996. *The National Training Policy.* New Delhi

Government of India. Training Division, Department of Personnel and Training. 2006. *Training Development Programme.* New Delhi.

Hooja, Rakesh. 2006. *Induction Training of IAS Direct Recruits: Some Views.* Jaipur: ASTI.

——. "Towards Excellence in State Government Services: Capacity Building and Training in Rajasthan." *Indian Journal of Public Administration,* 52 (July–September).

Hooja, Rakesh and Meenakshi Hooja. 2001. "National College for Higher Civil Services: Requirements and Positive Role." *The Administrator, 44* (December 2001).

LBS National Academy of Administration. 2007. Committee to Review the Syllabus of Induction Training (Vaidyanath Ayyar Committee). *Report.* Mussoorie.

National School of Government. 2008. *National School of Government Portfolio 2008–2009.* Ascot, UK: Sunningdale.

Annexure 1
Areas Requiring Focus While Imparting Long Training Course at a Proposed Higher Civil Services College

The critical areas, which require to be focused upon during training include:

- Policy making at state and national levels and coordination and macro monitoring of implementation of policies and programmes.
- Responsibilities with regard to parliamentary and legislative business, procedures and practices including facing of parliamentary committees.
- Preparation of cabinet notes.
- Drafting of bills and laws and constitutional amendments.
- Preparation of budgets and plans.
- Co-ordination with other departments, ministries and agencies.
- Conduct of inter-ministry/agency meetings, especially those involving other departments, ministers, and other institutions in the public and private sectors.
- Improving resources mobilization, including efficacy of taxation, non-tax revenue and user charges, loans and repayment.
- Manning higher level jobs in newly emerging areas such as regulatory commissions, financial institutions, international bodies in addition to the more conventional secretary level jobs in government.
- Interacting with international agencies with whom the central and state governments interact and deal.
- Actions required as per the Right to Information Act.
- Facilitating public sector – private sector partnerships in various fields.
- Innovative and creative ways of administration and management.
- E-Governance – its relevant use.
- Dealing with natural calamities and other emergencies/disasters/crises.

The course at Higher Civil Services College for officers at level of Additional Secretary, Government of India, or Principal Secretary to state government or senior-most Joint Secretaries in Government of India should contain a capsule on "Strategic Leadership in 21st Century" or on "Top Management and Leadership." The officers could also, as part of the training, be familiarized and re-familiarized with the working of:

- Planning Commission, Finance Commission, UPSC, Election Commission and other commissions set up from time to time.

- Judiciary and the legal system, functioning of tribunals.
- The organization and government structures at central, state, district, municipal and PRI levels and the corresponding roles and responsibilities, as they have evolved during the years.
- Government procedures of decision-making, approvals, purchase and procurement, expenditure, regulation of conduct, leave and service and personnel matters, as well as financial matters and facing audits.

Training of officers would need to facilitate an understanding, and appreciation, in a mature manner, of the following:

- The Indian society and its diversity and unity.
- History, culture and literature.
- Social changes, including new movements regarding civil society, consumer movement, women's power, user or beneficiary participation, etc.
- Steps to increase community cohesion.
- Functioning of the polity and the processes of devolution and decentralization.
- Developments in the economy in various sectors and dimensions, including steps for inclusive growth.
- Emerging role of private corporate sector.
- Developments in science and technology, including IT, BT.
- Programmes and policies of the government in social and development sectors.
- Fostering food and livelihood security.
- Changing role of the state and government including its various organs, in the Indian and the comparative contexts.
- Emergence of regulatory and other commissions.
- The role of the defence forces and civilian agencies, including the police, in national security.
- Functioning and the role of the media.
- Ethical dilemmas that civil servants face in contemporary society.
- Modern techniques of administration, management, analysis, decision-making, motivation, etc., and of interaction between politicians, opinion 'leaders, scientists and civil' servants as well as the media and community groups, which are essential for a modem administrator.
- How India can and should respond to the challenges of globalization, seizing opportunities which have arisen, and taking steps to protect

vulnerable sections of society, vulnerable sectors, and all potential sufferers, from threats emanating from globalization impulses.

In the present 21st century 'globalized world', the trainee officers could widen their perspective by learning more about:

- The international and the global environment.
- Trends in distribution of wealth and power in the global context.
- Military and economic alliances.
- Governmental and economic systems being followed, and successful developmental initiatives in other countries.
- The international economic and financial system.
- International commodity markets.
- Population dynamics, migration, etc.
- Trading and intellectual property regimes.
- Sustainability, global warming, climate change.
- Role of UN and other international organizations and agencies.
- Possible science and technology breakthroughs in the near future.
- Global and meta-theories and worldviews of man's past, present and future.

(*Note:* The above annexure has been adapted and developed further from Meenakshi Hooja and Rakesh Hooja, "National College for Higher Civil Service: Requirement and Possible Role", in *The Administrator,* Vol. XLIV, December 2001)

Annexure 2
Possible Types of Short Courses at the Proposed National School of Governance-Cum-Higher Civil Services College for Persons at Joint Secretary (GoI) Level and Above

- Public Policy Analysis and Formulation
- Strategic Leadership
- Macro Monitoring of Implementation of Government Programmes
- Concurrent Evaluation of Programme Implementation Impact
- Large Scale Public Procurement
- Practical Financial Management/Public Expenditure Management
- People Management
- Sustainability Issues
- PPPs and Public-Private Community Partnerships
- Leading Multi-skilled Teams
- Strategic Thinking
- Turning Policy into Law
- Risk Analysis in Policy Areas
- Working with Ministers
- Managing Change
- Ethics in Government
- Human Resources and Organizational Development
- Capability Reviews of Government Departments/Agencies
- Working with Economic Advisors/Consultants
- Preparing for Top Management
- Organizational Leadership and Governance
- Human Development and Achievement of Millennium Development Goals
- Accountability in Government
- Improving Public Service Delivery
- Use of *'Sevottam'* (Charter Mark) Scheme for Improving Public Service Delivery by Government Agencies
- Total Quality Management
- Government Process re-engineering
- Natural Resource Management
- Food and Livelihood Security
- Infrastructure Development and Financing

- E-Governance
- Comprehensive District Planning
- Budgeting and Planning
- Good Governance
- Leveraging Urbanization
- Government Support for Large Public Organizations

Annexure 3
Trainer Development Programme

Recognizing the importance of trainers in the training function, the Training Division started the Trainer Development Programme in the early 1990s. Initially, faculty members of various training institutions were developed as Master Trainers and Recognized Users of various training of trainers (ToT) packages in collaboration with the Thames Valley University of UK. Over a period of time, indigenous mechanisms were evolved for developing a cadre of professional trainers and resource persons in the country to create a cascading and multiplier effect. The programme has gone a long way in embedding the Systematic Approach to Training (SAT) into the process of designing and imparting effective training to government officials.

Currently, the following programmes are sponsored under the Trainer Development Programme at selected training institutions across the country:

- Training Needs Analysis (TNA)
- Design of Training (DOT)
- Direct Trainer Skills (DTS)
- Evaluation of Training (EOT)
- Management of Training (MOT)
- Experiential Learning Tools (ELT, earlier known as DTS-II)
- Mentoring Skills
- Distance Training Skills

Training Division is currently having a pool of about 50 certified Master Trainers (MTs) and 200 Recognized Users (RUs), who can conduct various ToT programmes. Every year, about 150 such courses sponsored by the Training Division are conducted by premier training institutions across the country, in which around 2,700 officers are trained and experienced trainers are also developed as MTs and RUs.

It is proposed to significantly scale up the extent and coverage of these courses to provide opportunities to a larger number of faculty members working in the various central/state level training institutions to undergo these trainer development training courses in order to improve the overall quality of training programmes in their respective training institutions.

2 Civil Service Training in India

Some Issues

Ramesh K. Arora

The training of administrators has been recognized as an important instrument of administrative change in most developing countries. In fact, the whole process of development administration, which has as its dominant premise a directed, planned and goal-oriented change in a society, assumes that enhancing the capability and capacity of administrators is a requisite, if not a prerequisite, to any worthwhile attempt at modernization. The present Indian civil service structure, which evolved and matured during the British rule lays considerable stress on preparing civil servants for the jobs that they have to perform in varied segments of national life. In this paper, a few important aspects of civil service training are being examined.

Training Policy

Most developing countries have failed to formulate a "systemic" policy that would promote integration of training with the rest of the public administrative system. There is a conspicuous absence of clarity of priorities, strategies and foci in the training enterprise. As a result, the training system in these countries has been characterized by *ad hocism*. India's position is somewhat better than the one prevailing in the most other emergent nations but, even here, no attempt has been made to integrate training with the macro-level planning effort. Whatever references one finds in the various plan documents are, at best, "indicative" in character, and these broad guidelines have not been adequately operationalized at the middle-range and micro levels.

Once a national training policy and, based on that, a training plan, are formulated, it would be expected that the various ministries and departments of the central and the state governments and public enterprises put in their best efforts to implement them. This would certainly require a mechanism of monitoring and control that is presently conspicuous by its absence.

Training: An Integrationist View

Presently, in India, as in most developing countries, the training function is not adequately linked with educational planning and structure, the process of administrative reforms, financial administration and public personnel management. The output of the investment in training can be enhanced to an optimum level only when the training strategies and programmes are attuned to the needs of socio-economic and technological development and the country's manpower is prepared to accept the challenges of change in an appropriate manner.

While it is generally accepted that both the formal educational system and the training practices are integral components of the broader socialization process, very little has been done in India to create an "organic" relationship between the two. It has been observed, for example, that, occasionally, the contents of foundational training programmes overlap the knowledge that has already been attained by a trainee officer through his formal higher education. Even the mode of training, which is generally the lecture method, makes training prosaic. This is not to deny, however, that training is a specialized and continuing education and, therefore, needs to be properly linked with the educational system as such.

A broader view of training would also take on-the-job training into account, since training is an ongoing exercise that does not end with the completion of a specific formal programme. Ironically, however, the chasm existing between a formal training programme and the prevailing administrative practices is wide enough to make both of them appear disjointed. A clear need, therefore, exists to bridge the gap between the two. This, however, will depend upon the success in creating a favourable climate for training in the entire administrative system.

The Committee on Civil Service Reforms, headed by P.C. Hota (2004), has recommended strongly the creation of a 'learning environment' in all organizations and that senior officers should act as mentors to junior officers. The Hota Committee has strongly come out in favour of massive foreign training for civil servants, backed by the Department of Personnel and Training of the Government of India. An innovative approach to training, with considerable emphasis on the assessment of training needs, can go a long way in creating a substantially professional environment for civil service training.

One particular dimension of an integrationist view of training relates to the interlinkages between the process of administrative reforms and the training system. It is generally recognized that training can and should act as an instrument of administrative reform, and as an effective intervention strategy in this sphere. Yet, no serious exercises have been undertaken to use training as an intervention device for administrative change in India. New policies, plans, programmes, projects and procedures are initiated without adequately training the people who will be responsible for their implementation. As a result, "innovations" are introduced in a "routine" manner, with little concern for change in the design and functioning of the administrative system.

Paradoxically, a curious imbalance can be seen in the process of modernization of training in India. Sometimes, there is a misplaced overemphasis on introducing newer management techniques, even when such techniques may not be quite relevant and useful in a particular administrative context; while, at other times, even the foundational training in basic laws, rules and procedures is not adequately provided to the "grassroots" administrators.

It would appear quite reasonable to suggest at this point that administrative training should become an essential part of the total career planning of an administrator, whether he is placed in higher, middle or lower positions. A person should be sent for a training programme immediately after his recruitment and after his promotion to a higher position. Even a transfer to a new position, whose job contents are markedly different from those of the position held previously, should, as far as possible, be followed by a short-term orientation programme. However, these aspects of training have been neglected in the Indian personnel system. The situation appears to be a concomitant of the "generalist" character of the administrative services which assumes that the administrative acumen of a bureaucrat will remain at a constant level in any type of job situation. No wonder, the best state-level service officers are rarely or never deputed for training courses, while some others are nominated at such great frequency for all types of programmes that they give the impression of being roving trainees, whose supervisors probably find their presence in offices unnecessary or uncomfortable. A corrective device, therefore, would be to plan the training pattern of each department in a manner that every officer should be able to attend a refresher or orientation programme suited to his job needs, once every five years. This feature should become an integral part of the scheme of universalization of training that would involve all the officers of the government at various levels.

The pattern followed for the IAS, whose officers with certain seniority are expected to attend refresher courses in eminent training institutions, could be ideally followed for the state general and technical. For instance, in Rajasthan, starting 2001, public policy courses have been made compulsory for all state service officers and a similar plan has become operational since 2004 for the state technical officers. Of course, such an ideal situation would require an adequate training reserve and massive financial resources, which a developing country like India cannot always afford. Hence, efforts in this direction need to be made in stages.

A disquieting feature of the training system in most developing countries, including India, is an almost total absence of a link between training and the placement policy. Officers trained in certain specialized areas are rarely positioned in organizations where they can utilize the additional knowledge or skills acquired through their training. While making nominations for foreign training, the aptitude or the needs of an officer are rarely kept in view and, in many cases, on his return from foreign training, an officer is not given an opportunity to utilize his newly acquired talent for long, rendering him unable to sufficiently experiment with and apply whatever newer skills he has obtained abroad. Nevertheless, the situation seems to be changing for the better with an increasing awareness among the nominating officers of following a more rational policy of post-training utilization.

It is necessary to link training and performance in another sense at the time of considering officials for promotion, the training that they have received during their career should be a reasonable criterion for selecting them for higher positions. In fact, in most cases, a separate column on the training received in a particular year forms part of the annual performance appraisal of a government official. Since everyone in the government cannot or does not get the opportunity of having in-service training, this particular criterion cannot be used for determining the potentiality of an officer for promotion. Notwithstanding these handicaps, it would be worthwhile to examine the possibility of providing incentives to trainee-officers on the basis of their performance in a training programme, judged through an end-of-the-course examination.

Training Evaluation: A Complex Process

Perhaps, the knottiest aspect of training administration is the evaluation of effectiveness of a training programme. While the short-term impact of a training course can be judged by an end-of-the-course evaluation sheet or programme comment sheet filled in by each trainee, the long-term impact can be seen only in terms of the difference it has made in job performance and behaviour of a trained officer. And, obviously, this is difficult to measure because a complete picture of performance and attitudinal change can emerge only when the trained officer, his superiors, subordinates, peers and the clients he interacts with are interviewed after an adequately long interval. This is a most difficult task to undertake, particularly on account of paucity of time and manpower and the frequent transfers of officers. Nevertheless, some evaluation exercises should be undertaken for different types of training programmes at different intervals.

A note of caution may, however, be added here. Performance and attitudinal change may not be the function of training alone. A host of factors – environmental, organizational, interpersonal, and even situational – interact to promote or hinder administrative change, whether at the middle range or at the micro levels. This complexity of interdependent variable, however, should not deter an attempt to provide a rational and continuous system of training evaluation. Informal feedback from trainees, though educative, may not always be adequate.

Professional Training Faculty

Most apex government training institutions in India at the central as well as the state levels are headed by generalist administrators, many of them belonging to the Indian Administrative Service. These officers are believed to have a sound grounding in general administration as well as in development administration and, therefore, it is taken for granted that they would be in a position to appreciate the requirements of the professional training of administrators. Further, in most of the training institutions, there is a "floating" faculty to assist the Director, who himself is generally placed in this position for two to three years. "Floating" faculty here means officers belonging to state general services who are placed in training institutions for short-term assignments in the same manner as they are positioned in other government departments. Though experienced in government functioning, most of these faculty members do not have special background or aptitude in training and they cannot be expected to wear the mantle of a trainer, with any noticeable commitment and profundity. And, training, it is generally stressed, is a function requiring specialized competence and specific commitment. It is in this background that several state training institutions have created permanent positions of professors. The Lal Bahadur Shastri National Academy of Administration and autonomous organizations such as the Administrative Staff College and the Indian

Institute of Public Administration have also such permanent academic positions that are designed for research as well as training functions. The civil service training structure in India, however, is still generally characterized by "generalism". No doubt, even among the generalist administrators, there are a few most outstanding trainers and training administrators, but such officials are only exceptions. It will hardly be disputed, though, that training is a specialized function and requires a professional outlook and a deep commitment to the training enterprise.

There is a clear need for having on the faculty of the training institutions a happy blend of academics as well as persons having field experience. But, in the latter case, only those officers who possess an academic bent of mind and an inclination for training should be selected for training positions. Former Prime Minister Rajiv Gandhi emphasized the desirability of providing special incentives in the form of extra pay to those officers who are posted in training institutions, but soon this idea lost its shine and could not be implemented with sincerity.

Keeping in view the prospective development of their administrative structures, developing nations need to create a separate professional pool of trainers. A specific number of generalist administrators at the central and the state levels may be asked to opt for joining this training pool which would also permit lateral entry of experts and teachers who want to make training their career. Such a pool of competent and professional trainers could facilitate the manning of important top and middle level positions in training institutions by training professionals who are likely to help promote the status and quality of training. A system of appointing only professional trainers to the training institutions will require on-the-job training of the trainers through field trips and surveys and even by positioning them on short-term administrative assignments in the field, thus facilitating cross-fertilization of ideas between the trainers and the practicing administrators. These programmes should gradually increase in number and should also become more specialized in content and focus. They need two components: first, exposure to important training methods and organizational skills, and second, a focus on specific subject areas in which the trainers are expected to train other officers. The programmes on training of trainers need to be provided a big fillip.

Training for the Lower-Level Bureaucracy

In the pyramidal structure of the Indian bureaucracy, the *babus* form the base if we include the assistants, office superintendents and the section officers in the clerical class the "*babu* bureaucracy" moves a little higher up in the pyramid, say, up to the lower middle level. The ministerial staff, as it is usually called, is essentially the backbone of Indian public administration. It is a reservoir of experience and the memory bank in the government organization. Its efficiency and competence considerably affect the quality of Indian public administration. Yet, the most neglected segment in the Indian training system is this very ministerial class. It appears that a major portion of resources for training is reserved for officials at the top and the upper middle levels of administration. As a result, almost all training programmes in the national and state level training institutions are designed for "senior" executives. This is true of programmes in the areas of skill improvement and attitudinal change. Ironically, however, training at these higher levels is seen more as a "refresher programme" than as a corrective device. Training can produce maximum results at the lower levels and, therefore, it is time that the clerical class be given its due place in the training superstructure. This might require the creation of new training institutions for ministerial staff and the expansion of the activities of the existing training institutions to cover the ministerial staff training within their ambits. A massive round-the-year programme of training, organized by training institutions specially created for this purpose, is essential to meet the needs of ministerial staff trainees. Universalization of training is possible only through adequate decentralization.

Above, then, are a few issues that deserve attention of policy makers in the domain of training systems at the central as well as the state levels.

3 Role of Training in Governance

An Outsider's View*

R.N. Gupta

The word 'governance' has replaced 'management' and 'administration' in academic circle for various reasons, the main being that it carries a clear connotation of socio-ethical responsiveness rather than simply of efficiency or even effectiveness. Governance goes beyond the concept of accountability to, and performing for, a particular organization and extends responsibility to society and other stakeholders. Training then needs to be relevant to good governance. There is a tendency, however, to treat training as simply an adjunct to good management and administration, and worse, sometimes an end in itself. More alarmingly, the resources deployed for the purpose of training and the results achieved tell a story of waste and non-achievement. My informal calculations show that the government training institutions in India are spending Rs 5,000 to Rs 10,000 per lecture/per participant. Surely, this can hardly be called a model for efficient use of resources, even assuming that we are getting some results. The second proposition – of getting results – is even more doubtful. It is difficult to quantify the impact of training in achieving better governance. We generally agree that 'good governance' is receding rather than coming closer. Of course, this may be despite the factor and influence of training. Even insiders, however, will agree as a general proposition that things may not be much worse if there were no training at all (of course, training mostly of non-formal nature) given to government servants at pre-induction and in-service stages. The reasons given may vary. The 'poor relation' theory is the most common. There is, therefore, no alternative to optimizing the use of whatever resources (may be inadequate) are available, to prioritize the training

* I have not had the good fortune till four months back to work in a training institute. These views have been put from the point of view of an outsider who is in mortal danger of soon becoming (or at least considering himself to become) an 'insider'.

needs with reference to the objective of good governance and only after having achieved optimization of resources and programmes within existing constraints, should we build a case for supplementing available resources.

For the purpose of optimization of resources, it may be helpful to define different dimensions of training taken up in government-run public administration institutes. The first exclusion is obvious – any formal training leading to a certificate or degree is excluded. It may be desirable to take this up but considering that most of the institutions are neither doing so at the moment nor are they properly equipped to do so in future and some courses are better organized in academic institutions, this area can be excluded. The second area is that of technical training conducted by government institutions and geared to the needs of a particular profession or discipline, e.g., patwar schools, multipurpose workers training, etc. The third is pre-induction training for entrants in government service, which is now mostly confined to administrative and non-technical categories. Then, there are in-service training requirements, which cover both technical/professional as well as administrative personnel.

It appears that there are two areas needing focus from the government training institutions. One is that all persons entering government service must get training/exposure in

(a) the technical aspects in which they are formally qualified having earned formal degree/diploma, etc., and
(b) aspects of management in government to which they are not exposed while undergoing the technical courses in academic/educational institutions.

As regards general aspects of management in government, the most important are:

(a) customer orientation/public dealings,
(b) financial systems in government, and
(c) personnel systems.

For example, the role of a pharmacist in a government dispensary is very different from what he does in a private hospital or even in a private drug store, for example, in accounting for stores and patient records. Such differences obviously cannot be a part of formal training to function as a pharmacist and it is necessary to expose such persons to the systems of working in government, especially with regard to the three areas mentioned above. This appears desirable from the point of view not only of governance as such but even for the limited purpose of administering or managing or running public services for which personnel are employed in government.

The second issue is to carefully identify the personnel and the training needs. It is true that the optimum may not be achievable as enough resources in terms of manpower or infrastructure may not be available or sufficient time may not be given by an agency which needs to get going with carrying out of duties languishing for the absence of personnel. That is where a pragmatic plan would be necessary, requiring

(a) prioritization regarding personnel of different departments and agencies to be trained; and
(b) taking a pragmatic view regarding the period of training.

In the Second World War, teenaged boys were sent to war by many countries after barely few days of training instead of the required one or two years just because they could not afford to wait. Surely in times of peace better planning should be possible. One way could be – where government itself runs dedicated technical schools for Patwaris – integrating the general management aspects in the syllabus of the technical schools. The apex training institutions can play an important role in this regard without tying up too much resources. This is something missing at present in the apex institutes, which today do not have any interaction with other specialized training institutions under different departments of the government.

So far as in-service training is concerned, this also includes refresher courses in technical/professional areas. This is done by sponsoring technical training programmes within the state and other states in India and sometimes abroad. Training of technical personnel in general areas of management in government set-up has to be handled by apex training institutes at least till such time as the pre-induction training covers all existing employees of a particular agency. That is a long way off as induction of new employees is now practically a trickle especially with talks of downsizing and de-inventing the government. Here again, there is a need for prioritization regarding categories of employees/ agencies, which need to be the focus of attention for training.

Thus, TNA (Training Needs Analysis) needs to be confined to categories and agencies whose training we can effectively take up. Like training, TNA is not of independent value and is relevant only to the extent that it is an active input to training design. There is no point in having a comprehensive TNA without devoting adequate resources in translating the same in programme design and actual training. The issue of relevance and impact is of course a different one as indicated above and will arise even after one has done all that is indicated.

The problem regarding the outcome of training is that training is now a one-way process and no initiative comes from the persons to be trained. The position is just opposite of what happens in educational institutes where many aspirants compete for a particular seat or a course. There is need to devise ways to involve the employees and this cannot be done by TNA alone as that itself is a passive process imposed from the agency heads and so forth and is structured on organizational rather than individual needs. Some solutions are available now with new developments in electronics, communications and computers. It is time we switch to new methodologies of 'online' training and 'training at home' to suit the employees and match their motivation. Fortunately, putting courses online on CD ROMs does not cost much, especially as (mostly) one-time investment is required. This needs at least to be offered as a major alternative to 'face-to-face' training to infuse some motivation among employees and to ensure what sociologists call 'self-selection'. Such computer-based training courses supplemented by 'Help Lines' for government employees to meet their queries will not only be more effective for individual employees but will also indicate the response to different courses simply by the number of 'hits'. One important aspect which has not been given as much importance as it deserves (as given in the private sector) in the bottom up/quality circles/team work/consultation approach as compared to top-down and file pushing approach, dislinked from outcome and dedicated to routine. All agencies and employees exist not to do a job but to achieve some results and outcomes. While responsiveness to public is no doubt a lip service, what is surprising is the omission of what in business are called 'internal customers', i.e., employees who themselves need service from other departments (for pay and other personal matters). It is difficult to believe that the government employees who are insensitive to even their own colleagues working in different departments will be responsive to the public at large.

So far as the design of training programme is concerned, it may be appropriate to follow for in-service training the 'workshop' method which ensures much closer interaction between the trainer and the trainee as compared to normal lecture mode (however well delivered and audio-visual aided). That will induce a sense of involvement and engagement among employees. There would be a need, therefore, to have a mix of faculty combining academics and practical managers.

We, as trainers, should constantly ask the basic questions which any business spending money and committing resources asks itself that what resources are being deployed; what are their alternatives uses; are they being optimally deployed; and are their results the best possible under constraints and given circumstances? With the largest percentage of illiterate population in the world, the trainers in India need to be cautious in asking for resources without delivering results.

Section II

Training of All India and Central Services

4 District Training for IAS Probationers

Emerging Scenarios

V. Srinivas

District training in their respective state cadres is an integral feature of the two-year training course of IAS probationers. A broad pattern for district training has been firmly established by the state training institutes of the country over the last five decades. This has been developed with years of administrative experience and must satiate the intense ideological commitment of high potential young officers entering service with the specific objective of serving the nation. Training experiences are remembered throughout an officer's service tenure and have an enormous impact on his future performances. With the large-scale entry of officers with high technical qualifications, it is essential to ensure that the district training package is more than an exercise in skill acquisition, and also oriented towards the socio-cultural adjustments in attitude that an officer undergoes while familiarizing himself with the job requirements in what is very often a new environment for him.

District training must serve the primary objective of familiarizing the probationer with the socio-economic profile of the state, detailed subject knowledge of the status of land reforms, land revenue administration and the role of IAS officer in implementing land reforms in his first posting as Sub-Divisional Officer and Sub-Divisional Magistrate and District Collector soon after. The long-term global objective is to develop among officers professional skills and attitudes to handle a wide variety of assignments in senior positions in the government. Thus, the forty-week district training course under the direct supervision of the District Collector is divided into: (i) completion of assignments as laid down by the LBS Academy, (ii) attachments and independent charges with various offices like the Tehsil, Patwari, Panchayat Samiti, Police Station and Municipality, etc., and (iii) court work.

Over the last seven years, some major changes have been introduced into the training pattern of the IAS probationers, some of which have been brought about by amendments in the recruitment procedures by increasing the age limit. The assignments which laid greater emphasis on regulatory administration, which form the bulwark of first five years of service, with detailed assignments on land reforms, socio-economic surveys/village study, district planning, agriculture and daily diaries, have moved away to cover developmental aspects like innovative schemes, gender issues, watershed projects, etc. The probationer who was visiting at least 10 villages for in-depth study and interaction has now moved to specialized developmental projects which can be studied from offices and covers only two to three villages for in-depth studies. The clubbing of the socio-economic survey with the land reforms assignment and restricting both these to the study of only one village has reduced the impact that these assignments have had on the probationer's future outlook. Land-based issues like ceiling, tenancy, land alienation and restoration, land conversion for industrial/commercial purposes and land allotment for permanent and temporary tenancies have lost their pre-eminent status in the probationer's list of priorities. The present assignment on land reforms now consumes only 10 days of actual work while earlier it took over 40 days of effort. The probationer now submits only two other assignments: the district training assignment and the assignment on innovation in government which consumes an additional 15 days. This may be compared with the six assignments which took up 90 days of work. The probationer is left with a surplus of 65 days of time which was earlier being spent on assignment work. Reduction in the number of assignments has meant that the in-depth knowledge of the probationer on issues of vital importance is limited to only those which he observes rather than those which he analyzes and puts down on paper. The daily diary has also been replaced with a monthly report which is a one-line abstract of the day's proceedings. The earlier pattern insisted on one-page daily notes which he had to mandatorily undertake once probation is completed.

The increase in the average age limit of recruitment has resulted in the average age of the probationer in the district increasing from 23–25 years to 26–28 years of age. Several probationers are seen these days with their families and children undertaking tours only if absolutely necessary. It appears that the number of night-halts has decreased from 100 to 60 which is a 40 per cent reduction over the last seven years.

Similarly, there has also been a 33 per cent reduction in the court work of the probationer during the training period from 18 cases to 12 cases only

The average IAS probationer is thus saving about 80 days of work which he would have executed in accordance with the directions laid down by the LBS National Academy of Administration (LBSNAA) and instead is utilizing that time in accordance with the directions of the District Collector. This means that 30 per cent of the utilization of time is left to the discretion of the District Collector. Probationers are often seen utilizing this for varying purposes like officers incharge of Collectorate's sections to being attached with several campaigns like pulse polio, literacy, distribution of pass books, etc. Precious time of the probation period for training and learning is thus being used for actual execution of work which is a cause for concern. The probationer who was hard-pressed for time during the district training period earlier has now more time on hands to experience the authority syndrome.

Although no official demarcation of training districts has been made in the state, there has always been an informal delineation with the larger well-established districts receiving prominence in attracting probationers. The experiment of sending probationers to remote districts was also tried out in the year 1990 to provide them with greater rural exposure, but it was not repeated to avoid the numerous hardships which the probationers faced during their initial phase of posting. With improved infrastructure available presently this may once again be tried out.

There is also need to increase the workload of the probationer as laid down by the LBSNAA during district training. The inclusion of developmental projects as part of the assignments is a welcome initiative but it has come at the cost of assignments which were thought of as the basis for future growth of the officer. Probably, this is the reason why it is being felt that probationers are not maturing ideologically and instead return with negative impacts following district training. With in-depth studies on village socio-economics, land reforms and tenancy, coupled with strides made in agricultural development, district planning and the management module, the probationer would really be able to make an enormous impact in catalyzing social/economic change in rural India in the early stages of his professional career.

5 Training for the Indian Foreign Service

Issues and Perspectives

Siran Mukerji

Training is the systematic modification of behaviour through education, instruction, development and planned experience. The present-day functions of government are complex and of varied nature. It requires framing of plans and policies, designing programmes, coordinating various activities, supervising the duties and providing necessary resources for the successful implementation of these activities. All these functions have not only to be performed within a set of rules and regulations but by incorporating the required changes brought about by political, social, economic, scientific, and technological forces. All this calls for trained and efficient personnel who are capable of performing well and producing the results which are commensurate with the national requirements. And, this could be achieved solely through a well-developed training system which would look upon the enhancement of capabilities of the personnel and prepare them to face the future challenges.

Training of civil servants helps to promote, maintain or enhance the employees' effectiveness not only in their present assignments but also prepares them for future work or promotional opportunities, i.e., assumption of higher responsibilities through cultivation or development of habits, thoughts, actions, skills, knowledge, attitude, and, behavioural patterns. All this promotes organizational effectiveness because functional efficiency and the morale of the employees are reflected in the totality of performance of an organization.

In this context, it has been the constant endeavour of the Government of India to frame training policies and render adequate training facilities to its personnel so that they can handle the tasks in a more effective manner. The training system for the civil services has gone through a long evolution since independence. Various training institutes have been established by the Government of India for imparting training to different services, as, for instance, the Lal Bahadur Shastri National Academy of Administration (LBSNAA), Mussoorie, for the Indian Administrative Service, Sardar Vallabhbhai Patel National Police Academy, Hyderabad, for the Indian Police Service, Railway Staff College, Baroda, for the Railway Services, Institute of Direct Taxes, Nagpur, for the Income Tax Service, Departmental Training School, Simla, for the Indian Audit and Accounts Service, etc. The efforts made by the Government of India in this regard include setting up of the Foreign Service Institute (FSI) primarily for imparting training to the IFS officers besides conducting short-term programmes for the staff of Ministry of External Affairs and also for foreign diplomats.

Induction Training

A need was felt for having an independent training institute for the IFS probationers and this led to major changes in the induction training for the IFS probationers.

The present system of induction training for the recruits to the IFS covers a period of three years. It is completed in four stages which are as follows:

1. Foundation Course of four months at LBSNAA, Mussoorie.
2. Professional Course for the probationers of the Indian Foreign Service of one year.
3. Attachment with the Ministry of External Affairs for six months.
4. Language training at an Indian mission abroad for 18 months.

Foundational Course at LBSNAA

The Foundational Course, imparted at the LBSNAA, is designed to provide the probationers their first introduction to the ethos and values of higher civil services, especially the values of integrity, humanism service and professionalism. The course provided to the trainees of the All India and the Central Services Class I by LBSNAA is of four months' duration. This includes lectures on various subjects by eminent persons, case studies, examinations and extra-curricular activities. It aims at introducing the officer-trainees to various aspects of the Indian social reality, especially the problems of the most vulnerable sections. And finally, it aims at building an *esprit de corps* among officers of various services, a perception that although their specific roles may be different, they are partners in the wider enterprise of public service. While the Foundational Course is not a course that emphasizes learning of details of various subjects, it does attempt to give the probationers an exposure to a variety of subjects so as to sensitize them to topical issues in these subjects. The subjects offered are Public Administration, Management, Law, Constitution and Political Theory, Economics, History and Computer.

Apart from the academic inputs, the trainees are required to attend language classes, write a term paper and participate in external programmes. The probationers have to learn one language during the Foundational Course. This programme is for those trainees who are exempted from the compulsory Hindi classes. The exemption is granted on the basis of a written test held at the beginning of the Foundational Course.

The foundational training is considered to be effective in providing a base for future. This training gives a wide exposure through lectures from experienced officials, specialized administrators, academicians, and other prominent personalities. Hence, they all provide impressive intellectual inputs. These basic inputs give a fairly good idea about the Indian Constitution, History and Culture, Law, etc., which is very essential for the probationers coming from different parts of the country. Apart from the exposure that the probationers get, it is a very good platform where the recruits of different services interact with each other, promoting camaraderie, inter-service harmony and *esprit de corps*. Hence, the Foundational Course is considered to be very essential for all the probationers.

Professional Course

The IFS probationers undergo one-year Professional Course at the Foreign Service Institute (FSI) in New Delhi. This curriculum is intended to provide comprehensive training for professional diplomats, not only in traditional areas of political reporting, protocol and negotiations but in new fields as well, including national and international security, environment, terrorism and human rights. Since it is important for Indian diplomats to know India thoroughly before they can represent the nation's interests abroad, the focus of this training is therefore on India, its history, culture, geopolitics, natural and human resources, security, economic goals and foreign policy priorities. The training also equips young officers with the competence to face the challenges of the future.

The Professional Course consists of 26 modules. The course contains subjects such as International Relations, Indian Foreign Policy, Introduction to Diplomacy, Regional Focus, International Law and Defence and Security. Besides, the probationers have also to undergo an attachment with the armed forces to study the structure and functions of the Ministry of Defence, role of the Defence Research and Development Organization (DRDO) and Department of Defence Production, the potential for defence exports, role and organization of the armed forces and relationship between the armed forces and the civilian administration. An insight is provided on the role, functions, problems and future plans of the Army, Navy and Air Force. Apart from this, the attachment also includes site visits to units of the Army, Navy and Air Force. A part of the training at FSI also includes studying computer skills.

The course also comprises training modules on foreign languages which include basic French, a compulsory foreign language and an optional foreign language. The probationers undertake a tour of major centres of historical, cultural and commercial interest in India and this is known as *Bharat Darshan*. They also visit the countries of the South Asian Association for Regional Cooperation (SAARC) for familiarization with the common bonds, share problems and prospects for future cooperation.

It is to be noted here that generally there is no fixed itinerary for *Bharat Darshan* and it varies depending on the background of the probationers. Two factors govern the choice of places; firstly, the probationers visit those places in India which they are not familiar with, and secondly, those regions which they are not likely to visit during their diplomatic career. Apart from this, the 1998 probationers visited four SAARC countries, namely, Bangladesh, Sri Lanka and Maldives, and Myanmar.

Attachment in the Ministry of External Affairs

After having completed the Foundational Course at LBSNAA, Mussoorie, and the Professional Course at FSI, New Delhi, the probationers are sent to the Ministry of External Affairs (MEA) for an attachment with its various divisions for a period of six months. This provides them an opportunity for general familiarization with the functioning of MEA and on-the-job training in the divisions. The important divisions and bodies to which the probationers are attached for on-the-job training include Administration Division, Bureau of

Security, External Publicity Division, Consular, Passport and Visa Division, Indian Council of Cultural Relations, Economic Division, Protocol Division, Finance Division and Cypher Bureau. Apart from the attachment with the specialized and support divisions, the officer-trainees are required to spend two months in their respective territorial divisions taking into consideration the foreign languages allotted to them and their language postings. During the attachment in the MEA, the performance of the probationers is assessed by the Joint Secretary of the division where the probationer is attached and is recorded in the ACR for that year.

Language Training at the Mission Abroad

Language training abroad is the final phase of the three-year long probationary training for the IFS officers. The probationer is posted as Third Secretary in the Indian mission in a country for study of the language which has been allotted to him by the Ministry. This allotment is based on the officer's preference and depending on his/her ranking in the UPSC merit list. The probationer learns the language for 15 months and continues to stay on till the completion of the posting which is generally for two to three years. When a probationer is sent out on his first posting, the MEA impresses on the head of the mission to take a personal interest in the training of the prospective officer and it is believed that "the success or failure of junior officers depends on the amount and the quality of guidance given by superior officers".

It may be pointed out that languages like French and Spanish are taught in India and after an initial training, the probationer is posted to the country where these languages are in vogue. But for other difficult languages like Russian, Chinese, Japanese, etc., the probationers are sent straight away to the respective countries for language training.

In-service Training

Instruction received later in the career, intended to impart new knowledge or to develop additional skills, may easily be recognized as in-service training. In-service training in the IFS is an area which is in the process of growth and is yet to gain a concrete shape. Immediately after completing the probation period, the officers are generally expected to implement the instruction given by their seniors but by the time they get into the mid-career, they start handling issues and taking important decisions. This is the stage when the officers would have completed eight years from the time of having gone through their

Foundational Course. Their knowledge base requires to be updated. Since they have to handle economic and commercial affairs, it is imperative that the officers are imparted in-service training to handle specialized subjects.

The Foreign Service Institute (FSI) has in the past tried to conduct a few specially arranged courses like the Orientation-cum-Briefing Programme for the Head of Mission/Head of Post. This high level course of ten days' duration was started at the behest of the Prime Minister of India primarily for the officers of the rank of Ambassador or High Commissioner in order to bring them abreast of the changing Indian economic policies. FSI also organized the Professional Course for the Commercial Representatives in collaboration with the Indian Institute of Foreign Trade (IIFT), New Delhi. This three-week long course is designed for the officers of the rank of Director and Deputy Secretary, engaged in trade and commercial work in the missions abroad. It offers opportunities for interaction with experienced officials of economic ministries, Chambers of Commerce and Industry, as also business representatives from the public and private sectors, for in-depth discussion on commercial techniques and procedures, and for updating on the government's economic policies and priorities. However, the FSI has not designed or launched any integrated course for mid-career training where the officers of certain seniority could be brought together and offered necessary training before being considered for the next promotion. Nevertheless, certain need-based functional courses have been conducted by FSI.

It has been proposed to start mid-career training course for the IFS officers with 10 to 12 years of service posted at the Ministry of External Affairs. The objective of this course would be to upgrade the skills of the officers and provide them up-to-date information on various aspects of their work like, science and technology, management techniques, commercial work, international relations, foreign policy issues, security issues and other relevant matters. There are also proposals for organizing tailor-made courses by seeking the involvement and opinion of HRD experts from the corporate world. This would help the FSI in getting their views on the training programmes.

However, the course for Head of Mission or Head of Post has not been conducted after December 1992 due to difficulty in assembling a large number of Heads of Missions/Heads of Posts from High Commissions/Embassies for quite a few days and because of the doubts expressed about the high cost involved in organizing such a programme.

Apart from the above mentioned in-service courses, officers have been undergoing other in-service training programmes such as briefing and debriefing sessions. In this programme, the IFS officers, before proceeding on postings abroad, are required to attend briefing session in the concerned territorial divisions in the MEA for getting acquainted with the facts, problems and issues, and other allied matters about the country where they are to undertake the assignments. This helps the officer to get familiarized with the place of posting. In this process, the officers are provided with fact-sheets, background notes, country notes, notes on living conditions, reports on various projects in which India is involved, and other files of interest. This attachment is normally of one month's duration, however, it may vary according to need and circumstances.

Similarly, the officers on return from their assignments to the headquarters are expected to call on the concerned division officer who is generally an officer of the rank of Joint Secretary for debriefing. The officers provide an updated account of the problems and issues and other latest information on the countries where they were posted. This system is applicable to the officers proceeding on direct posting from one mission to another. In such cases, the officer transiting through the headquarters undergoes debriefing and briefing sessions as mentioned above.

This is considered to be a significant feature of the IFS in-service training. This serves a dual purpose: one, it gives an opportunity to the officers to refresh their knowledge about the territory where they are going to assume office; and two, it promotes greater interaction between the officers abroad and the officers at the MEA.

There is also a practice of the Heads of Missions who, while completing their tenure in a mission, leave behind a detailed note about the country incorporating all relevant aspects for the benefit of their successors.

As a part of the in-service training programme, the IFS officers are also sent to other institutions in India or abroad for training.

Conclusion

In view of the above description of training in the Indian Foreign Service, here are some suggestions for improving the training system.

The foundational training at LBSNAA should be more oriented to the actual administrative responsibilities in the career. There need to be selective concentrated models on subjects keeping in mind India's national and international interests. Specific modules on macro-economic policies, which provide the backdrop for the new economic reforms, the role of banks and financial institutions, the problems of infrastructure in the economy and their resolution, major development projects, could be developed and included for coverage in the Foundational Course.

Since the Foundational Course is the first real exposure of a probationer in his career, there should be sessions dealing with the bio-profiles of civil servants who have in the past upheld the rich traditions of the country and the service and of neutrality and integrity. Besides, the modules should emphasize on the better understanding of tasks and functions that lie ahead and ensure all-round development of the trainee officer. Greater stress should be placed on significant national issues.

As already pointed out, there should be more focus on foreign policy in the Foundational Course also because this aspect is equally important and relevant for other All India and Central Civil Services. Visits of retired and serving Indian senior diplomats would prove to be helpful in promoting better understanding of the international issues.

There are a series of examinations at the end of the foundational training at the LBSNAA, Mussoorie, which focus on the six subjects on which the probationers have been provided academic inputs during the training. The officer-trainees should be assessed not only on the basis of knowledge gained but greater stress should be laid on evaluating the skills of the trainees. Emphasis should also be laid on performance during the course along with the examination at the end of the course. Evaluation could also take into consideration factors such as participation, team work, morale and motivation of the trainees during the course, and peer relationship. Along with the written examinations, the papers prepared by the officer-trainees should be circulated and a discussion on the topics of the papers should be conducted. A panel of eminent persons belonging to the various areas should then judge the officer-trainees. This would be a better and a much more practical approach to evaluation of performance.

There is also a need for having more interactive sessions, seminars on foreign policy and panel discussions on the various national and international issues. A panel could comprise senior diplomats and probationers. This would promote interaction between the senior diplomats and the probationers and also planning the training programmes, deciding who provides the training, implementing the training, and lastly evaluating the training.

Considering the importance of in-service training for the IFS officers, substantial planning needs to be done in this direction.

Training programmes should be organized after conducting a thorough identification of training needs. This calls for matching the objectives of the course with the needs of the trainees. Usually, training programmes are organized in FSI keeping in view the number of years of service put in by officer, and their career trajectories. Generally, on the initiative of FSI, the MEA, seeks participants for specific training programmes which turns out to be an *ad hoc* arrangement for training. Unfortunately, no serious attempt has been made by the MEA to identify the manpower requirements and to determine the availability of officers for training programmes. Hence, there has been no specific method of identifying the training needs and, therefore, the training programmes fail to have the desired impact on the trainees. This problem could be solved by conducting training needs analysis (TNA) on a continuing basis. Training needs analysis is concerned with defining the gap between what is happening and what should happen. This is what has to be covered through training, i.e., the difference between what people know and can do and what they should know and be able to do. However, it is necessary to avoid falling into the trap of adopting the 'deficiency model' approach which implies that training is only about putting things right that have gone wrong. Training is much more positive than that. It is, or should be, concerned more with identifying and satisfying development needs, people with multiple skills taking on extra responsibilities, increasing all-round competence and preparing others to take on higher levels of responsibility in future.

The Administrative Division of the MEA perhaps could institutionalize the mid-career training in collaboration with the FSI which should follow and guide the career growth of the IFS officers from the recruitment stage to the final phase of retirement. A step in this direction would be to link the appraisal process and the mid-career training with the career growth as is the case in the armed forces. Based on the appraisal of individual officers, steps could be taken to design training programmes. Feedback should be taken from the officers belonging to a certain seniority level and this feedback could be made the basis for organizing training programmes. It is not necessary that all the training programmes should be conducted by the FSI; in fact, the FSI could send the officers for training and necessary study programmes to other universities and institutes of international relations and diplomacy.

The next important factor is that of selection of the officers for the training programmes. Presently, the selection of the IFS officers for the training programmes is an *ad hoc* phenomenon with no specific method employed for this purpose. Though no uniform method can be devised in this regard, yet the academic background, the present posting and the potential of the officer help the trainees in imbibing practical knowledge about the service, besides improving their communication skills.

Those trainees who have passed the UPSC examinations through a language other than English pose a different problem of quality. Since English is the most important language of international diplomacy and commerce, systematic training in English language should be integrated with the other modules at FSI.

As a part of district training, the probationers should be exposed to the ongoing developmental projects in that area, and given complete information on the problems and issues of district administration. Then, the probationers should be asked to submit a report of their findings and experience along with the suggestions for improving the administrative set-up. This report should be considered while assessing the performance of the trainees.

The overall evaluation of the performance of a probationer should be based on the subject examinations at FSI, the report on district attachment submitted by the probationers, the paper on international relations, and a specialized testing of verbal and communication skills. There should also be a system of self-appraisal and peer appraisal which would give the officer-trainees an opportunity to make improvements as he/she goes along in the course.

As a part of the induction training, there is a usual practice of sending the probationer to a country where the compulsory foreign language to be learnt, is spoken. In order to make the language training more effective, certain measures need to be taken. The initial posting for language training should be followed by another posting to a country where the same language is spoken. This would enable the officer in attaining higher level of proficiency, i.e., near interpreter level, in that language. The MEA also needs to concentrate on languages other than French, Arabic, Russian, Spanish and Japanese. This would help the MEA in having an adequate number of officers in each important foreign language.

After the completion of induction training, officers are posted at the Indian missions abroad where they get an opportunity to utilize the knowledge and professional skills attained as a result of the initial training. However, there is a need for refresher courses to re-equip the officers having put in eight to ten years of service to reorient them and also provide them in-service training to stay abreast of the problems and issues of national and international significance.

The first thing which deserves the attention of the Foreign Service Institute is that there is a need for planned training which would necessarily mean having a deliberate intervention aimed at achieving the learning necessary for improved job performance. This would have the following steps: identifying the training needs, specifying the learning required, defining the objectives of training, annual performance appraisal should form the basis of specifying the objectives and contents of the training programmes. The heads of the MEA divisions should initiate this process for the concerned division as also for the heads of missions for their missions. The areas of specialized training should also be considered while selecting the officers for the training programmes.

The next issue towards institutionalizing the training system is that of frequency of in-service training. Though this should be a flexible arrangement, yet it is felt that an officer should undergo training after 10 years of service and again on having completed 20 years of service. The courses should, however, be at least for three months' duration, with the objective of reorienting the officer for his future responsibilities and challenges. This should be accompanied by short and comprehensive briefings before every new posting abroad. The officer proceeding to a new area or a new sphere of duties should always receive some "pre-posting" training in order to get acquainted with the nature and scope of his new charge. It has been observed that there is a system of briefing and debriefing for the officers returning from the posting and those going to the posting abroad but these briefings should be taken more seriously and the officer during this period should be directly assessed by the head of the division.

The present practice of sending officers for training to institutions in India and abroad is indeed useful for the officers in order to give them greater scope for understanding the complex, political, strategic and other international issues and also to provide them an opportunity to interact with foreign diplomats. These training programmes should be linked with the career growth of the officers. Besides, performance -related training should be stressed and be related to organizational needs. This should ensure that the personnel have the necessary knowledge and skills to be able to take on new tasks as the organization grows and faces new challenges. Performance-related training is competence-based. It starts from an analysis of the competencies required for successful performance, now and in future, assesses the areas in which competencies need to be developed, and plans and installs training programmes or processes, such as performance management to create the levels of competence required.

Yet another important aspect of in-service training is the evaluation process undertaken during the training. Since training has not been adequately linked with career growth, the evaluation of performance of an officer in the training programme does not seem to be taken seriously and to a great extent depends upon the institution imparting the training. It is suggested here that the parameters of evaluation should be defined and conveyed clearly to the officers participating in the training programmes. The results of the evaluation should become a part of the ACR of an officer. There is also a need for having post-training evaluation for getting the feedback of the officers on the training programme. Sessions for reviewing training programmes should be conducted wherein the officers should be asked for suggestions and feedback. These suggestions should then be assessed by the Dean, FSI, or the head of the institution imparting the training, and the training programmes should be modified accordingly. In this context, training evaluation reactionnaire should be developed for the training programmes and the feedback of the participants should be taken in these end-of-course reactionnaires.

Another issue in this regard is that the in-service training is not linked to any system of incentive. This becomes specially important for language specialization, where an officer is required to undergo an advanced course in the language learnt during the initial years of service. Financial schemes should be introduced for continuing language courses during postings abroad. This would motivate the officers to improve the foreign language.

Last but not the least, the FSI, which is responsible for planning and organizing training programmes, should have better infrastructure facilities. The increasing responsibilities and tasks of FSI call for having its own campus and a highly dedicated permanent faculty. Efforts should be made to acquire on deputation highly efficient IFS officers for the FSI for at least three years who should also be given necessary incentives. This would enable the officers to contribute towards the well-being of the FSI and share their experiences with the trainees. Steps should also be taken to make such arrangements that every officer of the rank of Joint Secretary would have to serve at FSI for a tenure of at least two to three years. This would create awareness amongst all the officers towards training and development. Initiatives should also be taken to provide permanent faculty members. The FSI should not only be a training centre but also a research institution for studying and analyzing crucial issues affecting the formulation and implementation of Indian foreign policy.

6 A Scheme for 52-Week State and District Training of Direct Recruits to IAS

Rakesh Hooja

One view of training of IAS officers is that the first 25 to 30 years of an IAS officer's career are a training for the last 5 to 7 years of his/her service when he or she is at top policy making and managing levels in central or state government and can provide the requisite administrative leadership to government and the civil services. Be that as may be, IAS officers throughout their service careers have a vital role to play in ensuring that government is capable of meeting the ever increasing expectations of the people in an optimal manner and that government can make the best of the opportunities being thrown up by technological change as well as globalization/liberalization while at the same time can take steps to prevent or reduce and mitigate the adverse impacts. Thus, an IAS officer is expected to develop expertise in good governance, policy formulation and implementation and the administration and management of governmental activities impinging on all the sectors of the economy, society and polity. One of the means of preparing IAS officers to play such a role is systematic and professional training.

Keeping in view the above, the induction or entry point training of an IAS officer is intended to prepare him/her for the various roles that he/she may be expected to play in the first decade of his/her life in the service.

This training includes a Foundation Course and Professional Course (in two phases) at Lal Bahadur Shastri National Academy of Administration (LBSNAA) and a 52 weeks' State and District Training, which is the focus of this opinion paper.

It is well recognized that there are many aspects of administration (including Acts and rules) which differ significantly in nature from state to state. Also, the nature of postings that a direct recruit may expect during the first ten years of service (i.e., two years of induction training and eight years of post-training service) differs from state to state. Thus, it is not possible for LBSNAA to cater during its institutional training (Foundation Course, Professional Course, Phase I and Phase II) to all the diversity of conditions that an IAS officer is likely to face and the roles that he/she may have to play in the first ten years of service which are normally spent in the state rather than on central deputation. This task of state-specific theoretical as well as practical training can be better taken up by state level ATIs (where ATIs do not exist, the SIRDs or other institutes of administration or training by whatever name as may exist in the state could be asked to take up such work). In fact, in many states, the ATIs are presently providing such training (and have built up training material accordingly) to state service officers, or even to IAS probationers, and in such cases, the present ATI component for IAS probationers could be enhanced.

It has also been noticed that the period of district postings in the first ten years of service of an IAS officer has significantly reduced compared to earlier years and that many postings now occur as deputy/additional head of department or as deputy secretary to government at state headquarters, or in a state public sector enterprise, or in an urban improvement trust, city development authority, or municipal body or rural development project agency. Training to prepare officers for such assignments cannot be ensured through district training, but the state ATIs can serve such a purpose through a combination of theoretical and practical training. IAS probationers also need to know how the reports and proposals sent by SDMs and Collectors-cum-District Magistrates are dealt with when they reach the state government level and the state-level ATIs could cover this aspect during the institutional state-level training.

This indicates a need to enhance the duration of institutional training through the state ATI and to correspondingly reduce the existing period of district training.

Presently, some ATIs are providing up to eight weeks of institutional training in two or three instalments, some arrange for one to two weeks of "Rajya Darshan" tour, and the remaining period is kept for district training. On the other extreme, in some states, the IAS probationers do not go to the ATI at all and spend the full year on district training.

It is suggested that at the all-India level there should be prescribed a uniform pattern comprising a period of 15 weeks of state-level training at the state ATI (or if no ATI exists in the state at any other state-level institute like, for example, the SIRD) and a period of 37 weeks for training in the district. Since some state-specific and state-level inputs, traditions and conventions are required to be imparted to IAS probationers when they first reach the state, the initial stay at the State ATI could be for 10 weeks. In many cases, the IAS probationers would want to be able to review and discuss their experiences during training in the field (district) and to link them with theoretical aspects. Thus, after 37 weeks of district training, the IAS probationers should again return to the state ATI for five weeks of further state-level training and also to appear at the state-level departmental and revenue laws examinations, which are prescribed for IAS probationers in most states.

The entire training at state ATI and in the district needs to be planned keeping in mind that now-a-days most IAS probationers are from IITs, IIMs or from engineering or medical backgrounds while in administration it is social science related skills and knowledge – political science, public administration, economics, sociology, psychology, organizational behaviour, development studies, rural development and law, etc. – which are more relevant.

Thus, the scheme for a 52-week state and district training of IAS probationers could be as follows (which is an indicative list which could be slightly modified from state to state to meet state-specific requirements provided that the broad framework is adhered to).

Institutional Training at State ATI - Phase I (10 weeks)

(i) Introduction to the state, its traditions, geography, special characteristics, system of administration and administrative culture, civil service traditions of the state, etc.

(ii) Calling on Governor, CM, CS, important functionaries and senior officers.

(iii) State-level laws, minor Acts.

(iv) Laws relating to Panchayati Raj, cooperatives, urban administration and municipalities.

(v) Land revenue system, land records, land reforms and revenue laws.

(vi) Analysis of the state economy and society – social mores and peculiarities of state, etc. The social sector, infrastructure development, agriculture and rural development, industrial development, water management, power, communications, etc.

(vii) State-specific personnel-related rules.

(viii) Financial management in the state: general financial and accounts rules, management of budget, audit, the treasury manual, purchase rules, etc.

(ix) Livelihoods and food security with special reference to the state.

(x) Welfare administration: state-specific issues.

(xi) Development administration: state-specific issues.

(xii) The Secretariat Manual and working procedures in the state secretariat and executive departments.

(xiii) Administrative innovations tried out in the state.

(xiv) Attachment to a secretariat or administrative department (one week).

(xv) Attachment to an executive or technical department (one week).

(xvi) Attachment to a state level public sector unit (three days).

(xvii) Bureaucracy-politician-media interactions.

(xviii) Important development programmes being implemented in the state.

(xix) State-specific law and order issues.

(xx) State-specific experiences of interactions with NGOs, CBOs and use of participatory approaches.

(xxi) Special interaction sessions with

  (a) two IAS officers of batches of the 1970s of the state cadre;

  (b) two IAS officers of batches of the 1980s of the state cadre;

  (c) two IAS officers of batches of the 1990s of the state cadre;

  (d) two IPS officers serving in the state; and

  (e) two retired IAS officers of the state cadre.

(xxii) Visit to state-level Agricultural University.

(xxiii) Visit to a research institute concentrating on development studies, social sciences in the state.

(xxiv) Visit to State Legislative Assembly (Vidhan Sabha) and knowledge of legislative practices.

(xxv) Capsule on how to conduct court work as well as administrative enquiries.

(xxvi) Capsule on dealing with assembly questions, Public Accounts Committee, etc. and with audit paras.

Towards the end of the Phase I of the Institutional Training at State ATI, the Director General, ATI, should hold a training of trainers workshop with the Collectors in whose districts the IAS probationers shall be going for district training and with the course coordinator of IAS probationers' training in ATI. What is expected from Collectors during the district training, as well as ideas that the Collectors have, based upon their administrative experience and the special features of their district, about what to include in respect to the training of the particular probationer in each district should be brainstormed thoroughly so that agreement is reached between State ATI and the Collectors (who would function as the district training coordinators) about how the district training for IAS probationers is to be arranged and imparted in the particular year.

District Training (37 weeks)

1. Attachment with
   - (i) Collectorate and its various sections
   - (ii) Superintendent of Police/Police Stations
   - (iii) District Judge/CJM
   - (iv) District-level officers of PWD, Irrigation, Forests, Transport, Food and Supplies, Agriculture, Animal Husbandry and Dairy, Education, Health, Industries, Cooperatives, Jails, Power, etc.
   - (v) Zila Parishad/DRDA/Special Development Projects
   - (vi) District Treasury
   - (vii) Patwari or Talati, Tehsildar or Mamlatdar, Tehsil Office, land survey and settlement staff
   - (viii) VLW or Gram Sevak, BDO or Vikas Adhikari, Panchayat Samiti
   - (ix) SDM
   - (x) Municipality and Urban Improvement Trust
   - (xi) District Milk Union
   - (xii) Industrial Estate developed by government or public sector undertaking
   - (xiii) Tribal Development Project
   - (xiv) Agriculture Produce Marketing Society
2. Independent charge for predetermined periods as
   - (i) BDO
   - (ii) Tehsildar
   - (iii) Assistant Collector and Executive Magistrate/Judicial Magistrate (under training)
   - (iv) CEO, Municipality
   - (v) CDPO in ICDS project
   - (vi) SDM
3. Visit to
   - (i) An NGO active in villages of district
   - (ii) A known CBO (community-based organization) or user group initiative of the district

(iii) Prominent animal fair/tourism fair of the district
(iv) Site of any disaster
(v) Police stations
(vi) Jail
(vii) Sites where important government schemes are being implemented
(viii) Drought relief works
(ix) Important public sector or private industrial unit in the district

4. Study of
   (i) District manual and system of district administration
   (ii) District vigilance and public grievances committee and its functioning
   (iii) Conduct of elections
   (iv) Major law and order incidents
   (v) Poverty alleviation and employment generation efforts
   (vi) District planning
   (vii) Land survey and settlement work
   (viii) Revenue laws
   (ix) Disaster management at the district level
   (x) Internal security efforts
   (xi) Crimes in the district and how they are handled
   (xii) Handling of law and order or communal incidents
   (xiii) Working of SDM
   (xiv) How Collector conducts meetings and tours
   (xv) The farming and livestock breeding systems prevalent in the district
   (xvi) Employment opportunities in the district
   (xvii) Handling VIP visits in the district
5. Throughout his/her stay in the district, an IAS probationer should be (a) undertaking revenue/executive magistrate/judicial magistrate court work including deciding some cases and writing final orders or judgements, and (b) working as officer incharge of various sections of Collectorate. The probationer should be made officer-incharge of various Collectorate sections in such a way that during his/her stay in the district he/she deals with matters pertaining to each and every section of the Collectorate.
6. Participating in any special government campaign that may be held during the period of district training.
7. Self-study based on training material provided by state ATI for the state-level departmental examinations to be conducted during

Phase II of the institutional training at the state ATI that would follow the completion of the district training.

During district training, the Director General of state ATI should visit each district where a probationer has been sent and discuss both jointly and separately with the Collector as well as the trainee the progress of the training and as to whether any additions or modifications should be considered in the district training even at this late stage.

Similarly, during the district training, the Internet and a web blog could be used to enable regular interaction between the probationers in the district and ATI faculty at the state headquarters.

Institutional Training at State ATI – Phase II (5 weeks)

The Phase II of institutional training at state ATI should concentrate on the following:

(a) Clarifying doubts that probationers may have about various issues, procedures and conventions observed during the district and field training.

(b) Sharing of field experiences.

(c) Providing theoretical and conceptual back-up (including state-specific viewpoints) to the practical ideas, knowledge, skills, etc., picked up by the probationers during the Phase I of institutional training at state ATI and also during the district training.

(d) Preparations and guidance (including some classes to refresh the probationer's knowledge) for the state-level departmental and revenue laws examination, which is to be conducted at the end of the Phase II of institutional training at state ATI.

Some of the interactive sessions to be organized during the Phase II should include those on:

1. The rural delivery system as it has evolved in the state.
2. Administrative issues related to service delivery, managing problems and facilitating well-planned development of small towns.
3. Public interest litigation and judicial activism.
4. Media, media activism, yellow journalism and positive use of the media.
5. Regional and caste/class politics in the state.
6. Ethical issues in state and district administration.
7. Trends of economic development in the state and its regions; potential for future development and vision for multi-faceted development of the state.
8. Government-CBO (community-based organization) interactions.

9. Multilateral/bilateral aid and funding agencies and how the state government/district administration interacts with them and reacts.
10. Poverty alleviation, employment generation and area development programmes in the context of the state.
11. Scope for administrative reforms in district administration/state administration.
12. Role of banks in state's development and growth.
13. Inter-ministerial/inter-departmental matters and coordination at the state and district levels.
14. How to make the state more competitive in the fast changing world so that it can grasp the opportunities being thrown up by globalization and technological breakthroughs, while simultaneously mitigating the adverse impacts.

The departmental and revenue law examinations held at the state government level presently differ from state to state. A common list of papers in which the departmental examination at state level should be prescribed with some indication about the syllabus for each paper; however, there should be scope for flexibility and the state ATI and the Training Department/Division in the respective state government should be free to finalize the syllabus in view of state-specific priorities, issues and problems that need to be reflected in the syllabus. The common list of papers in which the examination should be conduced in future are suggested as follows:

1. General Laws and Rules.
2. Revenue Administration, Revenue Laws and Land Reforms.
3. Financial and Personnel Administration (with specific reference to state rules and laws).
4. The Administrative Environment and Administrative Issues at State and District Levels.
5. Development and Welfare Administration.
6. Economic Environment and Planning at State and Lower Levels.

For the sake of comparison, the papers presently prescribed for IAS probationers in the State of Rajasthan for such examinations are listed below:

(a) General Laws and Rules
(b) Personnel Administration
(c) Financial Administration
(d) Revenue Administration
(e) Land Reforms
(f) Planning and Development

Naturally, some of the classes during both phases of institutional training at the state ATI would need to be geared up for preparing the IAS probationers for the examinations.

The state ATIs would also need to provide the probationers with copies of all important state Acts and rules as also with training monographs, descriptions of best practices, case studies, "how to" booklets, commentaries on state laws, rules and procedures, training reprints, copies of relevant published materials, etc. The IAS Syllabus Review Committee could consider recommending to DoPT, Government of India, to provide each state ATI between Rs 5 to 10 lakhs per year for a period of say three years to prepare training material both printed and online and to build up a small documentation cell for IAS probationers in the ATI library of each state.

Similarly, each state ATI should be provided central funds to conduct training of trainers workshops for ATI faculty and other selected resource persons who are proposed to be used as guest faculty before the start of each year's IAS probationers' training at the state ATI.

While state ATIs normally have computer labs and some computers in common places like library, computers are normally not provided in the hostel rooms used by IAS probationers or officers. Central assistance could be provided by DoPT for provision of computers and Internet linkage in, say, at least five rooms per ATI for use of IAS probationers.

The Government of India could also reimburse to ATIs the costs (salary, etc.) for the one person who would act as course coordinator in the ATI for IAS probationers' training along with one supporting staff for such course coordinator.

Throughout the 52 weeks of the state ATI and district training each IAS probationer undergoing training should be asked to send a fortnightly report to the Director General of the state ATI of the activities she/he underwent and his/her analysis and comments upon the same. This would enable the ATI to consider if any additional aspect needs to be covered during the state or district training.

It is hoped that implementation of the above recommendations, along with corresponding changes in the Foundation Course and both the phases of Professional Course at LBSNAA, would ensure that IAS direct recruits of tomorrow would be better prepared and equipped to face and overcome the challenges of the first ten or so years of their service.

References

Hooja, Rakesh and Meenakshi Hooja, 1995, "Increasing the Capability of the IAS: Emerging Issues and Challenges", in Hoshiar Singh (ed.), *Higher Civil Services in India,* Nirmal Book Agency, Kurukshetra.

Hooja, Rakesh, 1979, "HCMSIPA and LBSNAA: The Complementary Role of Training Institute in Training of IAS Regular Recruits", *Indian Journal of Training and Development,* Vol. 9, No. 4, July-August.

Hooja, Rakesh (ed.), 2006, *Induction Training of JAS Direct Recruits: Some Views,* Association of State Training Institutions in India (ASTI).

Puri, Anshu, 2005, *Making of an IAS: Role and Impact of Induction Training,* Aalekh Publishers, Jaipur.

Srinivas, V., 2000, "Direct Training for IAS Probationers: Emerging Scenarios", *ASTI Journal of Training and Development,* Vol. I, No. 1, January-June, being reproduced in this book as Chapter 4.

Section III

Training for Change

7 Management Development and Training

The Indian Experience

R.K. Mishra

The purpose of this chapter is to discuss, in the backdrop of the socio-economic and political scenario of India, the role of management development and training in the context of the economic challenges confronting the country today and the opportunities arising thereof, critically analyzing the status of management development and training at the levels of the government, public enterprises and private sector, and offer a few suggestions to radically transform the management development and training in India.

India was, at the time of independence, a socially, economically and politically underdeveloped nation. This state of affairs was the consequence of the exploitative regime of its colonial masters. Two hundred years of foreign rule sapped the entrepreneurial initiative. The incidence of poverty was very high. The industrial base was very small and unemployment was a characteristic feature of the economy. The Indian economy was in isolation from the rest of the world. The masses did not have access to formal education and professional training. There were a handful of universities, engineering and medical colleges and institutions imparting education at the graduate and postgraduate levels. The country was divided into British India and several princely states. The country became independent in 1947 and chose to function under the Constitution adopted in 1950 which laid emphasis on all-round human development.

In recent years, the stress on human development has been tremendously enhanced owing to the realization of the fact that the educational and professional development alone can bring about a socio-economic transformation capable enough to place the country in the category of developed nations. There is a commonly held view that this approach can take India out of the vicious circle of poverty and underdevelopment and make it technologically strong due to a continuous availability of scientific and industrial personnel.

Management Development and Training: The Indian and Global Contexts

It is common knowledge that management development and training are two sides of the same coin, viz., human resource development (HRD). However, some experts draw a fine line of distinction between the two.[1]

They assert that training is a short-term facet of HRD concerned with the development of present skills of a job and also the future skills that would help in its efficient execution. Management development, on the contrary, is a long-term and continuing phenomenon equipping a person with skills and concepts that could prepare him to take up new responsibilities and challenges.[2]

Table 1 shows the approaches that could be adopted for management development and training for the different layers of management.

Indian economy is no longer a traditional economy. Not only its structure is undergoing a decisive change but it is also inculcating the features of the new economy that are prevalent in highly developed countries such as the United States of America and Japan.

Until recently, India treated its human capital as inert stock on the same lines as accountants treat the fixed capital. But, influenced by the Japanese, the US, and more recently the Chinese and the ASEAN miracle in the early 1990s, the political view of the human capital underwent a paradigm shift. The government reconstituted its administrative set-up and carved out a new ministry of HRD with a full-fledged senior minister heading it, and the administrative support extended by a permanent secretary. The central idea behind the creation of the ministry was to provide the government an integrated view of the human resources available in the country and plan and implement suitable schemes and systems to upgrade/increase the supply of human resources commensurate with their requirements for the development of the country, to meet the present and the future challenges.

Table 1 ***Approaches for Management Development and Training***

Global Visits for Sensiti-zation	Seminars and Con-ferences	Attach-ment to Eminent Institutions/ Experts	Round Table	Self-Study	Refre-sher Courses	Under Study Method	Formal Training	On-the-Job Training
Area of Impor-tance		Top Manage-ment						
		Senior Manage-ment						
					Junior Manage-ment			

A study of the key ratios relating to management development and training, forming a major part of the HRD, shows that the training and management development expenditure per employee in US dollar terms was 960 in Europe, 531 in Canada, 386 in Japan and 650 in USA. Of payroll it was 3 per cent in Europe, 1.5 per cent in Canada, 1 per cent in Japan and 1.8 per cent in the USA. The employee to trainer ratio was 257:1 in Asia and Pacific, 504:1 in Canada, 1706:1 in Japan and 400:1 in USA. The percentage of employees receiving training was 75.5 in Europe, 68.9 in Canada, 44.9 in Japan and 75 in the USA. The payment made to outside experts/training institutions as percentage of total expenditure was 45.4 in Europe, 27 in Canada, 31 in Japan and 27 in USA. The Indian proportions are minuscule and do not deserve any mention. This can be seen in the context of the expenditure on HRD as a percentage of GDP. While USA and France spend about 20 per cent of their GDP on HRD and a small country such as Belgium spends about 40 per cent on HRD, India pledged to spend a mere 6 per cent of GDP on HRD in 1986. Currently, it spends only 3 per cent of its GDP on HRD. All these countries spent about 1 to 4 per cent of their turnover on training and management development. They have integrated their management development and training activities with the primary, secondary and higher education. Motorola, a US-based company, spends about $1 billion on management development and training. The company proposes to hike this outlay. On an average, each employee spends about 160 hours per year on training. The company has set up a university and has adopted 32 districts in the USA to upgrade the standards of education. In Japan, informal management development and training is more widespread as compared to the formal, on-the-job and off-the-job training and management development as existing in India. An average Japanese employee spends about a 100 hours in training per year. Technologically, an average Japanese employee is conversant with the use of CD-ROM, e-mail and company Internet, although to a lesser extent than the average the US employee. It is claimed that India is emerging as an IT superpower. However, an average Indian employee is wide off the mark as compared to the US and Japanese employees.

The global competition, initiation of economic reforms and the country's ambition to join ranks with the developed countries require that its existing approach to management development and training should undergo a fundamental change as explained below in Table 2.

India is opening up. The challenges of opening up provide a wide range of opportunities subject to the acquisition of relevant skills, competencies and concepts. The management development and training in the pre-reform era of 1947–1991 required limited innovation and thinking dealing with the needs of internal progression within the organizations and the methods and techniques that could increase the production and productivity of workers and supervisors on the shop floor or offices. The present-day concept of management development and training envelopes an all-round development covering the needs of the individual, team, organization and society.

Table 2 ***Transition of Management Development and Training in India***

From	*To*
Conservative	Liberal
Specific	Generic
Functional	Cross-functional
Hierarchical	Participative
Periodic	Continuous
Risk Aversion	Risk-taking
Formal	Informal
Traditional	Modern and Topical
Unsystematic	Systematic
General	Goal-oriented
Closed	Open

Cont'd...

Cont'd...

Skill-based and Narrow	Concept-based and Comprehensive
Static	Dynamic
Ad hoc	Planned
Structured	Customized
Inorganic	Organic
Directed	Environment-driven

Status of Management Development and Training

The Indian economy is composed of three important organs: government, public sector and private sector. In this section, an attempt has been made to analyze the status of management development and training as related to these three organs.

Government

There are three levels of Indian administration – central, state and local. These three levels employ about 20 million personnel. At the central level, there are four classes of employees, viz., Group A, B, C and D employees. Group C and D employees provide support services to officers of Group A and B services which are 29 in number and of which the first 12 fall within the scope of the Group A and are considered to be the top-most central services.

For Group A personnel, recruitment is done by the Union Public Service Commission (UPSC) and the foundation training is imparted by the Lal Bahadur Shastri Academy of Administration, Mussoorie. The Department of Personnel and Training (DoPT) deals with continuous training of the officers of the Indian Administrative Service, which number around 6,000. A total of 83 institutions of higher learning and research have been identified to provide advanced training in policy, general management, functional management and technology areas. The advanced training varies from one to three weeks and is optional in nature. The government provides for the entire expenditure. There are some courses which are vertical in nature and admit participants of all the seniorities whereas other courses are demarcated for officers having a certain minimum experience of service. The central government officials are provided slots for management development and training under schemes such as the Colombo Plan which entitled them to receive education in management and undergo advanced training in general and functional management. They are also entitled for fellowship awards allocated by foreign countries. The state governments have also set up their own training institutions which train the officials drawn from the different services mostly selected by the State Public Service Commissions. These state institutes are funded by the state governments but receive a generous support from the central government. The local governments do not provide management development training opportunities to their employees as their own funding is very trivial.

The budget for management development and training is minuscule and the areas covered are negligible. The training needs are not taken into consideration. The behavioural training is the most important requirement which gets scant attention. The training in technology is another important need of the hour. Some states of the Indian Union have caught up with the idea and have taken up programmes in e-governance. Andhra Pradesh, Karnataka, Tamil Nadu and Maharashtra are making rapid strides in this regard. The central government in line with the move of these states has also started imparting training programmes in e-governance to its employees in select departments. The Subordinate Staff Selection Services Commission of the central government conducts a large number of training programmes for employees in the cadre of the section officers.

The salaries and wages as a percentage of the GDP for the country as a whole, as related to the central and state governments, is about 12 per cent. The money spent on management development and training is a meagre 0.1 per cent. The number of hours devoted to management development and training is less than one per year. Vast sections of the government employees, specially in the Groups C and D and constituting about 90 per cent, do not get any opportunity for management development. Their training is limited only to induction training.

Management Development and Training in Public Enterprises

There are about 1,400 public enterprises at the central, state and local levels organized principally in the form of government companies, statutory corporations, departmental enterprises, commissions, authorities, boards, mixed corporations and port trusts. These employ about six million personnel. The investment in these enterprises is about US $120 billion. The salaries and wages in these enterprises constitute 12 per cent of their turnover which may be as much as US $120 billion. The expenses on management development and training are only 0.5 per cent of the turnover.

Features

Management development and training is an important activity in public enterprises which is discernible from the following features:

1. There is a definite direction existing in relation to management development and training in public enterprises. The Department of Public Enterprises, Government of India and the nodal agencies in state level public enterprises have their respective policies incorporating guidelines on themes to be covered, types and number of training programmes to be conducted, duration of programmes and the resource persons to be deployed. The policy also covers items such as the remuneration for the resource persons and the evaluation of the training programmes.
2. In the management structure, at the board level, invariably the function is represented by Director(Personnel), who in turn is supported by Executive Director (Personnel)/General Manager (Personnel), Deputy General Manager (Personnel), Assistant General Manager (Personnel), Senior Manager (Personnel), Executive (Personnel), Personnel Officer, etc. In many a case, General Manager (Training) is appointed as in-charge of the training function. In other words, management development and training is a high level function in public enterprises. The state-level public enterprises also accord high importance to this function though in many such enterprises it is not placed at the level of General Manager due to consideration of size.
3. Separate budget provisions are earmarked for this function although they are very minuscule as related to turnover and expenses incurred on wages and salaries.
4. In terms of hardware, separate space is allocated for the functionaries dealing with management development and training, equipment provided and support structure created in terms of assistance, transport facilities, etc. It may, however, be noted that the quality of budget support and assistance differs widely from enterprise to enterprise.
5. A training needs survey is carried out once in 5 to 6 years on the basis of which a training calendar is formulated. The operating departments and the management services department/corporate strategy department are approached for obtaining appropriate inputs. Small changes are carried out in the training calendar depending on the feedback of the participants. The major gaps in different areas for the three levels of management are given in Table 3.

Table 3 *Managerial Levels*

Gap Areas	*Top/Senior*	*Middle*	*Junior*
Knowledge	Technology	Procedural Knowledge	Implementing Knowledge
Skills	Conceptualization Planning	Analytical/ Adaptive	Executive Skills
Attitude	Towards Environment	Logical	Towards Work and Organization
Performance	Target Setting	Application and Skills	Appraisal and Recognition
Policy	International Scenario and Public Policy	Sensitization	Nil

6. Training programmes for workers, supervisors and junior executives are organized in-house. For the middle level personnel, the programmes are also arranged in-house with a mix of internal and external faculty. For senior and top level personnel, slots are provided for training in external institutions and abroad.
7. Induction training/foundation training is a rule rather than exception. The period of the training varies from six months to two years at this level.
8. About 40 large central public enterprises such as Bharat Heavy Electricals Ltd., Steel Authority of India Ltd., National Thermal Power Corporation, Coal India Ltd., Electronics Corporation of India Ltd., Mishra Dhatu Nigam Ltd., Bharat Dynamics Ltd., Hindustan Aeronautics Ltd. and HMT Ltd., have set up their own in-house training institutes. These provide training to senior managers in general management, middle/junior managers in functional areas of management and specialized courses to senior and top managers in total quality management, quality circles, memorandum of understanding and corporate planning. These in-house institutes also run Junior Management Induction Programmes.
9. At the state level, in-house training institutes are also created by the state electricity boards and the state road transport corporations. The state financial corporations and the state industrial development corporations also take up the management development training activities on systematic basis, though they do not have their own in-house training institutions. For example, in

Rajasthan, training of PSU personnel is conducted at the Centre for Management Studies of the HCM Rajasthan State Institute of Public Administration.

10. The public sector banks form the lifeline of the financial system in the country. There are in all about 90 banks excluding the cooperative banks. Most of these banks have their own training departments. The large banks such as the State Bank of India, Punjab National Bank, Central Bank of India, Bank of Baroda, Andhra Bank have their own in-house training institutes.[3] In a study conducted by Mishra and Ravishankar[4] about the Human Resource Development in State Bank of India, the largest commercial bank and one of the Fortune 500 companies with a sample of officers numbering 850 in senior/middle management cadres, it was noted that there was an urgent need to develop technical and managerial skills and bring about attitudinal changes in the work behaviour of the executives. The linkage of the training with the operation process of the bank was not complete. The deputation of trainees to a programme was not always on grounds of actual needs. Much subjectivity operated in the field. The managers at operational level felt that deputing personnel for training interface with the operation does not work. Moreover, the skills imparted and the change brought in the behaviour of the trainees fade out quickly and regression sets in once they face the operational realities and mounting scepticism from their colleagues. With the integration of information technology and banking operations, the banking training institutes have to now prepare a new syllabus. In fact, the experience emanating even from a country like the USA reveals that the bank personnel would like to redefine their operations and needs in view of information technology. They feel that the running of large number of training programmes is a mere waste of time. What they need today is an intensive understanding of information technology which can keep them relevant in the society.

Evaluation of Hyderabad Based In-house Training Institutes

Recognizing the importance of management development and training, 40 public enterprises have set up in-house training institutes, of which 10 are located in Hyderabad. The evaluation of these institutes in terms of faculty, infrastructure, library, research and consultancy, financial sources and composite score is given below in Table 4:

Table 4 ***Evaluation of Public Enterprises***

Name	Faculty	Infra structure	Library	Research/ Consultancy	Financial Sources	Total Score	Overall Rating*
Electronics Corporation of India Ltd.	1	4	2	1	3	11	Somewhat Acceptable
Mishra Dhatu Nigam Ltd.	1	2	2	1	2	8	Somewhat Low
Indian Drugs and Pharmaceutical Ltd.	1	1	1	1	1	5	Very Low
Bharat Heavy Electrical Ltd.	3	5	3	2	3	16	Acceptable
Bharat Dynamics Ltd.	1	3	2	1	3	10	Somewhat Low
Hindustan Aeronautics Ltd.	3	3	3	2	3	14	Acceptable
Hindustan Machine Tools Ltd.	2	2	2	1	3	10	Somewhat Low
Hindustan Cables Ltd.	1	2	1	1	2	7	Somewhat Low
Indian Airlines	2	5	2	1	3	13	Somewhat Acceptable

*Scale (Based on Total Score): 0= Poor, 3.5= Very Low, 7= Somewhat Low, 10.5= Somewhat Acceptable, 14= Acceptable, 17.5= Good and 21 =Very Good.

The reasons for nominations to the courses sponsored by the in-house training institutes point out that they do not conduct need-based training. Of the 500 executives who were trained by these institutes, it was revealed that 8 per cent were sponsored as per the training needs identified in annual assessment, 15 per cent due to changes in job content, 12 per cent due to initiative of the trainees who intended to upgrade their capabilities, 25 per cent to fulfil training quotas, 15 per cent to pacify their wishes of being sent for external training and the remaining 25 per cent did not know as to why they attended the training. Regarding the actual benefits from the training, 29 per cent felt that there was nothing worth mentioning about it and even a larger percentage felt that it was a retreat from the company work. Only 15 per cent felt that the training helped them in sensitization to changing roles and the remaining 21 per cent perceived that the training gave them new knowledge, skills and attitudes. The applicability/usefulness of the programmes was rated at 2.8 on a scale of 1 to 5.

Department of Public Enterprises

The Department of Public Enterprises (DPE) is the nodal agency for central public enterprises. One of its divisions deals exclusively with management development and training. It does get directly involved in these activities but operated through a network of about 75 institutions for the conduct of training programmes ranging from one day to one year. It organized training programmes on topical themes, functional areas and general management. The management hierarchy is given due consideration. It does not provide any financial help, faculty support and infrastructure assistance to the training institutes. It organizes a meeting on an annual basis of the training heads and sensitizes them about the training needs. On the basis of decisions arrived at in the meeting, a training calendar is prepared. The DPE issues a forwarding letter for each training programme which has to be dispatched by the respective institutes. In 1983, the DPE initiated an advanced management programme (AMP)[5] for general managers/assistant general managers/executive directors who could take over superior positions within the enterprise or shift horizontally. The AMP exposes the top level executives to emerging trends in management of enterprises as well as to the state-of-the-art management techniques in India and abroad. The DPE has conducted 34 AMPs between 1983 and 1999 with the premier management institutes such as the Administrative Staff College of India, Hyderabad, IIM, Ahmedabad, IIM, Kolkata and IIM, Bangalore. Recently, they have approached the Institute of Public Enterprise, which provided the initial inputs on AMP when it was being conceived in the early 1980s. The DPE also nominates a few public enterprise executives at the senior/middle levels to MBA programme run by the University of Hull (UK). In addition, executives have been recommended for training by DPE to Germany, Singapore, Japan and USA. The DPE's administrative approach and indifference to management development and training has not done any good to this very important instrument. A number of training programmes sponsored by the institute get cancelled/postponed. A large part of the remaining ones are unable to muster even a respectable number of participants.

Management Development and Training in Private Enterprises

Bitten by the globalization bug, the public sector is on the wane and a new private-public sector mix is emerging in which the public sector is required to play a supportive role. The private sector is on the growth path. It has a formidable challenge to reorganize its human resources to rise to the occasion. Family business will no more help a private sector enterprise to grow. Moreover, private sector has to move from old economy to new economy where owners and employees will be subordinated by the enterprise. The private sector, having taken a leaf out of the change book, is now going for employee stock ownership scheme, employee stock options, greater representation to the employees on the board and professionalization. Nevertheless, it has to be admitted squarely that the status of management development and training in private enterprise is no better than the public enterprise.

Some big business houses such as the Tatas (they run the Tata Management Centre), Birlas (they run the Birla Management Centre), Reliance (they run the Reliance Management Academy) and Kirloskars (they run Harihar Institute of Management) have their own academies catering to the needs of top and senior level personnel. Some business houses have set up management institutes/universities to integrate the requirement of management development and training with undergraduate education. These include the Tatas who have a major say in the running of Xavier's Labour Relations Institute and Institute of Management Technology and the Birlas (Birla Institute of Science and Technology). Recently, some big business houses in India with the support of the Andhra Pradesh government and in collaboration with Kellogg Institute of Management have set up an International Business School at Hyderabad which will impart education in management for MBA degree and doctoral degree. Though there is a technology boom in India and the TMT (Technology-Media-Telecom) business is on the rise, it has not led to any increased commitment to management development and training. Even Infosys, Wipro, Himachal Futuristic Communications, Bharati Telecom, Zee Tele, etc., have no academies of their own. Satyam Computers Ltd., a leading infotech enterprise, plans to provide a bold relief in this regard as it is in the process of setting up an e-business academy with a proposed investment of US $0.1 billion.

The All India Council of Technical Education (AICTE), Government of India has seen to the setting up of 700 management institutes in the private sector with an intake of 30,000 students per annum for MBA courses. A survey on the quality of education and infrastructure of these institutes point to a number of gaps. The private sector has not taken much interest in developing these institutes which is reinforced by the fact that some of the business houses have used these institutes as milch cow.

The private sector cannot make any meaningful beginning on the management development and training front unless it changes its philosophy of scouting for human resources afresh for meeting a challenge rather than developing the existing personnel.

Future Directions

The country has to change both its perception and approach to management development and training as explained hereunder:

1. The percentage of expenditure of GDP on education needs to be stepped up significantly, say, at least to 10 per cent. Some innovative methods and techniques may have to be evolved for financing the enhanced outlay. More importantly, the development strategists have to reformulate their preferences assigning a higher weightage to software rather than hardware. In line with the USA, Germany and France, the primary, secondary and higher education have to be integrated with the needs of management development and training.

   The Singapore experience needs a special mention here. It has set up a Skills Development Fund (SDF). Employers are required to contribute 1 per cent of their gross salary and wage bill to the fund. The companies get the value of their contributions back upto 80 per cent if they apply to SDF for grants for enhancement of skills and management development. They may also buy out of these grants more than training equipment, establish training facilities, spend money on overseas training or expand the existing facilities of training. The employers wanting to have access to the SDF submit the total training plan. Experience shows that the grants awarded are twice the amount initially requested. The fund has contributed towards modernizing the training establishments, infusing new skills and upgrading the conceptual abilities of executives aged 40 years and above. The fund has also been accessed for general development and to ensure continuity in competence of a cluster of industries which are globally competitive.
2. The public enterprises need to step up their outlay on management development and training. The number of hours devoted should be gradually increased from the present 10 to 100. The expenditure needs to be doubled from 0.5 per cent of the turnover to 1 per cent. The in-house training institutes have to tone up their work. The training contents must accommodate the inputs dealing with globalization, technology management, international business, quality management, cost leadership, enhancement of market share, improving interpersonal skills, team building[6], counselling, knowledge management, creativity and performance appraisal to mention a few. The training needs survey in each enterprise should provide for multi-skilling and the possibility of development of the

executives in diverse areas. Management development and training must cut across all the levels[7] including the top management, i.e., public enterprise boards.

3. The private sector, in order to gain tremendously to be globally competitive through a leading edge, must exploit the potent tool of management development and training. Instead of looking for new people to fulfil the requirements of the changes in a job, they should impart new skills well in advance to their existing employees. The minuscule expenditure and time spent on management development and training by the private sector will not go a long way in its professionalization.

To sum up, it can be stated that management development and training will play a significant role in the socio-economic and political emancipation of India, especially in the changed context of globalization. Bitten by the globalization bug, the government, public sector and private sector are redefining their vision of management development and training. Although the management development and training function has not made significant headway so far, the country is now well set to undergo a paradigm shift in this direction.

Notes

1. Alan Mumford, *Management Development: Strategies for Action,* Jaico, Mumbai, 1995, p.7.
2. N.K. Singh, *Human Resource Development in Indian Public Sector,* Standing Conference of Public Enterprises, New Delhi, 1987, p.10.
3. Anil K. Khandelwal (ed.), *Human Resources Development in Banks,* Oxford and IBH, New Delhi, 1995, pp.377–466.
4. R.K. Mishra, and S. Ravishankar, *Organisational Development in Public Enterprises: Perspectives for 1990s,* Vision Books, New Delhi, 1989, pp. 125–30.
5. Government of India (Department of Public Enterprises, Ministry of Heavy Industries and Public Enterprises), *PE Survey: 1998–99,* Vol. 1, 2000, New Delhi, pp. 132–35.
6. S. Ravishankar, "Training and Management Development for Higher Productivity", in Satish Pai, R.K. Mishra and S. Ravishankar (eds), *Reengineering Organisational Productivity, Challenges Ahead,* Himalaya, Mumbai, 2000.
7. Rolf P. Lynton and Udai Pareek, *Training for Development,* Vistaar, New Delhi., 1990, p.8.

8 Training for Behavioural Change

Udai Pareek

Training for behavioural change requires a different orientation compared to the traditional orientation to training and education. In addition to considering the major dimensions of training *per se,* it would be necessary to pay attention to some overall considerations without which training may only remain a ritual, and may not result in effective change of behaviour. The purpose of this paper is to draw attention to some such general considerations and implications for specific training strategies to stimulate discussion on these aspects.

General Considerations

The following aspects need to be considered by the organizations or institutions which are interested in designing training for behavioural change. Behavioural change is for a purpose and goes beyond the learning of principles and being intellectually convinced about the desirability of some behaviour. It should result in actual change of behaviour.

1. *Emphasis on and awareness of values:* Behavioural change involves change in values. Training which professes to be value-free is likely to run into difficulties because no behavioural change can be produced in vacuum. Any change in behaviour, in fact, attempts to bring about change in the underlying value. It would be necessary for those who are responsible for training to be aware of the current values underlying a particular behaviour, and changed behaviour, so that strategies can be evolved to move from one value system to another. Further, the training should also help participants become aware of such a process of change. It serves two purposes. In the first place, training, instead of degenerating into brainwashing, liberates the participants by making them aware through what Paulo Freire calls 'conscientization'. The participants then make a conscious choice of such a movement. In the

second place, this awareness may help participants see the need, relevance and context of the change being brought about. It is also necessary that persons responsible for training also examine their own value systems, and how they are operating and whether there is enough congruence between the values they want to emphasize for behavioural change and the values they practise in their own organization. This seems to be particularly important in India where coexistence of values preached and quite opposite values being practised is not infrequent.

2. *Congruity in the training organization:* Like examining the values being emphasized as well as practised in the training organization, training organizations should also have a hard look at such congruence at other levels, like the types of behaviour being emphasized and the types of behaviour shown in the institution itself. The way the training institution runs, and the way people in the training institution behave with each other and with participants, communicates and influences much more than what may be taught there. Congruence should be attempted in the organizational and administrative practices and the values and behaviour being emphasized. Similarly, congruence between values and behaviour on the one hand and the way of living of people in the institution on the other would also be important. Training in how to work with the poor or self-help, being given in a posh air-conditioned setting, is an example of lack of conformity. The entire climate should reinforce the messages which are emphasized in the training itself.
3. *Building linkages with organizations and society:* Since training for behavioural change has to be for a purpose, the training organization or institution should necessarily build strong linkages with those organizations and communities from which the participants come for training. The linkages should not be only in the form of casual and occasional visits. Organizations and communities should not overburden the facilities of the training institutions, but attempts should be made to draw on the resources of those organizations and communities. Active participation should be sought from them in building curriculum, examining the needs for change, developing a programme of training strategy to maximize the effects of training, developing strategies for follow-up and providing support so that behavioural changes can be sustained later on.
4. *Relationship of mutuality with the participants:* Training for behavioural change can be attained only through a process of mutual growth. The basic approach should be to create a situation in which all those who are involved influence each other, and the process of

learning is shared, rather than being monopolized only by one section of people. Freire stresses this point by emphasizing that the participants should not be treated as objects but as subjects. The teachers and trainers should equally be prepared, open for and look forward to learning from the participants. It is only in such a climate that training can be effective in producing behavioural changes.

5. *Use of modular approach:* In order to increase the effectiveness of training, minimum concentration of a package which produces behavioural change has to be achieved. Experience and research have shown that without such minimum concentration, the change cannot be produced and sustained. Thus, depending on what kind of behavioural changes are being attempted, various modules can be prepared, and different training programmes can have different combinations of such modules. This approach also ensures that a particular package or a module is self-contained and is planned in such a way that the objectives are achieved to which both the sequencing and concentration of the various items contribute.
6. *Emphasis on experience, experiment and practice:* Behavioural change cannot be achieved unless the person is able to both experience and experiment. For a person to learn to swim, it is necessary for him to get into the water and experience the act of swimming and practise swimming so that he may be able to behave differently in water. This is true for all kinds of behavioural changes. Experiencing helps the person to make a choice; experimenting helps him to seek feedback and make a choice; and practice helps to internalize what he has chosen so that it becomes a part of his regular work and way of life.
7. *Establishing innovative tradition:* For a training organization interested in producing behavioural change, it is necessary that it has innovative character and is prepared to examine critically the experiences it has been having, and reviewing these experiences to bring about necessary changes. This kind of renewal is necessary for the institution also in addition to this being emphasized as an important value for behavioural change.
8. *Developing self-renewing system:* Not only should the training institution establish self-renewing mechanisms within its own system, it should also build and develop them in the client organization. The relationship of dependency on the training institution should cease as soon as possible. It is, therefore, necessary that the training institution works out a strategy of such termination and setting up of monitoring and self-renewing system for follow-up and sustained behavioural changes.

9. *Participation in action:* When we talk of behavioural changes, we are referring mainly to changes in an organized system. This may be a family or a work organization like school, factory, office, etc. Most of the time people work in such organized sectors. If changes are to be planned for persons belonging to such organized systems, it is necessary, as already stated above (pt. 3), that linkages be built between the training institution and the client system. These linkages should go beyond merely getting the help of the client system in designing programmes or arranging follow-up and reinforcement. The training institution should take active part in diagnosing problems, solving problems, and take some responsibility for effectiveness of such an effort. Without such direct experience, the capability of the training organization to work on behavioural change will be highly limited. This is being done through what is usually known as consulting work or institution building work in some organizations. Training cannot be effective without the trainer's participation in such specific problems-solving activities.

Training Inputs

Training for behavioural change has three main phases: pre-training phase, training phase, and post-training phase. These have been dealt with in detail by Lynton and Pareek. Each phase has implications for what needs to be done at the level of the training institution or at the level of the client organization. Briefly, these phases are described as under:

(a) *Pre-training phase:* Pre-training phase is concerned with necessary motivation of the person to learn from training and to use the training experience to maximum extent to try out and learn new behaviour. This phase can be made very productive by emphasizing four things: (i) dissatisfaction with the present state of affairs; (ii) hope that something can be done to remove such dissatisfaction; (iii) perception that resources are available to use for working on the problems; and (iv) self-motivation to change in order to remove the dissatisfaction and increase satisfaction.

(b) *Training phase I (behavioural inputs)*: During the training phase of programmes, which are meant to influence and change behaviour, the following conditions should be fulfilled for an effective training programme: (i) helping the participants experience various phenomena during the training programme; (ii) helping them to experiment with their behaviour; (iii) helping them to seek feedback on the experiments they perform; (iv) helping them to give feedback to other participants; such feedback should be useful and effective; and (v) helping them to use feedback which may help them to accept change. These conditions can be achieved by necessary inputs by the training institute.

(c) *Training phase II (to support inputs):* In addition to the conditions to be fulfilled in making training effective for behavioural change, some substantive inputs are also necessary and some other conditions should be fulfilled for making use of the opportunities the participants get. These would include: (1) some knowledge about the various theories underlying what is being done and attempted in training so that the participants may be able to build conceptual linkages on which experiences and skill in training can hang; (ii) helping them to understand linkages between the experiences they have and the theories which are discussed; (iii) helping them to understand the linkages between what is done during training and what actually exists in life; and (iv) utilizing their desire to belong to valuable reference groups. In fact, such reference groups should also be developed.

Table 1 ***Training Inputs Relevant to Factors of Behavioural Change in an Individual***

Factors at Individual Level	*Training Inputs*
(a) *Pre-training*	
Dissatisfaction	Feedback on behaviour through instruments; exposure to mass media describing alternative forms.
Hope	Exposure to how things have been done elsewhere.
Perception of resources	Image building of the institute.
Motivation to change	Pre-training activities like microlab, training (or learning) group, etc.
(b) *(i) Behavioural Training*	
Experiencing	Less lectures, more simulation exercises and games.
Experimenting	Opportunities for experiments, like role playing, field work.
Seeking feedback	Climate of psychological safety; organized periodical feedback exercise.
Giving feedback	Same as above.
Using feedback for change	Emphasis on action planning; concurrent evaluation with emphasis on behaviour.
(ii) Training support	
Knowledge of theory	Concept sessions; self-study.
Understanding linkages of experience and theory	Concept sessions with discussions.

Cont'd...

Cont'd...

Understanding linkages of these with actual life	Sharing of experience by insightful guest speakers.
Desire to belong	Helping set up an association or study circle in the client setting.
(c) *Post-training*	
Continued experimenting and learning	Preparation of action plans at the end of training.
Examination and change	Refresher and follow-up programmes.
Self-monitoring	Designing such programmes at the end of formal training.

(d) *Post-training:* Training for behavioural change cannot end with what happens during the formal training programmes. Strong linkages should be built even after the formal training is over with the participants and their client systems. Post-training aspects would include the following as far as individual participants are concerned: (a) their desire to continue to try and experiment; (b) their inclination to examine their behaviour, styles and values and change through experimentation; and (c) their self-monitoring skill so that they are able to use resources needed at various stages of change, and are able to continue to grow. The various inputs are shown in Table 1. In the first column are listed various dimensions of training inputs as far as the individual participant is concerned and in the second column are given the implications for training institutions. The training institution should ensure that the various conditions are achieved both at its own level as well as at the level of client organization. Such a collaborative approach can bring about effective change in the behaviour.

In short, training for behavioural change requires reorientation of attitudes of people who are involved in training, redesigning of the system and organization sponsoring such training, reformulation of strategies of training with necessary linkages with various systems, and ensuring effective partnership with those for whom such training is meant. The last one is extremely important. Unless the training organization has genuine respect for the users, the resources available with the participants, training for behavioural change cannot be effective.

9 Training for Organizational Change

Neeraj Gupta

In past few decades, we have witnessed some exceptional and incredible kinds of changes. From international to the local level, there has been a sea change in our environment: Berlin Wall was pulled down after the German unification; end of the Cold War resulted in disintegration of Soviet bloc into many smaller nations, which have strong armament including atomic power; and European Union has emerged as a unified force tilting the economic centre of gravity of the globe. Likewise, in the East, many nations emerged as tigers but after a few years ended up purring like a domestic cat. World got together to sign a trade treaty. Advancements in information technology and transportation technology have made this earth a global village. Today, globalization, liberalization and privatization have become buzzwords. Many more such changes in the environment affecting organizations have happened before us. Not only have these environmental changes been more rapid but also the nature of changes has become more complex. Environmental changes have forced organizations to a corner where they have only two options: to either change or perish.

In today's turbulent environment, the success of any organization lies in changing itself holistically to meet the market demands and effectively managing the change process. The top management has to play a crucial role in terms of interpreting environmental signals, making strategic changes ensuring that transitional phase of organizational change is smooth and organizational members willingly embrace change. Such changes cannot be sustained unless accepted by the organizational members. All this requires substantial amount of learning and attitudinal change at all levels through training. In present-day chaotic environment which threatens the very existence of the organizations, there is only one way to survive both at the individual as well as organizational levels – continuous learning and updating to face the challenges posed by the external and internal environments. This is possible only through systematic training.

Training of organizational members is, thus, important so that they acquire knowledge and skills to manage change while maintaining a positive attitude towards the change process. Since change affects all cross-sections of the organization, training for change must encompass all its members from the top management to cutting-edge level functionaries. In this paper, we will briefly discuss, in a generic manner, issues concerning change, implications of change for organizational members, role of different levels of management in the change process and training for organizational change.

Organizational Change

On change, Peter F. Drucker says that in a period of rapid structural change, the only organizations that survive are the 'change leaders'. It is, therefore, a central 21st century challenge for the management that its organization becomes a change leader ... Being a change leader requires willingness and ability to change what is already being done just as much as the ability to do new and different things. It requires policies and practices that make the present create the future."[1]

To survive in the future, holistic changes may be required in the organizations. The concept of organizational change is in regard to organization-wide change, as opposed to smaller changes such as adding a new person, modifying a programme etc. It might include a change in mission, restructuring operations, new technologies, mergers, major collaborations, rightsizing, new programmes such as Total Quality Management, re-engineering etc.[2]

Organizational changes are product of two forces for change: the organization's top managers and the organization's environment.[3] Usually, external forces drive organizations to change, e.g., change in government policies, emergence of new markets, takeover threats, technological changes leading to product obsolescence, etc. Results of A. D. Chandler studies on American firms suggest that in the early part of 20th century, majority of the firms did not really manage change but were rather managed by it. Changes in the external environment forced changes in the external strategy and these in turn forced changes in the pace of internal configuration. Later, because of the accelerating environmental change, many organizations began to develop know-how to manage change through anticipation and preparing for it. Earlier, the focus was on external strategy due to the belief that the internal structures of the organizations did not require change and that new strategies could be chosen to capitalize on organization's inherent strengths and avoid its weaknesses. However, it has since become increasingly clear that in the present tumultuous environment, both the external strategy and the internal structure need to be changed substantially. Today, the change managers are not only concerned about the strategy to be developed to enable organizations to succeed in a changing environment, but also with the kind of structure to be installed to support the strategy and how to ensure a smooth transition from one structure to another. The nature of change is becoming more and more complex and turbulent. In fact, the change itself is changing.

The fast changing nature of today's organizational environment is largely a consequence of two factors: (i) the increasing effectiveness of information technology (both communication technology and computing technology), and (ii) the increasing effectiveness of transportation technology.[4] Increasing complexity and turbulence in the organizational environment makes it imperative that organizational processes change. This means that decision-making must be more frequent, decision implementation must be more rapid, information acquisition must be continuous and wide ranging, information distribution must be more directed and organizational learning must be more managed.[5]

Organizational change is, however, not a one-time activity. Successful change is a continuous journey of learning, growing and improving. However, organizational change is not easy for it affects people and they tend to resist. Understanding change and its effect on people and the organization is essential for successfully managing change. It can help in minimizing the disruptive aspects of the change process. Developing skills to plan for, manage, and cope with change is essential for survival of organizations.

Need for Training

Organizations are required to change in the wake of increasing competition, economic crisis, structural adjustment, technological innovation and many other external forces. Organizations must continuously learn to keep pace with the long-term process of development. These requirements have created a need for training for organizational members who both understand and can contribute to organizational change and development.

Various factors affect performance of an individual at workplace.[6] Employees must have a clear picture of the organizational objectives, people must be able to engage in behaviours that are necessary to achieve the objectives despite the changing circumstances and environmental disturbances. There must be adequate feedback mechanism, which gives information about actual conditions in relation to intended results so that corrective measures can be taken. There must be adequate motivation for employees to perform and the organizational environment should have an enabling effect on the performance. All these factors have a strong bearing on the training systems in the organization. Making planned efforts towards systematic training and creation of suitable environment for learning by the employees is thus crucial for successful organizational change. Management must also carefully isolate training and non-training interventions. It must be remembered that training is not a panacea of all organizational ills. If the organization's environment is not supportive of the empowered employee, it may lead to frustration and may end in increased employee turnover. A learning employee needs to be nurtured by the organization more so during the transitional phase.

Alan Down, writing in *Training* magazine, has suggested that the key employee trait in the 21st century will be willingness to learn. With it employees will be more likely to adapt as their jobs change and to experience change as a challenge to be mastered. They will flex and grow, thereby ensuring their own success and success of the organization.[7] Employees must be both willing and able to perform in the changed environment, which essentially means that they must be educated about new designs and empowered so that they can work more effectively and are willing to assume the responsibilities and burdens of change.

Training Need Assessment

The method of choice for determining who needs what training is usually called "training needs assessment" or just plain "needs assessment".[8] Since the transformation process is unique to every organization, the exact training required to orient and educate employees is also unique. This requires systematic analysis of training needs, preparing a training plan, implementing training and evaluating training. Training needs assessment must be carried out for training to be more focused and cost-effective. Needs assessment can help in establishing the nature of training, the purpose the training is to serve. It can help in design and development of training and may govern the methods and techniques to be used for training. Needs assessment helps in identification of the problem, establishing the performance gaps and, thus, helps in getting down to the basic reason for training. In order to properly target the training, one must know the results it is expected to produce and how achievement of these results will be evaluated.

Role of Different Levels of Managers in Organizational Change and Area for Training

Resistance to change is a natural instinct and it must be managed well to implement the change programme. One of the biggest problems faced in organizational change is the anxiety of the persons. This is largely due to uncertainness and the fear of the unknown. Employees are apprehensive about the changed environment in terms of the power and position, which they will have in the changed structure of the organization. Some may lack the skills and the confidence to cope with the technological changes. All these factors contribute towards increasing resistance to change.

Effectively communicating the details of the change process helps in reducing anxiety levels of the employees and consequently lowering the resistance to change. Organizational members must be convinced about the necessity of change and the positive implications it will have for organization's growth. It is also necessary to build their capacity to cope with the change. These issues can be effectively addressed through well-thought-out training plan.

Thus, it may be seen that the most important part of change management plan is an effective approach to training employees. This would involve:

- general orientation;
- communicating details of change process;
- developing employees' skills commensurate with changed technologies; and
- influencing behaviour that is appropriate in changed condition.

Area of training is required to be seen in context of role of different levels of management and desired competencies. In the context of change, though the top management's role is crucial, the middle and lower levels of management are also required to perform specific roles and as such they need to develop their competencies through training. Though the specific training plan will emerge after training needs assessment (TNA), the focus areas for training for different levels of managers are summarized in Table 1 below and discussed later.

Table 1 ***Roles, Competencies and Focus of Training for Organizational Change at Different Levels of Management***

Level of Management	*Role*	*Core Competencies*	*Focus Area for Training*
Top Level Managers	• Visualizing future	• Inspirational leadership	• Futurology
	• Sensing and anticipating change	• Visioning	• Strategic thinking
	• Interpreting environmental changes	• Analyzing	• Spiritualism
	• Influencing external environment	• Public relations	• Ethics and values
	• Redesigning organization	• Managing dynamic systems	• Organizational re-engineering
	• Leading the organizational change	• Sensitivity	• Creativity and innovation
	• Devising transition schedules	• Emotional intelligence	• Lobbying skills
	• Ensuring ethical practices in the change process	• Political acumen	• Stress management
Middle Level Managers	• Comprehending change	• Participatory and affiliative leadership	• Leadership skills
	• Influencing the organizational process	• Analyzing	• Monitoring and controlling skills
	• Learning to adapt to change	• Technological/subject expertise	• Team building
	• Implementing change	• Expert communicator	• Decision-making in uncertainty
	• Ensuring quality processes	• Team builder	• Listening and feedback skills
	• Receiving and giving feedback	• Human resource developer	• Stress management
	• Developing human resources		• Creative problem-solving

Cont'd...

Cont'd...

			• Knowledge about technological advancements • Training skills • Supportive supervision • Total quality concepts
First Line Managers	• Ensuring smooth readjustments in processes	• Technical expertise	• Role clarity
	• Giving feedback	• Skilful communicator	• Customer orientation
	• Commitment to improvement and growth	• Team worker	• Knowledge about new processes
		• Openness to new ideas, readiness to learn	• Communication skills • Learning skills • Self-motivation

Top Level Managers

Top management must function like a sophisticated weather forecasting system sensing remote changes in the environment, interpreting the data, analyzing information, setting or resetting organizational goals as per environmental demands, implementing organizational changes and leading the organization through the change. Top managers must, thus, possess certain additional competencies in today's violent environment, which probably was not so important about 50 years back. Top managers must be on a continuous learning spree in the present era of global competition and they must hone their skills to attain the requisite level of competencies. This requires learning through focused training.

Environmental changes lead to organizational change but top managers play a vital role in influencing organizational changes. They influence organizational change in four ways. The first way is through their belief system – their values, ideologies, and mental models of cause-effect relationships. Belief system of top managers determines organizational strategies, structure and culture and in this way they are the sources of change. Quite often organizational changes happen when a new top manager with a different belief system than his predecessor enters an organization. Their belief system can also have restraining effect and, thus, top managers can be inhibitors of change. Top managers may not be capable of recognizing the need for change or may not have competency to implement the change. Thus, he or she may serve as an undesirable constraint to change. The third way that the top managers impact their organizations is as interpreters of the organization's environment. Top management may see the environmental stimuli as either a problem or an opportunity and these labels affect organizational actions. Finally, the top managers are manipulators of organization's environment. They advertise, lobby and educate to make the environment hospitable for their organization. Lee Ioccoca's success in influencing creditors, unions and the US government exemplifies a top manager as a manipulator of the organization's environment.[9]

Manipulating the environment and influencing changes and implementing organizational change may throw up many ethical issues. These may be related to societal concerns or fair trade practices or to employee welfare. Largely, the issues are related to employees' rehabilitation in case of downsizing. Likewise, ethical issues may be concerning the responsibility of the firm to its owners and shareholders in terms of reaping adequate profits. Top management has a key role to play in ensuring that change is ethical and value-based. Top managers' belief system can be source of inspiration for the whole organization. Belief system sometimes undergoes changes as managers learn and unlearn. At the top management level learning events focused on ethics and values, thus, have great relevance.

Ethics training is fast becoming a part of regular management training in the corporate world and government systems. In India, the traditional system of education heavily emphasized on ethics and values but this thought seems to have lost relevance under the influence of new education systems and changing values of the society. Fortunately, ethics and values are formally gaining ground in management training systems once again, thanks to some non-resident Indian gurus and adoption of subjects like ethics in the western schools of management.

Ethics programme may broadly focus on either developing employee awareness of business ethics or addressing a specific ethical issue. By helping to develop employee awareness of ethical issues in decision-making, for example, organizations hope to[10]

- Enable recognition of ethical components of a decision.
- Legitimize ethics as part of the decision-making process.
- Avoid variability in decision-making caused by lack of norms or awareness of rules.

- Avoid confusion as to who is responsible for misdeeds.
- Provide decision-making frameworks for analyzing ethical choices.

In the context of change management, training must also focus on specific ethical issues in conflict of interest situations discharging one's job responsibilities not only strictly following the legal framework but also ensuring that the spirit of law and the societal needs are also honoured. Issues like developing employees for rehabilitation in case of downsizing or issues related to sexual harassment are important specific areas to focus on in ethics training.

When the world has become a global village and competition has a tendency to come unannounced from any direction, the organizational sensors need to be very sensitive. Remote sensing mechanism of organizational leaders must be of high resolution. In addition, it may be essential to gather greater amount of data from different (and even unconnected) fields on continuous basis. The huge volume of data thus generated must then be analyzed extremely quickly and decisions must be made in rapid-fire sequence to ensure organization's survival and growth. In such a scenario, top management must possess high level of sensitivity. Training in futurology and strategic thinking is important for the top managers and it can help them increase their visioning capacities.

Top managers often are required to take major decisions without any logistic support and these seem to come from the inner core of wisdom the top managers may possess. The decision may be termed as intuitive in absence of any explicit and obvious logical answer. In Indian context, the concept of inner source of wisdom is not difficult to accept and comprehend for we know that *Vedas,* written thousands of years back, offered solutions to many mysteries of the universe, which remained a puzzle to modem science. This inner wisdom is now being accepted even in the western world and is being referred to as emotional intelligence. Emotional intelligence is an important skill which top managers must possess. This can be developed through training in spiritualism and alike. Yoga and meditation have been known to benefit persons to achieve higher levels of efficacy and productivity.

The changed environment and top management's perception may lead to organizational redesign. At times, the new design may begin with rewriting goals of the organizations and may extend to changes in technologies, processes, and structures, which must be well suited to each other and also to external environment. Organizational redesign requires professional skills in re-engineering and restructuring. External consultants are required for redesigning so that they may look at the organization in an objective manner. Nevertheless top management plays a crucial role in rediscovering the organization goals, visualizing the position of organization in the future scenario and transforming the organization to meet the future challenges. Training in restructuring and re-engineering skills is, thus, important for the top management.

Since the top management has to lead the change process, large proportion of training for top management will be taken up by leadership skills besides political skills. Any person who has reached the top management level would naturally possess leadership traits required for the job. However, in the present violent environment, it is important that the top management is able to provide inspirational leadership to all the employees of the organization. A sensitive and caring top management sends positive signals to all the organizational members and helps in reducing the anxiety of employees during the change process. Training in ethics and values, spiritualism and similar behavioural subjects helps managers to reach new heights from where they can provide inspirational leadership to the organization.

Since the role of top management may extend to influence the external environment they must possess political acumen. Public relationship skills and lobbying skills are very important for top management.

Top management must also be competent in managing dynamic systems in transitional phase wherein various control mechanism are lax. The top management must also possess knowledge to cope with technological advancements, which may be required in view of the change. These competencies essentially require structured learning environment for top management.

In the competitive environment, top management must not only innovate they must consciously strive to generate creative ideas in the organization. Generation of new ideas requires encouragement and also creative conversation. Creativity has a role to play in developing our conversational skills. The way we think affects the way we converse and our mental patterns are affected by the nature of our conversation. A creative conversation encourages discussion, which facilitates thinking and evaluation of ideas, which can be developed into working plans. Any conversation includes listening. Creative listening involves listening to what intuition might be trying to say; carefully watching for creative triggers, for example, metaphors, analogies, evocative and emotive words and providing encouragement to the speaker without being judgmental or critical. This requires patience and an attitudinal change. Creative listening skill is an art that top managers must learn to master.

Any training package design for top management would, thus, consist of modules, which cater to the aforesaid competencies, while final design of training may emerge after the TNA exercise. Training modules focused on training different subject areas as listed in Table 1 could be considered as the basic input for top management.

Middle Level Managers

While the top management plays a crucial role in terms of initiating the change process and leading it through, the middle management's role is critical in terms of carrying the burden of change through the transitional phase and working as a linking pin between the top management and the first line managers.

Middle level managers unfortunately seem to be bearing maximum brunt of the change as 21st century organizations are becoming leaner and flatter in an attempt to be more agile. Advancements in information technology have given opportunity to the top managers to directly maintain contact with line managers and conveniently obtain data related to various activities of the organization, thus obviating the requirement of middle level managers. Further, this level of management does not enjoy the support and the protective cover of trade unions, which first line managers may enjoy.

In such a scenario of uncertainty, it is also in the personal interest of the middle level managers to continuously upgrade their knowledge and skills and continuously be on a learning spree. This can help them increase their employability and thus reduce the level of anxiety. With expanded knowledge base and skills beyond their requirement for routine job, middle level managers also gain foothold in the organization and in case of restructuring, they can be easily shifted to another division within the company.

Middle level managers perform a vital role in change plan. It is for them to comprehend the change, devise ways for smooth implementation by influencing various organizational process. They play an important role as feedback agents. Middle level managers can easily sense the difficulties, which the change plan may experience in implementation and, thus, can keep the top management abreast about required changes, if any, in the change plan.

Middle level management must, thus, possess analytical skills to judge the pros and cons of possible implementation strategies and the subject expertise to adapt the technological changes in their respective spheres. Change process demands decision-making beyond the routine and all this needs ingenuity and creativity on part of the middle level managers. Besides the technological knowledge, the middle level managers must possess creativity to solve problems that may crop up during change process. Training in creative problem-solving is highly relevant for the middle level managers.

High levels of communications skills are essential for the middle level management. It is for them to inform the first line managers and supervisors about details of the change plan, convey benefits of the change and avoid undue anxiety. They are also required to receive feedback and communicate it to the top management. During the change process, they are in fact required to overcommunicate so as to avoid any ambiguities and avert distortions in the communication.

The middle level managers in normal circumstances must exhibit participative and affiliative leadership skills, more so during change. In the transitional phase when decision-making is based on uncertainty and factual information may not be readily available, it is important that the managers make best use of participative approaches to learn more about the organizational processes and ground realities and plan their action with bottom-up approach rather that force down own decisions made in isolation. Participative leadership is a matter of attitude, which can be changed through training.

Middle level managers need to be trained for building and working in teams consisting of members from different subject specialties. Future organizations are not going to be hierarchical. They are going to be flatter, structured around core processes instead of separate departments. Managers must be trained to work in the changed paradigm of organizations whose essence is core processes and networked responsibilities. The challenge before the training managers is to develop a cross-functional development programme that can prepare managers for rotational assignments covering multiple processes. Middle level managers must be trained in the art of supportive supervision so that they can empower employees and motivate them to work as self-managed teams.

Mantra of organizational change and re-engineering is empowerment of employees. Empowered employees are expected to be more knowledgeable to have increased authority. They may be expected to challenge processes and solve problems independently or as a team. Technocrats, who have traditionally performed limited functions, may be called upon to perform various managerial functions also and assume expanded responsibilities. Some of them may feel intimidated with the expansion of responsibility and they need to be encouraged and motivated to learn and increase their capacities.

Capacity building of the human resources in the organization is by and large the responsibility of the middle level managers. All middle level managers irrespective of the department they lead must possess core competencies as human resource developer. They must through training acquire knowledge and skills in various aspects of human resource development. They must take care of their first line managers' growth and development. Middle level managers must also be trained in basic training skills and management of training so that they can plan and arrange requisite training programmes for their team.

Driven by the competitive forces, the organizations are becoming more conscious of quality aspects. Quality consciousness has increased even in the public sector in recent years. The concept of total quality, by whatever name it may operate, is something that all organizations will have to embrace if they have to survive. This is another important area of training for middle managers. The culture of value-laden, ethical practices that percolate from the top leadership must be translated into quality output at the middle and lower managerial levels.

First-line Managers

First-line managers and supervisors come in direct contact with the employees and the organization's customers. If they are not clear about the change plans in terms of proposed systems, organization's new processes and policies and their role in the changed situation, there is all likelihood of the workforce getting confused and customers feel misinformed. Thus, they must be well-informed about the change plans not in the form of occasional mass meetings but in structured informative training programmes. Training for role clarity is the first and foremost step in implementation of the change plan. Training for customer orientation is also necessary. In the 21st century when markets have expanded beyond the national boundaries, customer satisfaction assumes new relevance. All employees, especially first line managers whose interface with the customers is quite high, must be oriented towards high quality customer service.

First-line managers play an important role in the success of any planned change. Lowest managerial rung is at times not taken in confidence while implementing change plan. The line managers are in touch with the ground realities. Their working at grass roots level gives them an edge above other managers in pointing out operational difficulties in implementation of the change plan. If the ideas concerning change are thrashed out with the involvement of line mangers and then the change plan is evolved, it has better chances of being accepted at the operational level. Line manager's most important contribution to organizational change is giving feedback.

Giving feedback is a skill which needs to be developed through training. Many a time information about problems being faced at the operational level may be taken as excuses or complaints if not communicated properly and objectively. Also, such communication may be construed as resistance to change and, thus, send wrong signals. Line managers need to be trained to perform the role of spokesmen amidst the operational functionaries. Training in communication skills is, thus, important from this point of view also.

First-line managers are often too engrossed in the operational working and hate to even listen to new ways of doing things. They must develop an attitude to listen and be open to new ideas. In fact, learning things is also a skill which needs to be mastered by one and all. Quite often the first line managers fresh from the business school are so confident of their knowledge that they are not open to new learning. This can be quite detrimental to their growth and development. Learning to learn is an art, which young managers must master. Managers must continuously strive to learn more and more and upgrade themselves.

Line managers must upgrade their knowledge and skills to be able to quickly and efficiently master the technological and process changes in the organization. Substantial amount of resistance to change is due to the anxiety caused by the fear of failure in the scenario of advanced technology. Skills specific to changed processes must be developed so that employees can contribute effectively to achieve the desired results. Training in self-motivation is essential to motivate the employees and keep their morale high in difficult circumstances of change. Commitment of the first line managers would help in gaining confidence of all operational functionaries.

Evaluation of Training

The process of training is a continuous cycle of identifying needs, delivering training to fulfil these needs and then evaluating what has been provided. However, evaluation of training for organizational change is not an easy task. In the final analysis, if it is found that organizational change has been implemented smoothly without undue costs then it can be said that training has achieved its goals. Cost is to be seen not only in financial terms but also in terms of socio-economic costs, which may include loss of productivity due to anxiety or lack of appropriate communication or costs of increased employee turnover and alike.

Evaluation concentrates on judging if the objectives of the training have been achieved or not. It gives information that can help in improving training processes. The process of evaluation begins as soon as the training plan is formulated. Evaluation of the training objectives in terms of measurability and achievability is the first step in this regard.

This is difficult to quantify when it comes to imparting knowledge and experience in a specific area but attempt must be made in this direction. For example, evaluation of customer orientation training could be based on perceptible attitudinal changes and by observing the decrease in number and nature of complaints.

The training plan must include schemes that provide for ways for comparing results with objectives. Opinion forms, feedback procedures, questionnaires, checklists and other assessment procedures must be designed beforehand. Training inputs can be appraised through short questionnaires circulated at the end of the training or exit interviews to assess the effectiveness of the actual training experience. The outcome of evaluation must contribute to improvement in the training sessions and is critical for restarting the training cycle.

The training evaluation must also involve other stakeholders like members of related work teams, top managers and customers, The evaluation must take the long-term outcomes of training into consideration. The outcome of the training evaluation must be viewed with an open mind. At the same time, it should not be taken at face value as in the process of organizational change though training plays a critical role there are many other non-training interventions which have vital role to play.

Conclusion

In the present era of political, social and economic turmoil, there is only one thing constant, i.e., change. Change has become a constant companion of today's' work environment and it is adaptation of change that alone can bring relief to the beleaguered managers. The changing environment is compelling organizations to redesign themselves, globalization, liberalization and rapid developments in information technology have made it imperative for organizations to change and incorporate dynamism in their systems, which can quickly match the changing market needs. It is easier said than done. It may be easy to evolve new organizational designs but to implement them is not simple for it requires people to comprehend and accept the change.

There are two forces of change: the external environment of the organization and the organization's top management. They cause departure from the status quo or smooth trends, which is termed as 'organizational change'. From the viewpoint of general management, there are two basic types of change. First is the change in operational level and conditions in terms of budgets, sales, profits, labour force, inventory, etc. This kind of change does not affect the basic nature of the organization; it only expands or contracts its activities. The other type of change transforms the organization: its products, markets, technology, culture, systems or its structure.

Implementing organizational change is not simple; it demands concerted efforts in the shape of training interventions. Training interventions must be directed at all levels of management and they must be able to prepare the organizational members for change. This requires taking a realistic look at one's organization, a comprehensive understanding of the proposed change with a focus on various processes, identification of training needs and implementation of the training plan. Training is, however, not a one-time activity. It is a means towards an end. It is a process, which helps in achieving the organizational goals. For change to succeed it is essential that training is dovetailed in the change management plan.

The focus of training must be on general orientation of the employees towards change, communication of the change plans, upgrading the skills to meet the challenges thrown by environmental and organizational change. Organizations can meet today's challenges if they have a critical mass of skilful, informed people with positive attitude for growth and action. Competent, positively inclined people with good information can successfully leap to new ways of thinking, being and working and can, thus, take organizations to new heights.

Notes

1. Peter F. Drucker, Change Leader, *Inc. Magazine,* June 01, 1999.
2. Carter McNamara, Basic Context for Organizational Change, 1999 www.mapnp-org/library/mgmt/org, change-htm
3. George P. Huber and William H. Glick, Sources and Forms of Organizational Change, *Organizational Change and Redesign: Ideas and Insights for Improving Performance,* Oxford University Press, p. 3.
4. Ibid., p. 4.
5. Ibid., p. 8.
6. Fred Nickols, *Five Factors Affecting Performance,* 2000.
7. A. Downs, "Planned People Obsolescence", *Training,* February 1995, p. 57
8. Fred Nickols, Who Needs What Training?
9. George P. Huber, and William H. Glick, op. cit., p. 9.
10. Susan J. Harrington, "What Corporate America is Teaching About Ethics", Academy of Management Executive, February 1991, p. 23.

10 Public Policy and Strategic Management

The Bridging Role of Training

Gitika Kapoor

The Emergence of Discontinuities

The nature, role and pace of changes, whether political, social, economic, technological or competitive, that have taken place in the last two decades, have been unprecedented. The cumulative effect of these changes has created conditions of global-level competition, fast rate of technological change and obsolescence, better systems and speedy communication, coexistence of homogenization of tastes/preferences with cultural and ethnic diversity, emergence of the young, restless, impatient, demanding population and the demystification of the belief about immortality of institutions – social, public, private or government.

These changes have opened up hitherto closed societies and markets. China and India are examples of this opening up. The opening up has put the customer and civil society in an important position. No longer can corporate or public institutions underestimate their expectations or power. Global competition encourages a customer to demand cheaper, better quality products, sooner than before. The centrality of customer-focused strategic and customer relationship management in marketing decisions bears testimony to this.

On the other hand, the citizens want impartiality, simpler procedures, respect for law, efficient service delivery, accountability, delivery on promises made and transparency. The effort by public services to initiate better governance and the stated commitment of governments to this bear proof to the acknowledgement of power of civil society.

Table 1 shows the select major changes and their impact on public and private organizations:

Table 1 *Select Major Changes and their Impact on Public and Private Organizations*

Change Zone	*Old Era*	*New Era*
Economy	• Agrarian	• Services dominant
	• National	• Global
	• Slow changes	• Fast changes
Politics	• Single ideology	• Multiple ideologies
	• Dominant party	• Coalition
	• Independent	• Interdependent
Technology	• Breakthrough inventions with long gaps	• Innovation in processes/application
	• Slow commercialization	• Faster commercialization
		• Dispersed use of technology
Social	• Simple stratification	• Multiple stratification
	• Homogenous cultural context	• Coexistence of homogeneity and heterogeneity
Competition	• "Big eats small"	• "Fast eats slow"
	• Predictable	• Unpredictable
Communication	• Few means	• Many means
	• Controlled	• Interlinked and dispersed
	• Uncomplicated	• Complex
Change Impact	↓	↓
Growth Drivers	• Large manufacturing units	• Innovative entrepreneurial organizations
Management Administration	• Through command and control	• Through teamwork, cooperation and mentoring
Skills	• Standardized	• Multiple flexible
Knowledge	• One-time learning	• Life-time learning
Service Expectations	• Minimum	• Maximum
Public Policy	• Inward looking, regulatory	• Outward looking, facilitating
Public Service	• Delivery and performance, expectations low	• Rising expectations
Public Sector	• Stand alone	• Partnerships
	• Government ownership	• Disinvestment

Today, there is perhaps no organization in corporate, government and public policy domain which is not undergoing chaotic transformation and finding ways to effectively respond to the change.

The changes mentioned in Table 1 have created situation where the question before companies and governments is not "should we respond?", but "how do we respond?"

The Darwin observation, "It is not the strongest, nor the most intelligent of species that survives. It is one that is most adaptable to change" seems to be proving true for organizations as well.

Strategic Management Process

In the past, organizations have orchestrated their response to the environment through rational, analytical approach. Experience has shown that these approaches may be inadequate to deal with hitherto not experienced changes. The complexity and magnitude of discontinuities require strategic thinking, direction and leadership, commitment to implementation and putting in place co-ordination, motivation, reward and communication system and managerial infrastructure. Managers under such conditions are perplexed. They need guidance to allocate resources to situations/events/issues when returns are uncertain and outcomes shrouded in ambiguity. Decisions are taken under conditions of risk. One cannot foretell what will happen in future but better information and preparation help in remaining focused. The strategic management process is about managing discontinuous change in the organization. It develops the right set of attitudes, skills and knowledge within the organization about change. Its objective is to link strategic and operational decision-making so that along with a strategy for future being made appropriate corporate values, managerial competencies, organizational resources, systems and processes that respond to uncertainty are also put into place. Change is not a one-time phenomenon, therefore, the issue is not about change response only but about preparedness for response as a choice all the while.

The strategic management process includes external analysis, internal assessment, strategic direction, strategic plans, implementation and performance evaluation. Figure 1 shows these elements:

Figure 1

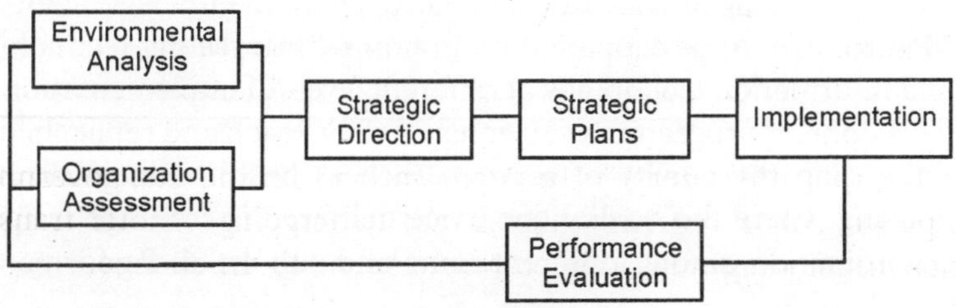

Strategic management helps answering questions such as what is our role, our mission, where are we, what are the most significant changes that impact us, what is our preparedness, where will we be twenty years later and are we giving attention to the factors that impact our future?

Take the case of Shell Oil – a fossil fuel exploration-based multinational conglomerate. Strategic management, through scenario building, helps it retain its pre-eminent position in the industry. At the same time, it also enables us to understand its future when a substitute to fossil fuel is available.

Toyota, an automobile manufacturer, on the other hand, works to retain its dominant quality position while mapping the ecological impact of fossil fuel on a decadenal basis and designing different fuel-based automobiles.

Does Public Policy Need Strategic Management?

The extensive interrelatedness of inputs and outputs, the diversity of stakeholders, the quantum of resources committed and the extensiveness of results sought also make public policy decisions very complex. They are strategic as they involve:

- commitment of large amount of resources;
- have long gestation periods;
- outcomes are uncertain; and
- involve a certain degree of risk.

Strategic management is a useful approach for public policy formulation and implementation because it is an approach developed to adapt to complexity and ambiguity. Strategic management has been used for managing complete projects like the Delhi Metro Project (see Box 1). The areas where strategic management can be used within the public policy domain are:

1. Management of infrastructure and public-private partnerships for infrastructure development. These are emerging areas with comparatively lower levels of competencies and preparedness that strategic management can help to strengthen the management.
2. Management of development programmes. Integrating technology and information technology at different levels of implementation in development programme can enhance their reach and replicability.
3. Enhancing the quality of services such as health, education and housing where the quality of service delivered is contingent upon co-ordination among different units and sub-units. Performance

measures can be developed for service delivery. The implementation can be improved.

4. Creating an understanding about the impact of global trends on hitherto inward focused sectors like agriculture and tertiary education. For example, is the country prepared to be a dominant player in the knowledge economy? What changes does tertiary education need for attaining that position? This provokes different type of thinking and the policy apparatus can indulge in new thinking.
5. Management of foreign direct investment. It calls for extensive inter-ministerial coordination at national level, between industry associations, departments, state governments and many other stakeholders. A national strategic perspective helps more than a regional one in highlighting conflict areas and resolution techniques.

Box 1 ***Strategic Project Management for Delhi Metro***

- Mission
  - To offer attractive mass rapid transportation system and to de-choke Delhi roads
  - To provide comfort to citizens
- Targets
  - 2.2 million commuter trips/day
  - 245 kms network of lines to be completed in four phases
  - Cost control + + +
  - Timely completion
  - Minimum bottlenecks for citizens
- Important Stakeholders and Manageable
  - Public expectations
  - Governments (Central + NCR)
  - Civic bodies
  - Politician-bureaucrats
  - International sanction
  - Technology
  - Process
  - Consultants
  - Systems structures process

Adapted from *A Dream Revisited Delhi Metro Rail Corporation: An Archival Journey into the Making of Delhi Metro Rail*, DMRC Ltd., New Delhi, 2003.

6. Creation of entrepreneurship opportunities and tapping sectoral interrelatedness. The interrelatedness of handicrafts, tourism, basic and information technology linkage can do so much for rural and urban entrepreneurship. A strategic perspective towards rural development and industrial development is needed.
7. Cluster management with clear identification of goals, resource mapping, skill mapping, stakeholder expectations and a five-year perspective can lead to development of sustainable small and medium enterprise clusters.
8. Disaster management requires preparedness planning akin to the contingency approach in scenario building.
9. Expectation mapping in different programmes. This helps in understanding and articulating mission and output for different programmes.

Training for Strategic Management

Training will develop the requisite knowledge, skills and attitudes for strategic management among public service providers.

To begin with, training for strategic management perspective can be designed within the structural learning system already in existence for public services. Later, strategic management specific programmes for projects/departments can be initiated as a capacity building approach among senior- and middle-level public officials, both horizontal and vertical programmes. The management institutes, state training institutes or other agencies can implement these. The performance mapping of these programmes in terms of efficiency and effectiveness can at the third stage be a policy input to a comprehensive project for strategic management in the pubic services domain.

The strategic management focused training will be multi-method, multi-context. Training objectives for strategic management focused programmes can be to:

- develop among senior public officials and career bureaucrats a perspective about their role as change agents;
- promote the holistic, unified view as opposed to departmental budget-centric view among decision-makers;
- develop competencies for expectation mapping, environmental analysis, internal analysis, etc. Training can enhance use of computer-based simulation models for analysis, trend forecasting of complex systems;

- develop strategic thinking capacity even at middle levels within the government;
- develop capacity for negotiation, consensus building, chaos management;
- develop the capacity to dream and the wherewithal to deliver among public officials;
- in a workshop mode of training, as a vertical programme, develop commitment and results orientation across the board;
- develop the competencies to rigorously analyze and question what do they imply, what is the impact, how can we cope to service factional considerations and bottlenecks; and
- redesign services/departments to suit current realities.

In the present scenario, strategic management is given limited time in training programme. If it can be coupled with specific issues for a common pool of officers, results from training may be forthcoming sooner. Global experience has shown that strategic management is being pursued at the highest level to re-engineer the public services. The Irish model is one such example. Box 2 shows the salient features of the model. Till such developments occur, strengthening the strategic management component in ongoing programmes is required.

Box 2 ***Irish Civil Services and Strategic Management***

The strategic management approach has been used to initiate change in the Irish civil services. It was influenced by the new trends in Public Management and Developments in other countries. It evolved in 1988 and was finalized in 1994. In 1996, the process was codenamed DBG – Delivering Better Government. Strategic management approach is regarded as "taking a view of what we should be doing and how we might go about it".

The process is overseen by a coordinating group of nine Secretaries-General and Prime Minister's Office. It aims to address following key issues:

- contribution to national development
- provision of quality services to the public
- effective use of resources
- improve linkage between ministries and with agencies
- extend public services

References

Delhi Metro Rail Corporation, A Dream Revisited: An Archival Journey into the Making of Delhi Metro Rail. DMRC Ltd., New Delhi, 2003.

Hax, Arnold C. and Nicholas S. Majluf, *Strategic Alanqeinent: An Integrative Perspective,* Prentice Hall Inc., Englewood Cliffs, NJ., 1984.

http://www.aipa.net

Kramer, Fred, *Perspectives on Public Bureaucracy: A Reader on Organization,* Winthrop Publishers Inc., Massachusetts, 1973.

Venugopal, R., "New Directions in Strategic Management: Insight from Literature and Case Studies", *Vikalpa,* Vol. 26 to 30, July-September, 2001.

Zajee, Edward, Kreefz Mathew and Rudi Bresser, "Modelling the Dynamics of Strategic Fit: A Nominative Approach to Strategic Change", *Strategic Management Journal,* 21: 429–453 (2000), John Wiley and Sons Ltd.

11 Management of Change through Human Resource Development in Government

The Case of V-Governance Training of Government of Gujarat

Anita Karwal

Gujarat state is situated in the western part of India and boasts of the most enterprising populace in the country in terms of business acumen. The state has a population of about five crores scattered in 18,000 villages, 147 municipalities and seven municipal corporations. The feudal system, which lingered on in most other states during the post-independence period, has been severely diluted in this state mostly due to its 'cooperative' spirit. The state also boasts of a strong workforce of five lakhs in the government, which is responsible for giving it the plausible reputation of having the best environment for industrial promotion, high growth rate, most widespread ICT infrastructure and e-governance practices, etc.

Of late, there has been an intensification in concerns for redefining the role of this workforce from one that is controlling, negative, protective and procedural to one that is positive, effective and efficient managers of change with a citizen-centric approach towards delivery of services. Generally, it has been assumed that the general changes in the socio-economic environment would automatically rub off its effect on the public servants and result in their smooth adaptation to the changes. That is to say that it is assumed that no interventions are required for ensuring a smooth transformation to attune public servants to the changing environment. Historically also, there has been no culture of looking at capacity building and training as facilitators to ensure such role makeovers in the government. Naturally so, as in most governments, training consists of routine orientations for entrants, or updated rules, procedures and standards and perhaps some annual seminars and workshops on new policies. In fact, training systems within governments are yet struggling to evolve sufficiently clear training objectives out of inadequately defined needs. Training needs in developing countries are considered especially difficult to define and the problem gets compounded because even the public servants themselves mostly suffer from the general assumption (though superficially arrived at) that training cannot change their attitude, or redefine their roles. The realization that the private sector is much less flexible than the government, and that there is more scope for innovation in the government, has yet to touch the mindsets of most public servants.

With this background, it was decided by the Government of Gujarat to undertake a massive training and empowerment exercise for all its employees, of all categories, with the firm conviction that an innovative methodology of training and well-designed content can incorporate the practice of positive attitude as a habit in the work culture of public servants and smoothen the process of adaptation to change. The training programme thus undertaken is known as the 'v-governance training', or vibrant governance training programme (see Annexure 1 for milestones of this programme).

Analyzing the Need for V-Governance

The shifting of an organization to a new culture of openness, to learning and changing, usually presents the greatest hurdles, unless the problems plaguing the organization and its workforce are clearly established and understood. An analysis of the mindsets of the workforce of the state government pointed to the following problem areas:

- The increased use of new technologies, particularly ICT, had brought in a sense of insecurity towards a wholly unknown future.
- Skill development had not matched the pace of developments in the field of management and information and communication technologies.
- Somewhere along the way, interpersonal relationships were shown the door in favour of the cut-throat competition at workplace to obtain due and undue favours in terms of good postings, promotions, rewards etc.
- Little or no training has been imparted to most categories of employees of the state government. In fact, as per available figures, the Sardar Patel Institute of Public Administration (SPIPA, which

is a premier training institution of the state) had trained approximately 2 lakh employees in the last 20 years or more. Therefore, a workforce of 5 lakh (this number has remained more or less static during this period) can be assumed to have received training at the rate of per cent coverage per year, which is dismally low.

- To top it all, a historical disappointment with training, its standards, its middling designs and methodologies ensured an active hostility towards it.
- Creativity had been posing a problem in training programmes and a multidisciplinary approach was yet to evolve.
- The work culture of most governments is such that it hardly provides any scope for self-development.
- The above-mentioned point necessarily leads to the fact that there is a negative attitude towards change and its management.
- A general lack of motivation had been experienced by all functionaries, either intermittently or constantly. To initiate the process of result orientation in work rather than being process or procedure-oriented appeared to be a herculean task.

Identifying the Strengths

Since the very beginning of undertaking this programme, it was very clear to us that the shift we are looking for is a shift away from treating training as a resource first and last. In this context, an analysis of the available potential and strengths revealed the following:

- After the introduction of the compulsory training policy by the state government in early 2004, the employees of the state were already prepared for towards the need to be trained though the willingness may or may not be quite genuine at that time.
- The turn around of the umbrella training institute of the state, i.e., SPIPA, was being closely watched and encouraged. From an institution imparting routine and listless training programmes, it was now emerging as a leader of innovations in training and capacity building, in approach, methodology, content, design and scope of training. A visible transformation was taking place in this organization with the main objective of establishing the positive role that effective training can play in the management of change, leading to efficient delivery of services to the citizens.
- Many innovative projects undertaken by enterprising public servants were being actively supported by the government. The success of these projects had a ripple effect and many public servants showed inclination to replicate or partner such processes.

The state government actually institutionalized the concept of undertaking innovative projects by individual officers under the scheme of "Swantah Sukhay".

- Several initiatives of good governance of the state of Gujarat had been receiving accolades nationally and internationally, which prepared the background for extensive review of routine policies and developing innovative approaches for their future implementation.
- All in all, an enabling environment had already been created to usher in transformation through a process of discovery, practice and internalization of new skills and attitudes.

Aims and Objectives of the V-Governance Training Programme

With the above background and context, the v-governance programme was launched. It is a unique, innovative programme of the Government of Gujarat in Human Resource Development, and is based on the premises that "governance is as good as the human resource employed". This training initiative has been conceptualized as the first step forward to bring forth desired changes in the work culture by turning positive attitude into matter of practice and habit. The objectives of the programme were designed as follows:

- To expose government personnel to the need of being responsive to changes and to inculcate the ability to adapt them meaningfully.
- To usher in a paradigm shift from process orientation to result orientation.
- To ensure redefinition of perspectives and contexts as individuals and also as government employees. Cultivating a positive approach, proactiveness, and better work processes etc. are also envisioned.
- To facilitate attitudinal/behavioural changes to enhance personal and professional growth to fit in with the changing organizational needs.

Scope of V-Governance Training Programme

In terms of numbers it was decided to initially cover 1.25 lakh employees of all ranks, i.e., class I to class IV and all categories including police, technical, non-technical, executive etc. (see Annexure 2).

- The locational spread includes all the 25 district headquarters and 184 block headquarters of the state.
- The time period for the first phase is one year. The second phase covering approximately 70,000 employees began on 15th June, 2005, and will be completed in March 2006.
- The programme aims to cover all employees of the Government of Gujarat in its ambit.

The Programme Concept

The programme framework builds ownership among employees for the transformation and also helps them explore different options for responding to situations/issues while reflecting on better performance through positive attitude and high motivation. Thus, the v-governance programme is not a routine or technical programme limited to an understanding of rules and procedures for everyday work and functions. Rather, it aims to bring about a transformation in the following key areas:

- Role effectiveness, i.e., understanding one's role in creating an enabling environment.
- Customer orientation, i.e., a shift from "processes" to "results".
- Effective communication, i.e., for getting better cooperation from others.
- Personal and interpersonal effectiveness, i.e., for improving interactions.
- Self-motivation, i.e., being proactive rather than reactive.
- Improved work processes.

Programme Design and Operation

The nodal organization for implementing, monitoring and continually improving the v-governance training programme in the state is the Sardar Patel Institute of Public Administration (SPIPA), which is the premier training institute of the state government. The training programme is implemented in partnership with a private agency, i.e., IL&FS Education and Technology Services Ltd., which has signed an MoU with the state government to undertake the need assessment, design the course contents, provide trainers, train the government trainers, take the feedback and appoint the impact evaluation agency from outside. The main features of the design and operation of the programme are as follows:

- Need assessment was carried out to design the course contents, structure, and delivery system through the help of intensive focus group discussions.
- The course contents are designed to make it very participative. Group exercises, success stories, role plays and discussions make the training highly interactive, contextual and applicable to everyday work.
- The role of the trainer in this programme is that of a facilitator. The trainers for each batch of trainees consist of two persons – one is

from the state government, who has willingly undergone a ToT programme specially designed for this programme; and the second one is a trainer of the partner private agency.

- Training of every batch of 25 trainees is for 25 hours, spread over four days, i.e., six hours per day (revised to six hours per day and seven hours on the last day, for the second phase on popular demand).
- Volunteers from class I, II and III are trained as trainers in a rigorous six-day (36 hours) module. These trained government trainers ultimately render training to other government employees and officers with assistance from trained IETS trainers, who only act as facilitators.
- The feedback is taken on the contents, design and usefulness of the programme as such, and also on the training skills of the trainers.

Expected Outcomes/Impact of the Training Programme

A positive impact is expected in the following three areas:

- In the area of *innovation,* it is expected that there will be more openness, welcoming of new ideas, acceptance of others' views and readiness for searching and experimentation.
- In the area of *implementation of change,* it is expected that while respect for tradition will continue there will also be readiness to blend the new with the old with creative adaptation.
- In the area of *personal and professional growth,* it is expected that a well-rounded individual will emerge.

Risk Factors

An exercise of such a large dimension cannot be impervious to risks or constraints in operationalizing and/or implementation. The following risk factors were identified and taken care of to ensure smooth implementation:

- The sheer number of trainees is itself a potential risk and can lead to problems if planning in advance is not done.
- The quality of training programme could suffer if there was slackness in selecting trainers.
- The number of locations/venues for training is very large.
- Pulling out many employees from the same department or office at the same time for training for four continuous days is difficult.
- Since each batch consists of employees drawn from different offices and categories (i.e., technical non-technical etc.), the risk of interpersonal conflicts in a training situation is very high.

- The contents of the training programme have to be relevant and interesting.
- If the programme is allowed to continue at its own pace without proper monitoring, then neither the targets in terms of numbers can be achieved nor the stated objectives of the programme fulfilled.
- It is always possible that the private partner, not having any exposure to government practices and systems, may not be sensitive enough to the problems that the public servants need to deal with and the solutions that can be offered to them. This could reflect in the training material if not addressed effectively.

Innovative Aspects

At the core of any training system is an institutional mechanism to orchestrate and integrate the diverse efforts in this area and to take primary responsibility for overall performance and to lead. The Sardar Patel Institute of Public Administration (SPIPA) has recently attained autonomy and it is also the "linchpin" in implementing the mandate of innovation by positioning training as a major ingredient for management of change. Its innovative efforts have enough scope and backing to enable commitment towards desired organizational transformation through training. The mammoth v-governance training programme undertaken by the state government and SPIPA is innovative in several respects:

- The reach of the programme is perhaps the most ambitious in itself in the country. This is so because it is on record that so far no other state government in the country has decided to train 100 per cent of its employees without discrimination of rank, categories, posting etc.
- The time period for the training programme is short and sacrosanct.
- Related to the above, the scale of the programme can be realized from the following figures: at any point of time there were a minimum of 100 batches of 25 participants each and a maximum of 315 batches with 25 participants each, being trained simultaneously all over the state of Gujarat. The figures are mind-boggling and obviously it required an immense amount of advance planning and subsequent monitoring for implementation.
- A majority of the beneficiaries of this training programme are being exposed to training for the first time in their careers.
- The policies existing in the central government and the state government for training government personnel have fixed the

age bar of 55 years for training. This, in effect, means that approximately five years before retirement from government services, the employee is expected to stop learning. The creative departure in the V-governance training programme is that this training is imparted even to those employees who may be retiring on the very next day after the training is imparted. This is done with the objective that an attitudinal change will not only positively impact on the self growth of the employee after retirement but will also help him/her to contribute in a positive manner to the society as a senior citizen.

- Unlike routine training programmes which focus on a typical given subject of policy, rules and procedures in government, the v-governance training programme focuses only on personal development, positive attitude and interface with the society.
- The preconceived notion that training can be imparted only by educational experts from the academic field is sought to be corrected by this programme which trains government employees themselves to further train the target group of employees.
- The programme relies heavily on the quality of the master trainers who are volunteers drawn from class I, II and III ranks of the state government. This has created a pool of approximately 2,000 willing trainers within the government from all over the state.
- The programme is being run in partnership with a private educational agency.
- The expected impact of the programme was clearly understood right from the beginning. That it would lead to enhancement of skills for functioning at workplace was never the goal. The programme only aims at personal growth with the full knowledge that the spill-over benefits would directly or indirectly impact upon the professional growth. This in itself has been a major creative departure from the existing system of training.

Organizational Changes Effected During Implementation

The climate of an organization is generally considered "as the internal environment of an organization that is experienced by its members, influences their behaviour and can be described in terms of the values of the particular set of characteristics/attributes of the organization". To put it briefly, in this case, it was felt that the internal environment was not changing at the pace at which the external environment was transforming. This was obviously resulting in rigid behaviour patterns opposed to reforms in governance, re-invention, re-engineering and other improvement initiatives leading to a non-conducive climate for change. The only expected changes were the changes in leadership. Certainly, this alone could not be expected to cause the organizational climate to swing noticeably. But, on the basis of several live examples in the government, it was soon realized that when an organizational culture has been altered in a desirable manner, beliefs, attitudes, values and behaviours do not revert back easily to the original state. With this backdrop, the following systemic changes were brought about in the manner in which the v-governance programme was implemented:

- The v-governance training programme was not imposed from above. It look a lot of consultations with various categories of employees to assess their real training needs.
- Outsourcing a training programme was unheard of. Normally, governments find it difficult to accept that they do not have the requisite capacity for performing any task, least of all training their own human resources, However, the success of the present experience has ensured that it will inspire such partnerships in future.
- The long pending request for autonomy by SPIPA was granted on 1st October, 2004. SPIPA is now in a position to decide its own course, pattern of funding and expenditure and initiate all-round qualitative improvements without requiring government sanction. This has 'trickled down' to the implementation of this programme as well.
- The state government has seen a turn around in the manner it looks at training and capacity building. The state government came out with compulsory training policy in April 2004 which makes it obligatory on class I and class II officers to take a minimum of three days' training in every blocks of two years. This itself has created a very positive climate towards training and acceptance of change.
- Training has become a professional activity meant to develop human resources.
- The remarkable growth of SPIPA, from a routine training organization of the government consisting of government functionaries on punishment posting to the institute, to an organization to reckon with in the field of scientific, creative and multidisciplinary approach to training is a success story, which is most talked about in HRD in the state government. It is inspiring other training institutions of the state government to emulate the success.
- Innovation in governance by all categories of employees is encouraged. It has been institutionalized in the form of "Swantaha Sukhay" scheme. There is a reward scheme also at district level for best overall performance.

Impact Analysis of the Programme

For a formal impact analysis of the entire v-governance training programme, the International Centre for Entrepreneurship and Career Development was appointed as the impact evaluation agency for this programme in November 2004. This agency was expected to examine and assess perceived usefulness and applicability of the training programme, use or non-use of learning from the training and impact on internal customers such as superiors, subordinates and external customers, i.e., the citizens. The components of the module to be examined included, among others, perceived effectiveness of roles, citizen orientation, impact on interpersonal relationships etc. The approach and methodology was to assess the same random sample during pre-training, post-training and 45 days after training.

The salient features of the analysis and the highlights of the findings are given below:

(a) *Impact Analysis-Sampling*
- Sample size: 2,500 trainees
- Sample coverage: All 25 districts
- Time span: 1st day, 4th day and 45 days after training
- Methodology: Random sampling method with structured questionnaires.

(b) *Highlights of the Impact Analysis Report*
- Has created a new confidence and established credibility of training within government.
- Desired impact on changing mindset definitely achieved to a considerable extent.
- Trainees and trainers are very enthusiastic.
- Many departments are continuing the process; many others need to play key role.
- Momentum needs to be taken advantage of and there should be immediate follow-up action.

(c) *Observations of the Agency Appointed for Impact Analysis*
- Effectiveness of training is a result of teamwork of trainers of IETS and the Government of Gujarat.
- Mammoth programme effectively planned.
- Competency level of trainers is the critical aspect.
- Refresher training/focus group recommended.
- Recommended that HoDs play an active and facilitative role post-training.
- Training should include extra time for experience sharing.

(d) Impact Analysis Concluding Remarks

The training programme has achieved the objectives for which it was designed. Further, immense benefit which is accrued through this pioneering effort needs to be institutionalized on sustained and long-term basis.

Conclusion

Recognizing the environmental changes and fed by global information, the governmental training system has shifted from a static training organization towards becoming a continuously learning organization. The learnings are being used for changing its culture and to enable continuous preparedness for using innovative inputs for improving performance of its functionaries directly and also for improving itself. The crux of this improvement is "motivation of all employees at all times". There is no golden rule for selecting techniques of motivation that would help any given organization to motivate any given employee, under any given set of circumstances. What is perhaps required is that the selected technique should mesh with our own situations, needs, values, past experiences and expectations of the employees. With this aim in mind, the v-governance training initiative has been undertaken to enlarge the competencies and responsibilities of the employees and facilitate the development of their own individual visions of a positive personal and professional growth.

In conclusion, the felt need to expose the government personnel to strategies for adaptation to changes in a meaningful manner has been translated in the form of this capacity building exercise. This is now being perceived as perhaps the only one of its kind in terms of number of trainees, the short time span, the large geographical coverage, significance of contents, professional approach and a timely, appropriate and innovative intervention for management of change. It is already creating a permanent positive dent in the work culture of the state government and the mindsets of its functionaries.

Annexure 1
Milestones (Time Period)

- Training needs analysis–January to March 2003.
- Formulating methodology and concepts–June 2003.
- Inviting proposals from private partners–June 2003.
- Presentation of proposal by private partner–June 2003.
- Designing contents of training–October 2003.
- Approval of contents by state government–November 2003.
- First Training of Trainers (ToT) programme for government employees–December 2003.
- First training programme of Class I employees–January 2004.
- First training programme of Class II employees–February 2004.
- First training programme of Class IV employees–February 2004.
- Launch of v-governance training programme at Gandhinagar for state secretariat staff–February 2004.
- Finalization of approach, design, methodology and signing of MoU between state government and private partner–March 2004.
- Appointment of State Level Steering Committee, headed by the Chief Secretary for monitoring progress of the training programme–April 2004.
- Expansion of the v-governance training programme to Ahmedabad–June 2004.
- Collection of database for the rest of the districts of the state through video conferencing–July 2004.
- Expansion of the v-governance training programme to all the districts of the state–August 2004 onwards.
- Meetings of the State Steering Committee were held in the months of August, November, December 2004.
- Direct evaluation and feedback session by the Chief Minister with government trainers of the programme–September 2004.
- Appointment of International Centre for Entrepreneurship and Career Development as the impact assessment agency for the programme–November 2004.
- Interim impact assessment report presented by ICECD–29 December, 2004.
- The first phase target of 1 lakh employees completed on 7 Jan., 2005.
- The second phase of approximately 25,000 employees completed during January 2005 to March 2005.
- Final report of impact assessment–April 2005.
- Third phase to cover approximately 70,000 employees began on 15 June 2005.

Annexure 2

Details of District-wise Participants in Training for V-Governance Training Programme (2004–05)

Sr. No.	*District*	*ToT*	*Regular Training*					*Total*
			C1	*C2*	*C3*	*C4*	*Total*	
1.	Ahmedabad	358	259	770	16082	2312	19423	19781
2.	Gandhinagar	299	255	721	5819	1683	84781	8777
	Sachivalaya	33	355	520	2597	661	4133	4166
3.	Vadodara	113	40	246	4831	877	5994	6107
4.	Junagadh	46	47	349	5409	1119	6924	6970
5.	Mehsana	20	33	188	2606	391	3218	3238
6.	Kheda	30	53	248	4382	675	5358	5388
7.	Sabarkantha	46	12	36	2145	339	2532	2578
8.	Anand	51	9	78	3709	468	4264	4315
9.	Banaskantha	86		128	6786	333	7247	7333
10.	Jamnagar	48	9	71	3147	537	3764	3812
11.	Amreli	35			3647		3647	3682
12.	Porbandar	17		48	770	207	1025	1042
13.	Bhavnagar	33		200	4210	514	4924	4957
14.	Surat	71	14	86	5446	673	6219	6290
15.	Navsari	22	33	88	2418	224	27631	2785
16.	Narmada	23	3	146	2018	448	2615	2638
17.	Godhara	68			3157	382	3539	3607
18.	Valsad	53	34	122	1736	301	2193	2246
19.	Kutch-Bhuj	49	34	136	2470	417	3057	3106
20.	Surendranagar	21	26	131	2810	386	3353	3374
21.	Patan	23		139	1572	223	1934	1957
22.	Rajkot	206	55	243	4442	1118	5858	6064
23.	Dahod	25		170	3039	178	3387	3412
24.	Bharuch	47	20	106	3784	400	4310	4357
25.	Dang	20	6	32	1824	206	2068	2088
Grand Total		1843	1297	5002	100856	15072	122227	124070

C = Class; TOT = Training of Trainers
Total number of trainers in the state government pool = 1,843
Total number of employees trained upto 31.3.05 = 1,24,070

12 Managing Change in Government through Capacity Building

Intensive Training Across All Levels in Kota District

P.K. Jain and C. Lobo

Globalization, economic liberalization and decentralization of development administration have generated widespread discussion on the need to reorient public administration capabilities to meet the emerging challenges. People, nations and societies have to find ways to identify the changes in the environment and come up with corrective systems and procedures in order to meaningfully address the emerging issues.

Governance is as good as the human resource employed. It, therefore, need not be overemphasized that human capital formation in the government is the most significant strategic initiative required to be undertaken. This can only be achieved with concentrated efforts by sensitizing personnel with regard to the internal and external environment within which they operate and the need for adaptation to the rapidly changing environment.

The public sector faces a major challenge in improving performance and producing customer-focused services. Motivated employees are an essential component of the drive to improve productivity and results. Maintaining the commitment of government managers and staff is central to delivering continuous improvement. Skills about how to motivate staff are no longer an optional extra for managers, but should be one of their core assets.

While it is true that organizations value people as one of their greatest assets, it is less clear how to turn good intentions into the reality of committed employees who are performing to the best of their

The views expressed are those of the authors and are not necessarily those of the agencies where they work.

abilities. Tackling this issue is essential to delivering transformational change.

Over the years, government staff 'culture' has been perceived as one that has a tendency to avoid risks, follow the rules, settle for less than high quality results and respond gradually to change. The need of the hour is to change the mindset of government employees from 'ruler' to 'facilitator'. This culture is difficult to modify because it is embedded in the habits, hearts and minds of employees.

There is no quick way to change administrative culture. But efforts can be made by developing strategies for changing habits and mental models of employees to develop a responsive and entrepreneurial culture. Employees may need to question and introspect on the basic factors that shape a culture – from tradition, to communication, to the way things are done. Employees should start thinking about efficiency, working together to solve problems, respond politely and be open to feedback from colleagues and citizens.

Need for Intensive Training Across All Levels

There is a need to make personnel at all levels, especially at the lower echelons of government, effective, efficient and sensitive to people's needs. Few efforts have been made to provide systematic training to government employees of Class III and IV cadres despite the fact that these cadres are the first point of governmental contact with the ordinary citizen. There are a few training institutes which conduct random, short courses for training of Class III employees and the frequency of a person getting trained is as low as once or twice before retirement. These institutions are also often cash strapped and not geared to meet the ongoing development needs of employees at different levels. Therefore, the quality of training lacks lustre.

In this context, a unique 'bottom-up' approach to training is required in order to bring about change in thinking and practice at the lowest levels of government staff. All government staff, across all levels, will have to be involved in this initiative. Only then will such a transformation improve services to citizens, business and industry.

Most states in India are now in the process of re-looking at their training policies to comprehensively train their employees and build human assets as per the requirements of new and changing environment taking shape in the wake of globalization and the growing awareness among the citizens of their rights.

The Government of India, under the UNDP project, had initiated through HCM Rajasthan State Institutes of Public Administration (HCM RIPA) and its Centre for Good Governance (CGG), Jaipur, a pilot programme in Kota district, Rajasthan, for capacity building in civil services for employees across all levels. The training has now been completed. It was a unique experience which can be replicated in other parts of the country for transforming the mindsets of the employees.

Good Governance Initiative in Kota District

The details of the Good Governance Training Programme, viz., objectives, structure, programme modules, implementation strategy and feedback have been described in the forthcoming paragraphs:

Objectives of the Good Governance Training Programme

The overall objective of the programme was to enable each employee to clearly articulate his/her role and understand the key behaviour involved in improving work effectiveness. Thus, the programme is not a 'technical' programme related to everyday work processes but propels the state towards better service delivery through greater responsiveness and citizen engagement. The detailed objectives of the programme were as follows:

- To expose government personnel to the need to be responsive to changes and to inculcate the ability to adapt meaningfully.
- To augment capacity building in order to ensure citizen focus.
- To usher in a paradigm shift from process orientation to result orientation.
- To ensure redefinition of perspectives and contexts, as individuals and also as government employees.
- To cultivate a positive approach, proactiveness, and better work processes.
- To facilitate attitudinal/behavioural changes to enhance personal and professional growth to fit in with the changing organizational needs.
- To share learnings through discussion of case studies and best practices.

Framework of Training Programme

HCM RIPA was appointed as the nodal agency by Department of Personnel and Training, Government of India, for conducting a pilot training programme in one district in Rajasthan and HCM RIPA chose Kota district for this saturation training in consultation with the State

Government. HCM RIPA, through its CGG, in turn, assigned IL&FS Education and Technology Services Limited (IETS) the work of saturation training in Good Governance for State Government employees of Kota district. IETS has successfully implemented similar training programme, viz., "The Vibrant Governance Training Programme" for all the State Government employees in Gujarat. This programme has been widely appreciated and has had a positive impact on the mindsets of the employees as per the impact assessment carried out by an independent agency.

The framework of this training envisages building ownership amongst the staff for transformation through a process of discovery, practice and internalization of new skills and attitudes. The stress is on changing the employees' mindsets, and also their attitudes to work, sensitizing them to people's problems, improving their interpersonal behaviour, infusing personal convictions and developing communication skills, rather than on covering certain subjects or topics during training.

HCM RIPA and its CGG associated the District Collector, Kota, to oversee the saturation training in the district and help in the logistics of the programme. The Collector appointed nodal officers to assist them and periodically reviewed the training through periodic review meetings and visits to some actual training programmes. CGG/HCM RIPA faculty and senior IETS staff also visited some training centres from time to time to review the quality of training.

Programme Design

The training programme was designed to be interactive and contextual making it interesting, real and applicable to everyday work. The training helps participants to learn simple and practical tools for strengthening individual and team work, discussing solutions to day-to-day issues, making learning a part of group culture and, in general, getting better at work. The programme also identifies significant leadership and team work practices and examines how these have been carried out, both in theory and in practice.

The programme content captures and delivers case studies of success stories within the government, and uses them as a basis to motivate staff to understand that they too can get success by responding to issues in positive ways. Activities, games, role plays, group work and group discussions form an integral part of the programme structure.

The programme recognizes that for successful implementation of change programmes, there is a need to rapidly increase the number of individuals who will act as 'agents of change'. As long as change projects rely only on a small number of prime movers at the top and senior levels, acceptance and sustainability of change will be extremely difficult. Therefore, one of the most unique features of the training programme was the involvement of selected trainers from within the government as change agents. The government trainers were selected by Collector, Kota, working jointly with HCM RIPA faculty. These employees were trained by IETS as certified trainers and they, in turn, facilitated and conducted the programme for other employees, supported by IETS Master Trainers. This training methodology allows for high delivery standards even if trainer quality is variant.

Rollout of the Programme

The various stages and activities undertaken in the programme are depicted in the flow chart below:

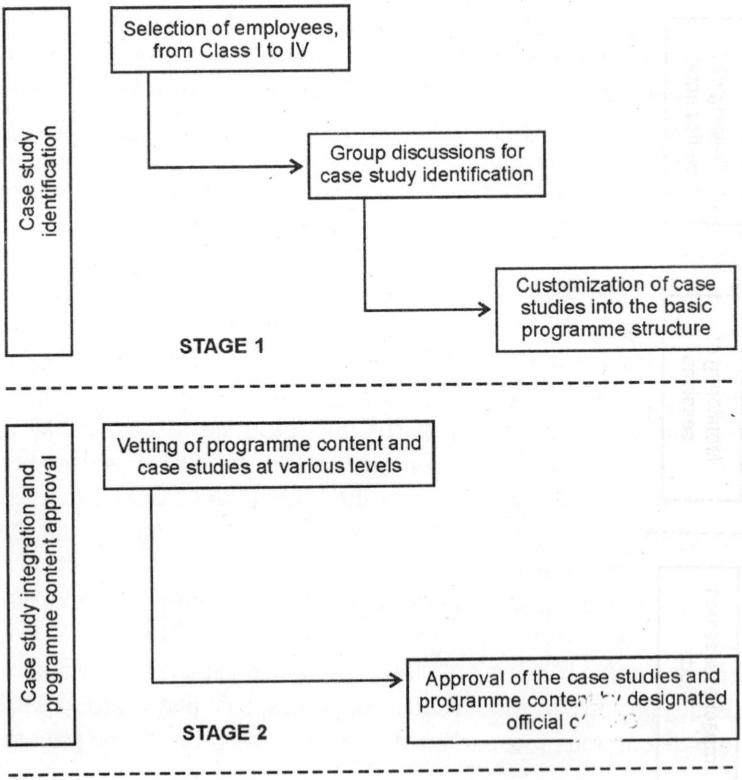

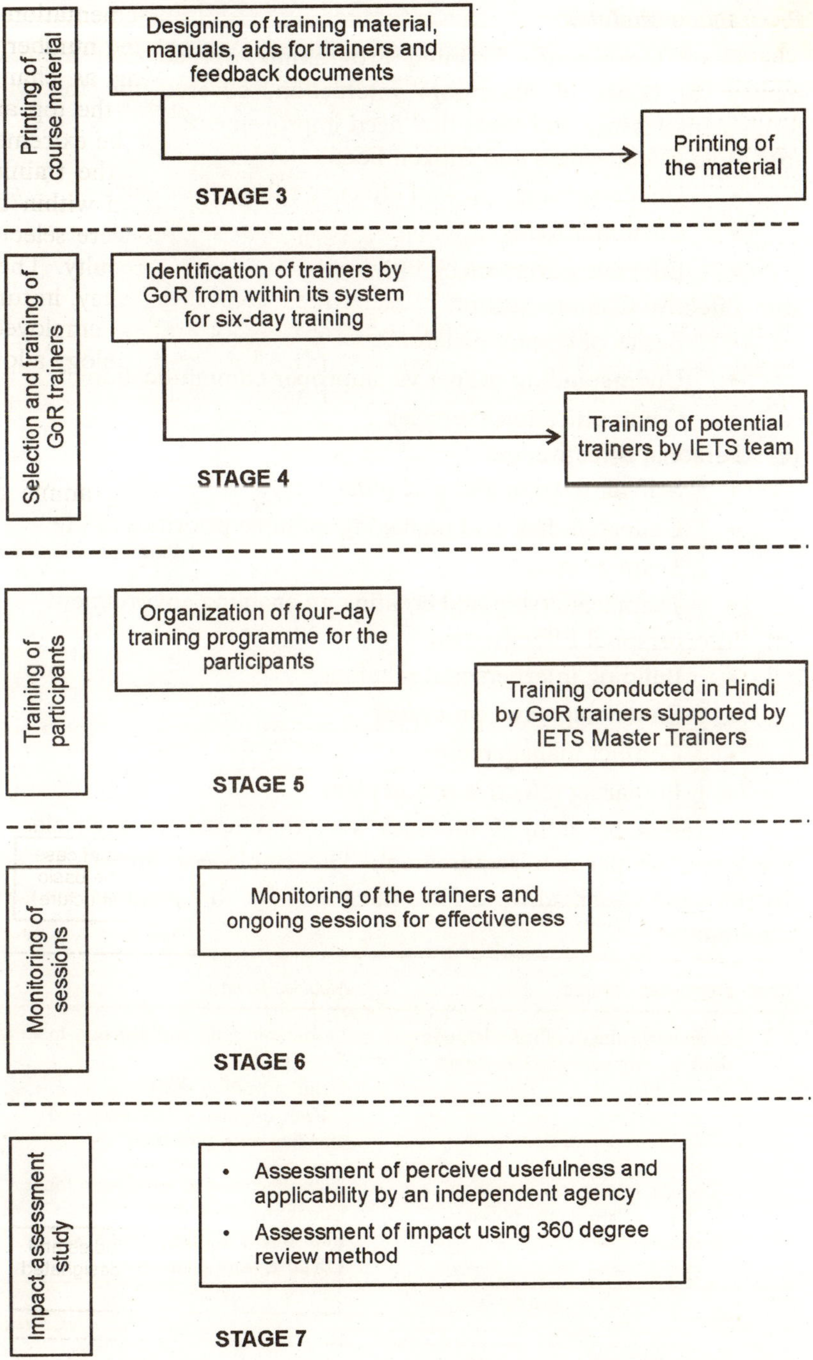
Printing of course material
Designing of training material, manuals, aids for trainers and feedback documents
Printing of the material
STAGE 3
Selection and training of GoR trainers
Identification of trainers by GoR from within its system for six-day training
Training of potential trainers by IETS team
STAGE 4
Training of participants
Organization of four-day training programme for the participants
Training conducted in Hindi by GoR trainers supported by IETS Master Trainers
STAGE 5
Monitoring of sessions
Monitoring of the trainers and ongoing sessions for effectiveness
STAGE 6
Impact assessment study
• Assessment of perceived usefulness and applicability by an independent agency
• Assessment of impact using 360 degree review method
STAGE 7

Programme Modules

The Good Governance Training Programme, spread over approximately 20 hours of classroom interaction, covered the following fundamental issues and areas that need improvement:

(a) Role Effectiveness and Citizen Focus
- Understanding role and effective role performance
- Customer focus
- Effective governance

(b) Effective Communication
- Basics of communication
- Understanding proper vs. improper communication
- Communication exercises

(c) Personal Effectiveness
- Self-motivation and discipline
- Understanding and managing multiple priorities of life
- Team work
- Team leadership and creating an enabling environment

(d) Interpersonal Effectiveness
- Building interpersonal relations
- Enhancing work processes
- Conflict management
- Preparing effective action plans

Different programme modules were developed for each class of employees as per job requirement. The employees posted in Kota district were classified in to four categories for this purpose, as given hereunder:

Class	*Employees Covered*	*Modules Covered*
I	State government officers including doctors, engineers and lecturers	Leadership skills and decision-making Team leadership Communication skills Citizen-oriented governance and effective work processes
II	Subordinate services including teachers, accountants, police personnel	Role effectiveness and citizen focus Communication skills Individual and interpersonal skills Effective work processes

Cont'd...

Cont'd...

III	Ministerial services like UDCs, LDCs etc.	Role effectiveness and citizen focus Communication skills Self-motivation Interpersonal skills
IV	Sahayaks, peons, drivers, etc.	Role effectiveness Communication skills Self-motivation Interpersonal skills

Programme Implementation

A total of 125 GoR trainers received training of trainers (ToT) training, the break-up of which is as under:

	No. of Batches Conducted	*No. of Trainers Trained*
Class I	1	22
Class II	3	52
Class III	1	43
Class IV	1	8
Total	6	125

Training in batches was conducted at select places in Kota city and was subsequently extended to Ramganjmandi, Sangod and Itawa sub-divisions. The total number of batches conducted and participants trained were as under:

	No. of Batches Conducted	*No. of Participants Trained*
Class I	73	1419
Class II	401	8711
Class III	111	1935
Class IV	154	3119
Total	739	15184

As per a conscious decision, teachers in government schools were not covered under the programme since the funds available and time frame of the pilot programmes were considered appropriate to cover 14,000 to 16,000 trainers.

Participants' Feedback

At the end of each four-day training programme, participants were required to fill a feedback form. Feedback was taken from participants on content, design and usefulness of the training programme, as well as on the training skills of the trainers. The overall feedback received from participants shows a positive orientation and the training was well received.

The charts given below depict the cumulative participant feedback:

Overall Programme

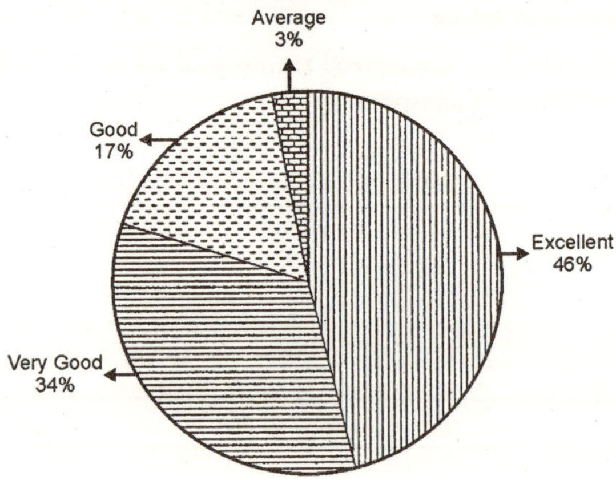

Usefulness and Practical Applicability of the Learnings from the Programme

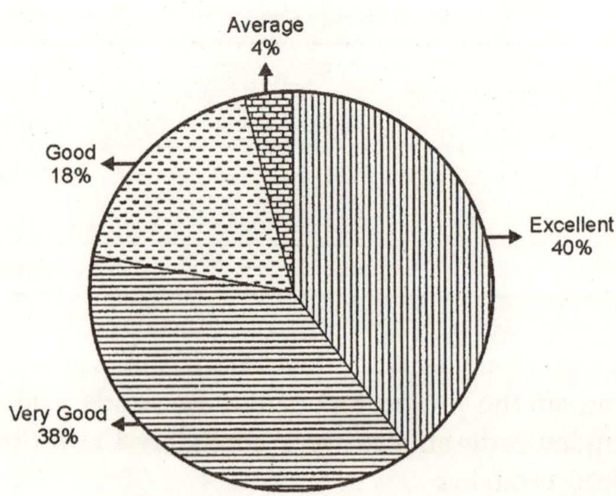

Structure and Design of the Programme

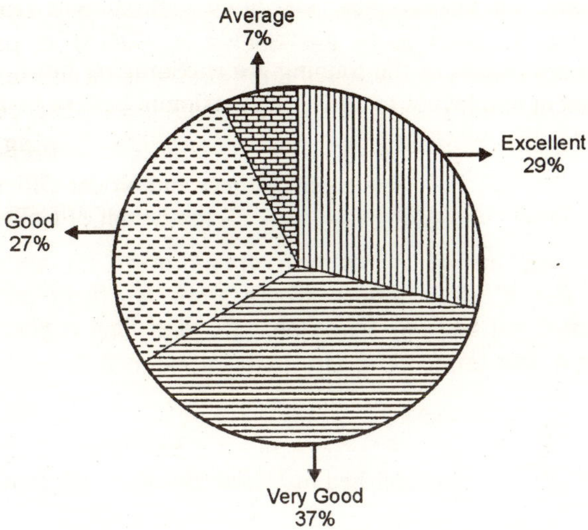

Course Content

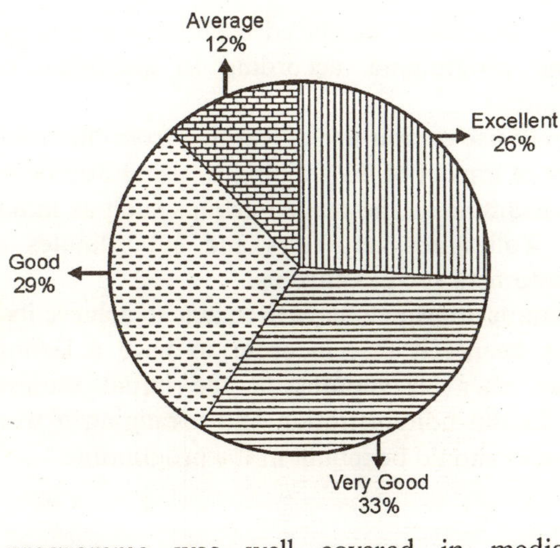

The programme was well covered in media and a few remarks/comments on the programme by district administrative authorities were as under:

"We often hear criticism of the style of working of government employees. To change this, the State Government has started a programme to teach good governance to officials and employees. Preliminary results of the training are encouraging but it is up to the government employees to derive the maximum benefit from it ..."

—Prathibha Singh
Settlement Officer and Nodal Officer Training
(on behalf of Collector, Kota)

"राज्य में गुड गवर्नेन्स के एक मात्रा पायलट प्रोग्राम की समीक्षा करने पर सरकारी क्षेत्र में इसके अनुकूल परिणाम देखने को मिले। अधिकारियों एवं कर्मचारियों में इस कोर्स को लेकर उत्साह है। कोटा जिले में सफल क्रियान्वयन के बाद इसे अन्य जगहों पर भी लागू किया जा सकता है।"

—Nirarjan Arya
Ex-District Collector, Kota
(published in *Dainik Bhaskar,* 4th January, 2006)

Impact Assessment of the Programme

An Impact Assessment Study of the training programme is also being carried out by an independent agency with a sample size of 3 per cent trainees across all levels.

This assignment would be carried out to address the following three aspects:

(a) To examine and assess perceived usefulness and applicability of the training programme, according to individual participants (self-evaluation)
(b) Assessment of use or non-use of learning from the training.
(c) Assessment of impact of the training by using 360 degrees review method to examine all the related groups such as family, internal customers, colleagues, superiors and subordinates as well as external customers such as citizens.

The programme appears to have been able to achieve its objectives. However, it has been felt that in order to have a lasting effect, a refresher course after six months of the initial training, remote monitoring by district administration and arranging a workshop for sharing experiences should be inbuilt in the programme.

13 Enhancing Skills and Capabilities in Government through a Regular Training Programme

Sanjay Kothari and Kiran Lekha Walia

The forces of globalization and liberalization and the consequent changes in the economic environment have created new challenges for the government departments the world over. In the case of planned economies such as India's, this involves a change in orientation from a command and control mode to a facilitative one, enhancement of technology, dissemination and improvement in the skills of its employees through regular training and education.[1] With the changing concept, the government personnel needs to be qualified and regularly trained in order that they possess the necessary knowledge about the government rules and procedures. The changing environment has led to increased mismatch between skills of the staff and the functional roles expected from them. The policy of time bound rather than competency and performance-based promotion has created a top-heavy organization with the number of field staff declining steadily. In the absence of adequate training opportunities, the competency levels in the government and its organization, especially in the matters relating to accounts, have gradually declined and need reorientation.

Management/accounts training and education has been widely accepted as a crucial input for improving managerial competency. The orientation training not only updates knowledge about the government rules and regulations but also increases organizational efficiency and effectiveness. It is general perception that the government functions on the basis of established procedures and knowledge and adherence to these procedures is essential for expeditious disposal of office work.

Background

To impart training to Haryana government employees in the matter of accounts, finance, budgeting and service rules and also to prepare the employees for taking Subordinate Accounts Services (SAS) (Part 1) examination held by the Government of Haryana, the Accounts Training Institute (ATI) was set up in the year 1969. The SAS examination is conducted in two parts, i.e., Part I and Part II, for government employees working as ministerial staff. The government employees on passing both the parts of SAS examination are given an appointment in the Treasury and Accounts Department as Section Officer. They have further promotional avenues as Accounts Officer, Senior Accounts Officer and Chief Accounts Officer. They work in different departments in different capacities as representatives of Finance Department and are responsible for proper implementation of financial rules, regulations and instructions issued by Finance Department from time to time. Thus, by passing SAS examination, a clerk can be promoted to a supervisory level, i.e., Section Officer, thus jumping a number of levels.

The ATI is a part of Treasury and Accounts Department and has a very small staff structure. It consists of only eight employees, including a Principal and a Senior Accounts Officer. It is a fact that the knowledge of up-to-date provisions contained in the Punjab Financial Rules (PFR), Civil Service Rules (CSR) and Budget Manual not only saves unwanted correspondence, wastage of time and public money but also helps the government in the best utilization of government resources for developmental activities.

In government departments, the main and pivotal functionary for all the financial matters is the Drawing and Disbursing Officer (DDO). DDO is a government servant who has been declared as such by the Administrative Department concerned in consultation with the Finance Department and who draws money for disbursement on bill, public cheques from the treasury.[2]

The DDOs play a vital role in the preparation of budget estimates, maintenance of departmental accounts and expenditure control on allotted budgets. They are also responsible for preparation of pension papers in time and sanction of loans and advances to government employees. The government has by and large streamlined the rules, procedures and instructions in order to ensure that the processing, preparation and submission of cases is carried out in a systematic manner.

The restructuring of government departments and public sector undertakings (PSUs) was started in April 2001, as per the directions of the government.[3] The state government issued detailed guidelines on restructuring of government departments/PSUs. These guidelines laid specific emphasis on reducing the establishment expenditure and reviewing the staff requirements, *de novo*. The main focus is on reduction of salary expenditure, which is the single largest factor responsible for the abysmal financial performance of the state government departments/state-owned enterprises. Stress was also laid on revision of work and efficiency norms, particularly in the light of information technology as a new technological tool and rationalization retraining and redeployment of staff and phasing out of commercial vehicles buses, trucks, tractors etc. The complete restructuring of 55 state government departments has been carried out with the above objective in mind.

The restructuring of state PSUs started way back in the year 1996 with the constitution of Ministers' Committee on Disinvestment/Privatization of State Public Enterprises. The state PSUs are smaller in size in comparison to the Central Public Enterprises, as such the scope for disinvestment was limited. Thus, the only options available were: (a) restructuring of potentially viable enterprises to make them self-sustaining, and (b) closure of enterprises which are sick and have no possibility of revival. The significant steps taken in this regard by this committee are as under:[4]

- The state government disinvested 51 per cent of its equity in two government companies.
- In some PSUs, the activities which had become redundant were closed down and the staff employed for these activities was rationalized.
- Six state PSUs, which were not doing well and had no possibility of revival were closed down. The entire staff of these organizations was retrenched in accordance with the legal provisions.
- Restructuring of the remaining PSUs was undertaken in accordance with the directions of state government.

During restructuring exercise, some PSUs pointed out that due to the lack of sufficient accounting personnel and awareness about the government rules and regulations, there has been persistent delay in finalization of annual accounts and other accounts related matters. It was also observed that the rules and regulations were not followed in letter and spirit. The financial monitoring is of utmost importance in

PSUs being commercial in nature. Hence, it was emphasized that DDOs, assistants and clerks should be deputed for accounts related training to ATI, Panchkula from time to time. This was also endorsed in the proceedings of the meetings of the respective PSUs. As such, training programmes to educate the DDOs, accountants and other personnel were started to upgrade the skills of the employees in various accounting and financial matters.

Structure and Functions of Accounts Training Institute

The restructuring of Treasury and Accounts Department was carried out in December 2002 and it was decided that the posts of Accounts Officer and Treasury Officer in the Accounts Training Institute (ATI) be abolished and that guest faculty be engaged for imparting training. This was proposed so as to reduce the burden of salary and pensionary benefits to be given to the regular employees. This also gave flexibility to the ATI to engage willing and motivated persons for training instead of posting unwilling staff in the ATI. The revision of pay scales and pension of the government employees after implementation of the Fifth Pay Commission had serious impact on state's financial health and if corrective measures are not taken at the right time, it may have serious impact on the state finances in the near future. Presently, ATI is conducting two courses simultaneously in a year with the faculty consisting of Principal, Senior Accounts Officer and guest faculty.

The institute was initially imparting training to the DDOs and clerical staff of different departments including Public Works Department. In addition, the ministerial staff of the state government was given training for taking SAS (Part 1) examination. Four different courses of the following durations were conducted as under:

Civil Course	42 days (clerical staff)
PWD Course	42 days (LDCs)
DDO Course	30 days
SAS (Part 1) Course	4 months

The training was basically on different codal rules as provided in various books, i.e., CSR, PFR, Subsidiary Treasury Rules (STR), Account Code(s) and also about the latest instructions of the state government issued on the various subject matters.

Need for Rescheduling the Training Programmes in the Changed Context

It was observed that in spite of directions from the Government of Haryana and Haryana Bureau of Public Enterprises to nominate employees for training at ATI, the response from the employees was poor. This appeared to be a weak spot in the process of building up the capacity of the government personnel in performing their functions. The role of the employees cannot be downplayed in the process of transformation as they are considered the mainstay in the government structure. Keeping in view the above fact, a meeting to reschedule the training programmes to suit the needs of each and every category of employees was convened in December 2002 under the chairmanship of Secretary to Government of Haryana, Personnel and Coordination Department wherein Principal, Divisional Training Centre, HIPA, Panchkula and Principal, ATI, Haryana, Panchkula and certain other officers from the secretariat and the departments were also associated to do a complete brainstorming session about training. After detailed deliberations, it was decided to introduce the accountants course for a duration of two weeks. The other courses being currently conducted were rescheduled as under:

Civil Course	2 weeks
PWD Course	2 weeks
DDO Course	2 weeks (DDOs/likely DDOs)
SAS (Part I) Course	8 weeks
Accountants Course	2 weeks

Civil Course

This course is for imparting basic training regarding codal provisions in CSR/PFR/STR etc. to ministerial staff promoted from Class IV employees and appointed under ex-gratia scheme etc. and will be of two weeks' duration. This training will be imparted again to the same official after a gap of two years.

PWD Course

The course is for imparting basic training regarding codal provisions in CSR/PFR/STR and PWD code to Lower Division Clerks (LDCs) of all the three wings of Public Works Department, i.e., Public Health, Buildings and Roads (B&R) and Irrigation, and shall be for a duration of two weeks.

DDO Course

This course shall be of two weeks' duration for the officers presently working as DDO and likely DDO. Those already trained shall again have to undergo one-week training after a period of five years. The reason for reducing the duration of this course from thirty days to two weeks was that it was not possible for the departments to send the DDO for a full month as a lot of work is held up in his absence. The officers likely to be promoted as DDO were also included so as to train them in advance before holding this important assignment.

Accountant Course

Keeping in view an acute shortage of accounts clerks and accountants in different departments of the state government and PSUs, this new course was started to impart training to the clerks with a minimum five years' service and also to the assistants for a duration of two weeks. The training shall include preparation of different kinds of bills, writing of cashbook and maintenance of different accounts books etc.

SAS (Part I) Course

Under this course, the training is to be imparted to the ministerial staff working in the various offices of Haryana government, its boards and corporations for a duration of eight weeks. This training is to facilitate the candidates to undertake the SAS (Part I) examination with determination and courage and on getting through the same, they are offered appointment in Finance Department as Section Officer.

Streamlining the Procedure for Conducting Courses

The procedure for conducting the courses was streamlined and it was proposed that two courses would be conducted simultaneously so that a total number of 24 courses can be conducted in a year. There would be eight sessions per day for two courses out of which three/four would be conducted by the regular staff and the remaining four/five will be conducted by guest faculty. The employees of the boards and corporations deputed for training are charged an amount of Rs 2,000 for Civil, PWD and DDO courses and Rs 4,000 for SAS (Part I) course. It was also thought to explore the possibility of engaging the guest faculty on contract basis at a consolidated amount as various universities and colleges in Haryana have already undertaken similar type of arrangements.

It was proposed that all ministerial staff and officers working in the capacity as DDO should be trained within a period of two years. The heads of the departments were requested to initially sponsor the names of those officers/officials who have not undergone any training in ATI. After the training, the trainees were required to undertake examination on the last day of their training period. In case of any candidate not passing the examination conducted by the ATI, he/she shall have to appear in the examination subsequently at his/her own expense, failing which, he/she shall have to undergo the training again. In such case, daily allowance would be admissible at 50 per cent for the actual period of training. This step was taken to make the participants serious about the training and avoid absenteeism in the class. A complete hard-bound manual was also given to the trainees for their day-to-day use in their jobs by the DDOs/accounts personnel, as this has to be frequently referred to for performance of their routine functions.

In order to finalize the schedule for imparting training to the DDOs/likely DDOs and officials, a meeting was convened in February 2004 to chalk out a departmentwise programme to suit the needs of each and every department. Directors, Additional Directors and other officers of various departments and officers of the boards and corporations were associated in order to obtain a first-hand information on the staff already trained and the staff which required immediate training.

Government Departments

Women and Child Department

In Women and Child Department (WCD), there are 19 Programme Officers at the district level and 116 Child Development Project Officers (CDPOs) in the department. The basic qualification of CDPOs is MSc (Home Science). They are provided induction training initially but there is no input on accounts in such trainings. As such, they have no knowledge regarding accounting principles. Only 30 CDPOs were trained at ATI. The training schedule was worked out in consultation with the Director so that the departmental priorities can be kept in mind. The Director, WCD, agreed that the dedicated courses be conducted for CDPOs during the months of April and May. It was decided that the department should sponsor a minimum of 35 officers. The reason for asking the departments to send 35 officers was that the class size becomes viable and the participants could also learn from the experiences of others.

The ATI has already conducted three courses of two weeks' duration till date. In these courses, 80 CDPOs have been imparted training. The ATI has also conducted three courses for accountants and has trained 68 accountants/clerks. This training should be of great help to the CDPOs in utilizing the funds in accordance with the rules and procedures of the government.

Health Department

There are about 400 DDOs and an equal number of likely DDOs, who are doctors in the Health Department. Of them, only 60 doctors have been imparted training in ATI. The state government has formulated guidelines for training and development of the staff posted in various health institutions. The training was aimed at achieving staff competence in accounting and related fields so that they gain confidence in utilizing funds in a proper manner. This was proposed as it was seen that even after delegating the powers of DDOs to the doctors, they were reluctant in utilizing/spending the funds due to the fear of their misutilization.

As such, the state government organized dedicated training programmes for DDOs of Health Department and directed ATI to conduct these courses. This was done as doctors, although competent, did not have the expertise to handle accounts related work very efficiently and effectively. The training schedule was worked out keeping in view the departmental priorities so that the official work does not suffer.

The ATI has already conducted seven courses of two weeks' duration each till date. In these courses, 125 senior medical officers had been imparted training uptill the time of writing this paper. It is felt that this training would help the senior medical officers in utilizing the funds in accordance with the rules and procedures of the government.

Animal Husbandry Department

There are about 80 DDOs working in the field offices and twenty officers are likely DDOs. As none of the DDOs, who are veterinary doctors, have been trained in financial matter at ATI so it was decided that such doctors be deputed for training during the month of June and July and in the subsequent courses conducted by the ATI.

The ATI has already conducted three courses of two weeks' duration till date. In these courses, 42 doctors have been imparted training till date.

Education Department

There are 3,000 DDOs and one thousand and 800 Headmasters/Vice Principals as likely DDOs. Five dedicated courses should be conducted for the Head Masters of the High Schools and Principals of the Secondary Schools in order to provide awareness and acquaint them with the accounting principles and the government rules and regulations.

The institute has already conducted four courses of two weeks' duration each till date. In all, 130 Head Masters/Vice Principals have been imparted training till now.

Sports and Youth Welfare Department

This is the only department where all the 22 DDOs have undergone training in the ATI. Accountants who assist the DDOs would be deputed for the accountants course, recently started by the ATI, to update their knowledge in accounting and other ancillary matters.

Public Sector Undertakings

Haryana State Agriculture Marketing Board

There are 106 DDOs and an equal number of Assistant Secretaries in the likely DDOs category in HSAMB. It was decided that keeping in view the nature of activities being carried out by the Board, dedicated course for DDOs and Assistant Secretaries be conducted in the months of March, June, July, August, October, January and February in the office premises of Agriculture Marketing Board Haryana at Panchkula.

The ATI has conducted two courses for these employees in which 68 DDOs/likely DDOs have been imparted training till date. The institute under the Accountants Course has also trained 33 employees.

Haryana Warehousing Corporation

Eight DDOs and accountants assisting them were deputed for training under the respective courses by the organization.

The ATI had already imparted training to 8,918 government employees uptill July 2004 in accounting and related subjects. Training is a continuous process and as per the schedule, a large number of employees would be trained during the financial year 2005–06.

Conclusion

In Haryana, the expenditure on salary and pension in 2002–03 was to the tune of Rs 3,958.25 crore, i.e., 44.43 per cent of the total revenue expenditure of Rs 8,908.68 crore. In the changed economic scenario with mounting salary and pension liabilities, the only way to restructure the economy is (a) training of employees, and (b) streamlining of government departments and PSUs. It is essential that in-service training is provided to the employees in order to update them on latest rules, regulations and government instructions issued from time to time. If they are not trained on the latest trends in the country, it is very likely that the employees who form the backbone of the government system would soon lose sight of the latest amendments and would be left behind. Greater emphasis is laid on dedicated courses so that they are acquainted with each other and it becomes easier for them to interact among themselves. The achievement, after the training was re-scheduled, was remarkable, as 942 employees had been trained during the year 2004–05 against only 149 employees trained during the year 2001–03. It is not essential that an employee continues to do the same work throughout his life. Change is the need of the hour, and to make an employee work in different capacities, which is not synonymous to his basic qualification, it is essential that he/she is imparted training to update his/her skills in that area. The whole exercise is a step in this direction and it is viewed that this will go a long way in orienting and enhancing the competency level and skills of an employee.

Notes

1. Paper presented at EROPA Conference in October 2003 at New Delhi by T.R. Madanmohan, P.D. Jose, Chiranjibsen Indian Institutes of Bangalore on Restructuring Government Services to meet Changing State Holder Needs: A Case Study of Department of Industries and Commerce in Karnataka.
2. Rule 2.16 of Budget Manual.
3. Chief Secretary's D.O. No. 2399-CS-2001, dated 27.4.2001.
4. Rightsizing in Government with Emphasis on Restructuring of State Public Enterprises of Haryana by Sanjay Kothari and Rajesh Barisal, *The Administrator,* Vol. XLVI, July 2003.

Section IV

Sector-Specific Training

14 Training and Rural Development

G.S. Narwani

The two major objectives of the British governance in India were maximization of land revenue collection and maintenance of law and order. India was more or less a 'Police State'. Dyad of District Magistrate and Superintendent of Police held sway in rural as well as urban India in terms of both power and authority.

Bureaucracy and Centralization in Development

Even after independence, when an independent development machinery was established, the Collector or District Magistrate continued to hold sway as head of the district for development works, acting as the chief instrument of the centralized state and central governments. This institutionalization of extra-local system of power and authority in post-independent India has been a critical factor in retarding grassroots democracy and empowerment.

Five-year plans for development were also highly centralized. Importance was given to non-local bureaucracy, rural subsidies and handouts, resulting in deteriorating social infrastructure and failed local governments. In the absence of financial autonomy, political autonomy proved meaningless. Moreover, when people are not part of a growing vital community, they gradually disempower themselves from the social process also.

Towards Decentralization

During the late 1970s, development thinking around the world moved in the direction of sustainability. Large-scale development projects came under scrutiny and smaller localized initiatives and decentralized planning emerged as the new panacea. During the 1980s, many developing countries encouraged people's participation and grassroots planning. In India too, there was a felt need to go back to the roots of local empowerment and in 1992, the 73rd Constitutional Amendment was promulgated to provide the first practical framework for empowering the local communities and their institutions. It provided for regular elections to local bodies every five years, reservation of one-third seats of members and chairpersons for women, reservation for scheduled castes and tribes in proportion to their population in the area, state finance commissions to strengthen their financial base and provide for district planning bodies for preparation of plans for economic development and social justice. Panchayati Raj bodies were to be created at village, block and district levels as the third tier of governance.

Though it ushered in an era of democratization, affirmative action, financial autonomy and decentralized planning in local bodies, disenfranchisement and disempowerment cannot be wiped away overnight by a change in the Constitution. It will still take a few more years to create awareness and desire for change and empowerment.

Prerequisites for Decentralization

Decentralization of governance demands responsive, accountable, transparent, decentralized and people-friendly administration at all levels. Delivery of efficient services and competence cannot be expected unless the elected representatives as well as officials are reoriented to meet current challenges with new approaches. Capacity building is needed to enhance competencies of such local level functionaries. Hence, efforts should be directed towards:

1. training elected representatives including women representatives and administrative personnel to increase their capacity and competence to manage local institutions;
2. enhancing institutional capacity for decentralized planning and implementation;
3. developing capacity to manage local resources;
4. enhancing interaction between stakeholders in local governance, specially the SCs/STs/women;
5. ensuring processes fully accountable and transparent to the people; and
6. improving systems and procedures for local public administration.

Core Problem

The 73rd Constitutional Amendment created a legal opportunity for the pursuit of local self-governance at the village level. While the ideals related to self-governance have been current in the Indian political thoughts throughout this century, their practice has been largely inadequate on the ground. Mahatma Gandhi had spoken at great length about the importance of self-governance by Gram Sabha in the 1930s. But, during the four decades after independence, the system of governance became far more centralized than was originally emphasized. This has been particularly so in the field of health, education, agriculture, rural development, drinking water, sanitation, forestry, etc. National programmes and policies have been periodically issued to be translated into budgets and targets at the state level and handed down to the district administration. In this process, not only was the participation of ordinary citizens in determining their own future completely ignored but traditional institutions of self-governance were systematically destroyed. Therefore, the current opportunity created by the 73rd Constitutional Amendment for holding regular elections through the State Election Commissions and infusion of new blood in the form of women, scheduled castes and tribes, other backward castes, needs to be seized in order to ensure long-standing commitments for decentralized, democratic governance in our society.

There are now more than 10 lakh official functionaries and 34 lakh elected representatives throughout the country at state/district/block /village levels. The representation of women at various levels in the panchayat bodies is almost to the tune of 11 lakh. The locally elected panchayats are expected to develop policies, prepare and implement plans and programmes to manage various functions envisaged in Schedule XI of the Constitution. The success of decentralization would depend on how well local government institutions are equipped to handle these responsibilities. There is a need to build all-round capabilities of local functionaries. Training of about 34 lakh public representatives and equipping them with suitable knowledge and skills in planning, management and delivery systems of the functional domain of panchayats poses a great challenge. The political space which is opening up through constitutional amendment requires careful and systematic interventions if the dream of local self-governance has to be translated into reality.

It has been realized that manpower becomes a resource only when properly trained and motivated. The effectiveness of manpower can be increased by improving human skills through well-tailored and job-oriented training programmes. Rural development in democratic societies is not a matter only of plans and statistics, targets and budgets, technology and method, material aid and professional staff or agencies and organizations to administer them. Rather, "it is an effective use of these mechanisms as educational means for changing the mind and actions of people in such ways that they help themselves to attain economic and social improvements. Hence, the process is one of working with people, not for them; of helping people become self-reliant, not dependent on others; of making people the central actors in the drama, not stage hands or spectators; helping people by means of education to put useful knowledge to work for them. This process is the essence of training for rural development" as described by Paul Leagans while advocating for extension education for community development.

The principle of self-help through training lies at the core of India's rural development programmes. It includes among other things:

1. *The objective: To* raise the economic and social level of the rural people.
2. *General elements requiring change:* Farm, home, public services and rural community.
3. *Specific elements requiring change:*
   (a) crops, livestock, soils, water use;
   (b) food, clothing, sanitation, comfort, appearance, etc.,
   (c) schools, health centres, wells, roads, cooperatives, etc.
   (d) organization, group skills, leadership, community spirit, cooperation, etc.
4. *Key element that must be changed:* People.
5. *Type of people that must be changed:* Men, women, youth and children.
6. *Voluntary agents of change:* Local leaders.
7. *Professional agents of change:* Village-level, block-level and district-level development officials/officers.

Rural Development Training

The need for training in rural development extends to all people who either have administrative responsibility or are people's elected representatives or who as volunteers seek opportunities to improve village conditions, including community-based NGOs. Change within democracy must be viewed and understood to be both a social and an economic process. The administrators, subject matter specialists and village development personnel as well as village leaders are all agents of social change and messengers of development. Village people also have to look at them not with suspicion but as their friends, as a resource that is helpful to them and provides answers to their problems. In this process of problem recognition and solution seeking, the government machinery is to perform a dual role. It must stimulate in the villagers the interest in the present and then bring them the resources to solve problems through participation of people in the rural areas.

Inspire and Train Village People

The success of development personnel will lie in inspiring and training village people to look to themselves, their leaders, their institutions and resources to solve most of their problems. Until very recently, they have been looking to the government to solve their problems. Gradually, the community has to take over the maintenance function of community assets created so far with government support and for that confidence is to be developed in them and they should be able to raise resources at the local level and become self-sustaining. This can be possible only through capacity building of village leaders.

A Passage to Empowerment

'Empower' means "to invest with legal power", "to authorize", and "to enable". The concept of empowerment has evolved from the bottom-up approach to development. Empowerment of grassroots level functionaries takes shape when genuine efforts are made to ensure autonomy, motivation and developmental opportunities for functionaries during their job performance. It is a process involving collective decision-making, collective action and popular participation. It creates a climate in which functionaries spontaneously develop a sense of fulfilment and ownership during the process of achieving institutional goals. It encourages teams to work together in a collaborative way. It has the driving force to reverse work style from dependency to self-initiative, from doing things right to doing the right things and from reactive to proactive posture. Human versatility, ingenuity and competence can do wonders when empowerment is focussed rightly and strengthened with conviction. The above perspectives on empowerment affirm the need to build the capacity of communities to respond to a changing environment.

True empowerment should focus on fulfilment of the following:

(a) Are we treating functionaries as assets rather than costs?
(b) Are we developing suitable institutional culture?
(c) Are we cultivating the climate of knowledge-sharing rather than information-sharing?
(d) Are we encouraging opportunity-driven excellence?

(e) Are we using power as generative rather than distributive?
(f) Are we really enabling functionaries to perform at higher levels by facilitating with necessary environment, tools, resources, etc.?
(g) Are we a favourably structured organization?
(h) Are we committed to the development of functionaries as much as to the development of organization?
(i) Are we reaching beyond the traditional approaches of motivation?

The practical thinking in the public sector and government still continues to treat human beings as public servants who are to obey government orders as committed servants and remain as silent spectators of policy dictated to them by the top bureaucrats and policy makers. Functionaries are hardly treated as partners in running the administration or as social assets who can really contribute in policy making decisions. Hence, the culture of participative management still seems to be a dream.

Training courses are generally to impart information rather than to develop human resources through participative processes and role-play or group discussions for exchanging success stories. The hidden potential is not driven out through brain-storming sessions. Instead of motivating people to perform better and encourage them, we still behave in traditional ways of disciplinary action and punitive measures only. It kills the initiative and proactive nature of budding youths and intelligentsia who become merely followers rather than leaders.

Empowerment should result in discharge of any or all of the following key roles:

(a) *Informal role:* To ensure that information at government, non-government, donor institution levels is shared to increase the combined knowledge power. People should have access to knowledge and skills.
(b) *Decision-making role:* To ensure that all people, particularly women and youth as well as marginalized classes, participate in decisions that affect them, they have autonomy in decision-making processes at village level and there is direct participatory democracy in governance.
(c) *Planning role:* To ensure people's involvement in setting their own goals so that application of indigenous knowledge is also possible in addition to theoretical/scientific knowledge.
(d) *Evaluating role:* To ensure a 'valuing process' and encourage people to take and ask for help.
(e) *Motivating role:* To ensure a sense of pride in accomplishment.

(f) *Developing role:* To encourage creativity and use all skills of people.

Such empowerment will lead to sustainable development. The thrust of empowerment for sustainable development approach is socio-economic, political, educational, technological, cultural and spiritual.

Humanizing through empowerment will have a remarkable impact on PRIs which will visibly grow in efficiency through the power of people, passionately committed to meaningful goals, acting in accordance with their own higher values, taking risks and demonstrating initiative and creativity in the service of these goals. HRD strength is developing leadership, confidence in power of people and competence of functionaries, role clarity, responding to change and working together by sharing responsibility and authority.

Major Actors in Empowerment Process

Groups that need to be strengthened for broad public participation in the decision-making process and for public access to information, include people facing poverty, marginalized peasant farmers, SCs/STs/OBCs, and women living in fragile socio-economic conditions. Non-government organizations (NGOs) are generally regarded as playing a responsible and constructive role in the process of empowerment. Some business houses also donate funds for development and empowerment of poorer sections of community in many states. Training institutions also develop people elected for PRIs through various institutional and field programmes. Some prominent NGOs, with the help of international funding agencies, have also created awareness among tribals who go the extent of preventing forest departments from using minor forest produce and prohibit the government from acquiring their agricultural lands for cement factories and other development projects without the approval of the Gram Sabha, specially after passing of the Panchayat (Extension to Scheduled Areas) Act, 1996.

Obstacles

The weight of tradition during the last five decades is going to make it difficult for local self-governance to succeed. The national and state governments, through political apparatus and bureaucratic machinery, are, by and large, going to resist any devolution of power. Their attempt will be to build PRIs in the rural areas as the third tier of government and decentralized development delivery mechanism. This posture will ensure that the Central Government remains the first 'tier' developing national policies and deciding on resource mobilization and allocation. Thus, PRIs will be the leftover residual category where plans made from the top level at the national and state levels will be merely implemented with the resources made available from 'first' and 'second' tiers.

Really speaking, the system of Panchayati Raj should be treated as the 'first' and fundamental tier. It is at the level of Gram Sabha where face-to-face and participatory democracy can be practised. It is at this level that all the available physical and human resources can be mobilized to develop priority programmes in social and economic sectors that first meet the needs of the families and community in the Gram Sabha. Thus, the base institutions of Panchayati Raj not only develop programmes but also govern their resources, inter-family relations and community as a whole. The areas and issues that require negotiations across the Gram Sabha may then be dealt with through representative democratic systems created at the block level. A similar approach can be taken to the issues that require the attention of panchayats at the district level.

As can be seen, this bottom-heavy model of local self-governance is dramatically different from what most governments would like to accomplish. But, it is a prerequisite for self-governance which requires space without external control so that village people can exercise their right of self-governance in the real sense.

The second arena that will require intervention in the process is building norms and institutions at the base level that will facilitate the practice of face-to-face participatory democracy at the Gram Sabha level. Since most of these traditional institutions have been destroyed and people's capacity to govern them systematically undermined by the top-down model of development practised by the state for almost five decades, it will need enormous support for rebuilding ideas, norms, capacities and mechanisms from the bottom-up. The attitudes and perspectives of the members of the village community have been so systematically conditioned that they continue to remain as passive recipients of the state support handed down to them as subsidy. This requires cultural transformation to inform, educate, inspire and stimulate families and communities to believe in their indigenous capacity and institutions of local self-governance.

It is in such context that educational interventions with village communities and newly elected representatives of PRIs become critical. It is likely that the state may also focus on propaganda for decentralization of powers but this major task cannot be left to the state alone.

Other institutions of the civil society need to seize this challenge in order to help utilize the space for local self-governance made available through constitutional amendment. The voluntary organizations, NGOs and training and research institutions all have to work hand-in-glove to achieve this gigantic challenge of participatory training and capacity building of functionaries of PRIs.

The constraints in the empowerment process mainly relate to lack of political will and paucity of funds required to develop the capacity of lakhs of elected functionaries in PRIs in India.

References

Balaji, C.S., Chandra Shekhar, S., Dutta Rajan, *Leading Change through Human Relations,* 1998.

Directorate of Extension, Government of India, *Extension Education in Community Development,* 1961.

Mahajan, Y.S., and H.R. Virmani, *Human Resource Management and Development,* 1989.

Saxena, J.P., Anita T. Kakkar, *Training and Development,* 2000.

Singh, Naresh, and Titi Vangile, *Empowerment Towards Sustainable Development,* 1995.

UNNATTI-Organization for Development Education, *Perspectives and Practices, Essays on Grassroot Development,* 1998.

YASHDA, *Capacity Building of Panchayati Raj Functionaries,* 2000.

15 Training for Participatory Irrigation Management in India

Rakesh Hooja

Introduction: Objectives, Approach and Contents of PIM Training

In many countries, irrigation sector reforms and Participatory Irrigation Management (PIM) with increasing transfer of management responsibilities from government agencies to farmer or user organizations are gaining momentum. Mexico, Philippines, Colombia and Turkey are some of the well-known examples of transfer of irrigation systems through PIM processes. In India, even though PIM is being promoted for some time, the scale and impact have been somewhat negligible.

The first shift in thinking on irrigation management can be traced to the multidisciplinary Command Area Development (CAD) programme in the 1970s, which envisaged optimization of irrigated agriculture in a manner that should improve the quality of life of the people within the Command Area, as opposed to the traditional approach of constructing canals, thus creating irrigation potential and hoping that it would result into increased area under irrigation which in turn would lead to increased agricultural production. However, after more than three decades of efforts under CAD, what is disturbing in India is the failure of even the best CAD organization to evoke much farmers' participation except in some rare instances. This could be attributed to attention being focused on hydrological, engineering, agricultural and economic aspects. Especially in official documents it has in the past been rare to find described, let alone analyzed, the human side of the organization and operation of irrigation systems. The management of those who manage water, the procedures of allocation of water to groups or individuals, and the distribution of water within groups, there may have been almost as many instances of those omissions as there are reports on irrigation. Hence, efforts to involve farmers in water management are like groping in the dark due to insufficient knowledge and understanding (Hooja, 1995).

PIM was introduced on a pilot basis as part of the CAD programme in various Indian states. Then, in 1996, the Ninth Five-Year Plan Working Group on PIM of the Government of India (GoI) suggested that irrigation schemes covered under centrally-sponsored CAD Programme or under World Bank-aided projects be taken up first for introduction of PIM. It also suggested mass awareness campaigns and large-scale training of farmers and government functionaries and corresponding training capacities for PIM to be built up. However, in most of the cases, these efforts have had limited success.

The inevitability of reforms and the urgent need for farmer participation led to renewed impetus for PIM. Andhra Pradesh became the pioneering state in India to bring about overall institutional reforms in the irrigation sector at the state level in 1997 with a 'big bang' approach (Joshi and Hooja, 2000). The Andhra Pradesh Farmers Management of Irrigation Systems (APFMIS) Act, 1997, became the model for reforms in Madhya Pradesh. Both Andhra Pradesh and Madhya Pradesh have witnessed two rounds of elections for Water Users Associations (WUAs). Some other states have opted for changes or replacement in existing irrigation legislation. In most of the states, however, the momentum for PIM has been slow.

The experience of the pilot projects on PIM under CAD, as well as the experiences of the various states, highlights the importance of training as an imperative component of any reform process, critical to the realization of the objectives of the programme. Through training, the farmers and the staff can be equipped to handle new responsibilities and to cope with changed job requirements. The limited success in many cases also suggests that training needs to be developed as an instrument of change in the reform process rather than as a support mechanism, which it is currently viewed as. Hence, the concept of training has to be broad based and flexible for incorporating new challenges.

The training needs for PIM in the country would vary from state to state depending on the progress of PIM and the changes that are envisaged, but for the country as a whole they are definitely immense. The report of the Working Group on PIM programme for the Ninth Five-Year Plan of the Government of India estimated that nearly 30,000 farmers and 2,000 officers would need to be trained during the plan period. These estimates were based on the proposal that 2,000 pilot projects would be taken up during the plan period and that at least 15 farmers and one officer would be trained per project. Further, the Working Group suggested the need for increasing the capabilities of the present training institutions and the creation of proper training modules (GoI, 1996: 47).

These estimates by the Working Group sound modest if compared by the magnitude of training man-days generated during the adoption of the new Irrigation Act in Andhra Pradesh. During March-April 1999 alone,11 intensive four-day training programmes were conducted for the training of trainers to become the district level trainers. Five officers, one each from irrigation and CAD, revenue, and agricultural departments, were trained as trainers for the districts. A "Trainers Hand Book" and a "Manual on Orientation in Training" were brought out for the guidance of the trainers. A special 'training kit' had been designed for training farmers with flip charts and a manual prepared in local language, During July-August 1999, the training programmes were conducted in all the districts at selected places for the training of 65,000 presidents and Territorial Committee (TC) members of Water Users Associations (WUAs). About 55,000 presidents and TC members were actually trained during this period. Further, these trainees were given a manual on WUA activities and details of the provisions of the APFMIS Act with description of the rights and responsibilities of the WUAs.

Given the aim of training to function as an instrument of change and to help shape the reform process, the issue of designing appropriate training programmes should be addressed so as to enhance effectiveness of the training programme. The design of the programme should clearly follow from the objectives of the training programme, and the follow-up and feedback received from previous programmes as a measure of the achievement of the programme objectives. A clear definition of the objectives for any training programme forms the first essential step for designing a training programme. A clearly spelled out purpose for the training could include objectives such as:

- To develop a cadre of committed people through the training programme with the conceptual know-how about PIM and the willingness to propagate it.
- To reduce the prejudices and problems through stimulation of modified attitudes and behaviour suited to the adoption of new paradigms in PIM.
- To enable participants to acquire practical knowledge and skills for various definite PIM related purposes, for example, for creation and management of WUAs or for the use of agriculture extension

and irrigation extension efforts of the government to facilitate, propagate and stimulate PIM.

The objectives of the programme would depend on the type of trainee group and the specific tasks that the specific group is expected to handle in the PIM process.

This paper adopts the view of training as an instrument of reform and stimulating changes in the existing systems and practices, thus removing it from the confines of the traditional, narrow outlook of training as a means to impart information and skills about particular aspects or subjects. Thus, in the context of this paper, training is being viewed in its broadest sense to include mass awareness building and attitudinal change in addition to imparting skills and knowledge related to irrigation, agriculture, participation, group dynamics, financial accounting, etc. The PIM training would thus need to:

(a) create a favourable climate within the country in general for the propagation of PIM,
(b) prepare water users to undertake PIM through Water Users Associations of some sort or the other,
(c) enable the government departments and agencies related to water resources and irrigated agriculture to reorient themselves and adopt new roles, organizational structures, processes and ways of functioning such that they can play a facilitative role for furthering PIM and joint farmer-government agency partnerships, and
(d) equip lower level functionaries of government, employees of NGOs, and others to facilitate PIM.

As has been indicated in Hooja (2000), training for PIM is too important to be left only to trainers in places like WALMIs. Multi-disciplinary teams of those knowledgeable about social interaction, irrigation, agriculture, groundwater, training, administrative coordination, rural development, extension services, etc., need to collaborate with government functionaries, farmers and NGOs who are intimately involved in implementation of PIM for imparting training in PIM. Thus, the multidisciplinary mobile PIM teams being used for implementing PIM programmes and government staff, Chairmen of WUAs, and community organizers involved in the PIM pilot projects should all be jointly used along with specialist trainers fully oriented about PIM to impart PIM training and orientation. The state-level PIM cell responsible for policy making and implementation of PIM should directly coordinate such training. Thus, a PIM Training and Orientation Centre should be placed under the direct control of the state-level PIM policy and implementation cell in the State Government Secretariat.

Sinha (2001) has suggested the following objectives of training in PIM:

- Increased participation of the farmers in every activity related to water management.
- Enabling farmers to identify the problems of the irrigation system to seek their own solutions and formulate and implement their own projects to set right the system.
- Rehabilitation of irrigation system, especially canals, through participatory processes.
- Operation, maintenance and management of irrigation system by farmers.
- Equitable distribution of water among all irrigators.
- Additional resource generation for irrigation management activities.
- Increased involvement of women and youth at all levels of irrigation management.
- Reorientation of irrigation bureaucracy, field staff of line agencies and high level policy makers including the government bureaucracy and politicians.
- Increased participation of NGOs, community organizers and voluntary organizations in PIM.
- Promote genuine NGOs, trainers and social activists who can facilitate the training objectives in PIM.
- Training of trainers in PIM.
- Environmental safeguards against waterlogging, salinity, alkalinity and water table recession.
- 'Social Capital' building in the form of Water User Associations (WUAs).

Hooja (2000) goes on to add that PIM training should include:

- efforts at general orientation about PIM and attitudinal reorientation about PIM,
- knowledge and skills in improved water and agriculture management, i.e., technical matters,
- PIM-related procedural, administrative and organization issues, incentives available, sources of incentives and funding,
- lessons (about both successes and failures) from a variety of projects in India and abroad, and
- commercial matters and accounting systems (e.g., 'bahikhata 'system) which local farmers can understand.

PIM training will be required not only for all farmers using surface irrigation, but also for all officers and staff of irrigation, agriculture and CAD departments (and perhaps even for groundwater department and district rural development agency staff).

Extensive use of mass media should be made. In addition to the Central Government generating and providing mass media packages, at the state level also video and audio cassettes, TV and radio programmes, newspaper articles, pamphlets, leaflets, posters have to be prepared and disseminated on a continuing basis. Schools and colleges could be tapped through debates and essays. Planning forums in colleges and the National Services Schemes could also be used to make people aware and orient them about PIM; its need, the problems in its implementations, as well as the likely benefits. Government agencies staff will also have to be convinced and motivated about the need for them to take a proactive approach to thc propagation of PIM, as would policy makers and politicians.

This paper aims to stimulate further thinking on the training needs for PIM in the country. Hence, the paper also identifies some policy issues related to PIM training at the national and state levels.

Identification of Trainees and their Training Needs

Capacity building constitutes an imperative component of an irrigation reform process (or a PIM adoption process). It encompasses all the stakeholders in the PIM process, from creating a supportive policy and administrative environment to building capable and sustaining organizations at the farmer level. A complete PIM training programme for a state should include:

- Appreciation workshops for politicians, bureaucrats, senior level officers including the ministers (especially Irrigation Minister), Secretaries of the State Irrigation, Command Area Development, Agriculture and Groundwater Development Departments, Chief Engineers, etc.
- Appreciation workshops for all officials of the irrigation department and other concerned departments.
- Specific capacity building workshops for community organizing teams of governments section officers and field staff as well as other community organizers.
- Specific training for the office bearers of the farmer's organizations/Water Users Associations.
- Training for local NGOs.

- Training of trainers for each category of trainee group and for skill development in the different subjects of training programmes including social sciences, agriculture, agronomy, engineering, etc.
- Case study exercises where participants' experiences and systematic examination of case studies would help to clarify concepts, issues and problem areas amongst the participants and show the way forward.

The training programmes would have to include various departments such as Agriculture, Irrigation, Groundwater, Command Area Development and Rural Development. Further, district administrative staff including the Collectors, Zilla Pramukhs and Divisional Commissioners should be involved in the PIM process. Their involvement and support becomes essential in arranging large-scale training programmes and awareness camps, dealing with extension efforts and aspects related to the collection of water fees and the various changes expected because of PIM. Farmers, members and the office bearers of Water Users Associations would need intensive training for handling new responsibilities and roles. Of special importance is training for trainers, researchers and scholars, evaluation experts, teachers in academic institutions. Civic society involvement and support needs to be developed by including NGOs, media personnel and the public at large with orientation training on PIM.

It is important to categorize these trainees into groups as per the roles they perform. The training and orientation needs of each category (or sub-category within it) may require different types and different modules of training. For example, Agriculture Department staff would require somewhat different training from Irrigation Department staff or from Command Area Development staff. Further, the categories of trainees would vary in different states, requiring the process of training needs identification to be based on detailed assessments at the state or regional level. However, a broad categorization is discussed below as an example:

Politicians

One of the major bottlenecks in the reform process is lack of political commitment to the reform agenda and lack of political leadership. The objective of having orientation programmes for the political leadership is to acquaint them with the developments in the field of PIM in various countries. These programmes would equip them with information on the process of irrigation reforms and the political implications thereof including possible benefits of PIM for the members of the WUAs, for other farmers, for the community at large and for the government. They may thus come to realize that good water management can also mean good politics as well as development of the area and its peoples.

Senior Management

The attitudes of the senior management are critical to the success of the PIM programme. Attitudes may be difficult to measure but make the difference in outcomes. This category of trainees would benefit from an exposure to the best practices adopted by other countries, and the progress of PIM in other areas. It is important to identify various departments like the Irrigation, Agriculture, Rural Development, CAD, etc., as the training needs would be different from one group to another. For the Irrigation Department, it would be imperative to stress on attitudinal change towards farmers, and for a movement from complete irrigation agency authority over management to joint management of the irrigation systems and the increasing role of the farmer associations, For the Agriculture Department personnel, they can be expected to have been more in contact with the farmers in their work than the Irrigation Department. Hence, the training would need to emphasize more on the technical aspects of water management and the problems of organization of groups in rural areas.

Middle Management

As key implementers of the reform process, they need to be convinced of the inevitability of the reforms and the training should focus on removing the fears and problems associated with uncertainty in the face of change. Again, there would be several categories within this group from different government departments or even specialties within them For example, the extension staff of the Agriculture Department may be sub-categorized not only for orientation training but also as trainers for the farmer associations.

Lower Management and Field Staff

These are functionaries who are directly involved as community organizers. They need to be informed about the thinking on PIM among the political leadership, and the senior management and how things would be changing with the implementation of the reforms. Again, attitudinal change would be extremely important, as they have to develop new relationships with the farmers and the WUAs. They would also require skills related to effective supervision for tasks that may be performed jointly by the WUAs and the Irrigation Department, or CAD and Agriculture Departments. Sub-groups within this category may be identified on the basis of project boundaries, regional differences or different systems depending on the nature of reforms and the progress of the reforms within the states. Also, for this category, training should be an ongoing process related to field implementation and not a one-time activity. Follow-up and post-training seminars, or repeated follow-up training would ensure that the participants have time to think and adapt to the changes and have access to regular upgradation of knowledge and skills as well as continuous impetus for attitudinal change. Agriculture extension, irrigation extension, on-field water application, rotational running of canals and water budgeting, under-taking of repair and construction works of a minor nature are amongst the subjects whose knowledge would need to be imparted.

Farmers

Training for the farmers is critical not only for the development of sustainable WUAs, but to bring about basic acceptance of the concept of PIM. Farmers should be able to discern that there are sufficient gains from assuming responsibilities that were previously thought to be those of the state. Because there are substantial monetary and non-monetary costs to the farmers for expanded WUA (Water Users Association) activities. Unless the anticipated benefits are also substantial, farmers would clearly choose not to get involved (Meinzen-Dick et at., 1995). Further, effective leadership among the community is a key factor for the success of the reform process.

Training of the users-cum-office bearers of the WUAs would need to incorporate several skills that are new for the farmers such as account management and book keeping, record maintenance or group functioning. This is the group that would require maximum training covering each aspect of training, viz., knowledge, skills and attitudes. They have to be encouraged to develop vibrant level local organizations through transparent management, group functioning and effective conflict resolution mechanisms. It is the development of a new rural leadership at the minor canal/distributory canal command level, which is likely to face problems both during its infancy as well as later. Unless sufficient time and resources are invested in building capacity at this level, it could become a threat to the entire reform process, as the farming community has to be prepared to take up the new responsibilities and to handle new challenges. The farmers would also need to be able to constantly update their irrigation and agriculture related knowledge and skills.

NGOs

NGOs can provide substantial back-up support in the form of training institutions and documenters of the reform process. At the implementation level, the NGOs could also function as community organizers. They could be involved as trainers to the irrigation, CAD and agriculture departments and of the farmers. They could facilitate the development of training material especially in local languages. Process documentation is another aspect where NGOs can function as effective observers and documenters. Hence, training of trainers would be useful for them, as well as equipping them with necessary training facilities.

Trainers

The training of trainers is a crucial activity in any training agenda for the state. There would again be several categories of trainers, who can train different categories of trainees and cover different subjects. Given the magnitude of training programmes that would have to be organized at the regional levels for imparting training to all the personnel concerned, trainers in significant numbers would have to be available for undertaking these training programmes. Hence, it would be imperative to organize several trainings of trainers to identify and train resource persons for the programme, implementers from various departments, from different states and sub-regions that have initiated reforms, especially Andhra Pradesh, should be involved for this activity, as they would be in the position to share actual experiences regarding reforms in their states.

Devising Training Modules

Given these different trainee categories with different training needs, it is important to devise training modules suited to their respective needs. David Groenfeldt and Peter Sun (Groenfeldt) briefly list them out:

- *For policy makers:* Awareness training to become familiar with the concept of PIM and the supporting policies it requires.
- *For mid-level officials:* Awareness training with detailed information about best practices from countries that have adopted PIM. It would be useful for them to tour successful areas in different states in India.

- *For agency* staff: Details on organizing and communication skills, legal and financial aspects of establishing WUAs, etc.
- *For WUA leaders:* Organizational and financial management.

This list, however, does not include the attitudinal and behavioural aspects that are critical components. The challenges is to train engineers, who have earlier been trained to think only in terms of number of hectares in command, storage capacity, length of canal, etc. One of the most important things, particularly for Irrigation Department officers, is how to start the PIM process and how to approach the farmers (Gupta and Srivastava, 1999). There is not only a change of attitude involved but also a reversal of roles. They have to build rapport with the farmer community, and to facilitate their efforts, patiently and persistently. Each individual staff member will have to understand his existing behaviour, attitude, role and perception, empowerment, and change, all along with working styles.

Annexure I gives some details on the topics that could be covered for training of different categories of trainees. The suggested topics are indicative and have borrowed from many sources. Each state, or sponsor of trainings, or training institution would have to design its own specifics course for each type of training objective and for each type of trainee category.

Categorizing Trainees

We may suggest categorization of trainees for PIM as follows: (1) politicians (at central, state and various sub-state/local self-government/Panchayati Raj levels), (2) farmers, (3) WUA personnel (elected office bearers as well as WUA employees), (4) NGOs (5) Community Organizers, (6) senior officers (in central and state governments as well as district collectors), (7) middle level officers (with generalists and specialists from agriculture, irrigation, CAD, groundwater, rural development, panchayats, etc., departments and from the district administration), (8) junior level officers (especially those related to irrigation, CAD and agriculture and such other departments with whom WUAs are likely to have regular interaction), (9) trainers (from WALMIs/IMTIs/WALAMTARIs or other training institutes related to agriculture, rural development, panchayats, etc., or for trainers picked from amongst government departments implementating PIM), (10) mass media or from amongst WUA chairpersons or from NGOs, etc., (11) professionals, and (12) the general public.

While the contents of the training programme should encompass various aspects, what needs to be investigated is whether such courses already exist, or, whether the existing course could be modified, or would totally new courses need to be planned for. What adds to the complexities of the various categories and their different training needs is that the needs would also depend on the stage of the reform process in a particular state or region, and that training is likely to be required as an ongoing process. The next section details some of these complexities and requirements for the training programmes.

Training: Aspects and Methods

Training for irrigation reforms is an extremely complex task of balancing diverse categories of trainees with experience in diverse hydrological settings and different historical water management regimes and the training needs of the region or irrigation projects. This necessitates the formulation of a detailed training plan at regional levels. Different states would have different focus depending on the following:

- *Nature of the reforms:* states that have new legislation, or those where existing legislation has been modified, or where no legislative changes have been affected, and
- *Stage of the reform process:* states that are just initiating the reforms and those that are now into second generation problems of the reform process.

Further, training should have to account for regional differences in irrigation and agriculture practices and the historical mindsets associated with each system. For example, North India *warabandi* states may require different type of orientation and training as the farmers and management both are against changes in the rotational water supply system and favour the functioning of the traditional *warabandi.* In states where *shejpali* is practised, there is greater scope of involvement of the farmers in management of water supply below the outlet and correspondingly the requirements for training would be different. Adding to the complexity is the diversity in the scales of the irrigation systems – major, medium, minor, tanks, etc., These complexities would decide the objectives of the training programmes.

For specific training programmes, the aspects of the training programme need to be based on a comprehensive exercise on the training needs assessment for the target group and the stated objectives of the training programme.

Aspects of Training

The different aspects that training should cover in three broad categories are as under:

- Knowledge and information for planning and appreciation of the programme.
- Practical guidelines and skills for effective implementation.
- Attitudinal change.

Attitudinal and behavioural change is an important component of the training for PIM. Most of the current training programmes encompass only knowledge or skills and do not adequately address the attitudinal components. The importance and need for attitudinal change was brought out effectively through a study that highlights that the irrigation bureaucracy is hardly aware of the variance between the department's own perception of its performance and the image as reflected in farmers' perception. These differences were effectively demonstrated by an exercise conducted separately with the farmers and the department officers in the Gujarat state. The results are presented in Table 1:

Table 1 ***Exercise in Perception***

Image factor	*Agency's self-image**	*Perception of the farmers**
Planning for irrigation	8	1
Adequate water distribution	10	1
Availability of water when required	10	5
Maintenance of distribution/sub-minor	8	1
Distribution of water according to turn	8	1
Recovery of water charges	6	10
Satisfaction of tail-enders	8	2

* Scores out of 10

Source: Anil Shah in a lecture delivered at International Training Programme organized by Indian PIM at Hyderabad January 2001.

Training Methods

Training methods vary with the aspect of training. There is a need to develop new methods of training. Given that the average age of the trainees would be fairly high, the methods used have to suit the age and the experiences of the trainees participating in the programme. It is now fairly well established that the usual classroom teacher-taught type of training is not going to have any lasting impact. Further, training material has to be developed to suit the methods employed for training.

Some of the considerations in choice of the training method include the objectives of training and the learner's needs. As stated earlier, the objectives for training different categories of trainers are likely to be different – the training of farmers and WUA office bearers could have specific objectives like building skills for record keeping and account management, while that of the politicians may be an orientation on PIM. Language of training may also differ according to category of trainee and type of training.

Further, the needs of the organization and the resource constraints, both time available and cost of training, have to borne in mind in the design of the training programmes and choice of methods. Exposure visits may require greater budget and training duration than classroom training. One of the limiting factors in the choice of training is often the non-availability of instructional materials or poor quality of material. Many of the training institutions have been using outdated training materials and well-circulated references. There is an urgent need to design suitable training modules, with acceptable standards and to identify material that could be used for developing session-wise training materials. This is especially relevant since individual training programmes may not have the time or the financial resources to support development of training materials for each training programme.

Some of the training approaches usually adopted and suggested are briefly summarized below:

Knowledge and Skills

For this component of the training programmes, it is an oft-expressed view that implementers should be involved in training as they can share from experience the process and problems in reform management. Also, the acceptability of the implementers is higher to the trainees, especially to the engineers of the Irrigation Department compared to NGO trainers who are essentially viewed as outsiders having little knowledge of what the job of the engineers or system management demands.

Where training is needed at the field level, for agency field operations staff or farmers, experience suggests that on-the-job or learning-while-training and peer training (such as farmer-to-farmer) often works better than theoretical training. Exposure visits to demonstrate what the situation after PIM reforms is in other areas is also an extremely powerful tool.

Another debate on training involves different views on the acceptability of traditional knowledge and procedures as against promotion of modern, scientific know-how. There is a view that knowledge of engineering concepts is essential for maintenance and operation of the irrigation system and modern knowledge is required also for other activities such as book keeping and financial management. Hence, training involves an effort to transfer these methods to the farming community without an effort to find out what methods they would adopt to achieve the same outcomes. For example, the rural communities could have their own accounting system or 'bahikhatas' which could perhaps be used for the purposes of the WUAs as well. This would not only reduce the pressure on the new office bearers of the WUAs to learn new skills, it would enhance transparency among the community as most of them would understand their traditional ways of doing things while new knowledge remains confined to a few. However, in absence of an open communication and an openness to discuss ways and means, developers of the training material remain unaware of these alternate ways of viewing and doing things. Hence, in developing training material and methods, an effort could be made to involve the trainee group and have a participatory development of the training. This kind of participatory training as compared to prescriptive training would enhance the effectiveness of the programmes and go a long way in making training an instrument of change.

Attitudinal Change

For effective attitudinal changes, which last beyond the training duration, it is suggested that training methods should include:

- small, informal, non-threatening, open-minded discussion groups with persons who are important and are respected by the participants
- role play enables participants to experience new attitudes,
- situation replays,
- interactive video tapes - feedback,
- simulation, and
- preparation and discussion of case studies.

Feedback from the international training course on 'Capacity Building for Participatory Irrigation Management', held at Bari, Italy, during September 11–20, 2000, suggests, that it is useful to incorporate exercises that stimulate the development of region/project-specific implementable plans by trainees and discuss these. Follow-up of the actual implementation of these plans after training has also been suggested as a mechanism to explore the usefulness of the training and to ensure continued support to trainees who are trying to utilize the training in their jobs.

Assessment of Training Programmes and Institutions

Limitations of Existing Training Programmes

Training is Low Priority

Training remains a low priority activity in the irrigation sector. Most of the training is mandated by donor agencies. This is also reflected in poor attendance and very often partial attendance on the part of trainees, thus resulting in failure to achieve the objectives of the training programme and also adversely affecting the morale of the trainers.

Training Needs Assessment

There is no assessment of training needs in terms of qualitative and quantitative requirements. There are two essential first steps. First, there is a need for an attitudinal survey of farmers, and irrigation department staff as well as other categories of potential trainees. Second, there is a need to conduct a Training Needs Analysis (TNA), because as regards PIM training, this being a relatively new area, the needs are enormous and their nature varied. This would also help the training institutions understand the requirements and the inputs that need to be built up.

Training Material

Training programmes are handicapped by availability of limited training material, especially in the local language. Efforts at developing methodology and curriculum are ad hoc, and often routine, with the result that both contact and style are pedantic and outdated. At best, training institutions evolve new training designs based on limited experiences and resources. Only a limited amount of feedback is obtained from participants, which could otherwise be useful in updating and improving the training materials. While this is true for written texts, audio-visual materials are very often not available at all.

Structural Problems

There are many structural problems generally associated with training. The location of training is a major factor affecting attendance as the key officials involved in field projects cannot afford to be away from their station for a long time. Hence, key staff members skip training (Oza, 1997). However, due to practicalities, training is organized at the training institutes away from field sites.

Lack of Proper Planning of the Training Course

In many of the training courses including those organized by some Water and Land Management Institutes (WALMIs) and by Water and Power Consultants Ltd. (WAPCOS), a comprehensive training schedule is not prepared by the core faculty of the training institutes but major emphasis is instead laid on guest faculty. The idea of inviting guest faculty is good so as to supplement with practical aspects and field experiences in motivating and organizing farmers and sharing of achievements. But such guest lectures are often not arranged in sequential order, nor is it ensured that a common approach is being followed and accordingly there is much duplication and even omission of important topics as the knowledge or specialization of the guest faculty available influences the topics included in the training schedule. The organizers should prepare a schedule course outline and detailed lesson plans in advance. They should ensure that the course is well structured and all the required topics and themes are covered in a proper sequence and indicate specific topics and lesson plans to the guest speakers, after ensuring that no gaps are being left in the course.

Failure to Use Evaluation of Training to Improve Subsequent Courses

Individual training programmes are sometimes evaluated at the end of course in a casual manner by getting an evaluation sheet filled by the trainees by the course sponsors or funding agency. Seldom is evaluation done to actually find out the trainees' perceptions of what the course achieved, or to use evaluation and feedback to improve subsequent courses. Impact assessment of the entire training effort in a particular state or a particular training institute via-a-vis objectives has not been done so far.

Limitations of Existing Training Institutions

Lack of Trainers

Most of the training on PIM is handled by the WALMIs and WAPCOS, the trainers being Irrigation Department engineers. They are deputed to the training institutes from the parent department, usually unwillingly. In addition to the lack of motivation for imparting quality training, they are themselves in need of training. They may lack exposure to multi-disciplinary fields and the dynamics of socio-economic aspects and organizational methodology. Further, knowing that they are likely to be transferred back to the parent department, there is little motivation for developing skills required for a good trainer.

There is little effort to involve implementers with experience who could contribute to the quality of the training programmes. External faculty is limited by the funds or convenience as regards their availability.

Funds

Financial resources usually are limited to the amounts required for class room training sessions with little support for exposure visits, development of new training materials, etc. Further, there is little support for any kind of post-training follow-up activity.

Lack of Post-Training Follow-up

Training by and large remains a one-time activity. The stress is on meeting the stated capacity of the training programmes, rather than on proper participant selection. Further, training is deemed complete after the schedule topics/lectures are over with very little emphasis on post-training follow-up and use of new knowledge and skills. WAPCOS conducts training for officers from various states. They have no idea who comes for training and where they go after the course (Gupta and Srivastava, 1999). As a result, much of the training conducted has failed to create the desired impart, in turn reinforcing the already poor perception of the importance of training activities.

Choice of Training Programmes and Clientele

There is little emphasis on training of trainers. Farmers are largely not much involved in any aspect. Workshops and conferences at the national, regional and project levels are often a forum for exchange of ideas and experiences, but are restricted in their impact due to attendance by the same officials, NGOs and consultants/experts. Very often this leads to little value addition, with repetitive examples and discussions. Exposure visits are limited to some officers and a few farmers or WUA chairpersons. Further dissemination of experiences of conferences, workshops and exposure visits remains limited.

Challenges for Training on PIM

The sheer magnitude, diversity, costs and benefits of Participatory Irrigation Management (PIM) in India suggest the immensity of training challenge due to the following reasons (Sinha, 2001).

- Irrigation not only requires much larger capital input than most other agricultural methods but also the largest input of trained and experienced human resources. The total manpower from irrigation, agriculture, command area development and land development organizations directly involved in irrigated agriculture in India, is probably the largest in the world. Besides these agency officials, nearly two-third of the country's workforce is still dependent on agriculture for livelihood. Therefore, the population size of the target group of PIM training is stupendous.

- The diversity of irrigation system ranging from small private wells, shallow and deep community tubewells, community tanks, small embankments *(bundhies)* to some of the most complex large-scale reservoir fed/run-of-the river canal systems further add to the training challenge.
- On an average, water use efficiency in the existing irrigation projects is put at 40 per cent which means that there is tremendous scope for water savings with introduction of improved irrigation methods, techniques and careful selection of less water intensive crops.
- The share of agriculture in total water use in India is estimated to come down from the present level of 83 per cent to the level of 73 per cent in the year 2025 due to competitive demands on water use from other sectors, particularly energy, domestic and industrial use. In view of such compulsions, the optimal use of water in agriculture sector will occupy centre stage in the PIM training strategies.
- Irrigation issues are intertwined with many sectors like rural development, agriculture, surface water, revenue, cooperatives, forestry, environment, energy, marketing, post-harvest processing, banking, transport, etc. As a consequence, PIM training strategies have to be truly multi-sectored in character.
- Regional differences have to be given due consideration. Problems profiles, and thereby strategies will exhibit fundamental differences from region to region. Different sets of interventions and customized approach are required for different agro-climatic regions.
- Language barriers between different regions of the country have to be acknowledged and education and training is to be conducted in regional languages.
- Training institutes and organizations have neither the inclination nor the resources to cater to such complex set of training needs.
- In the absence of focused government policies for the same, the necessary coordination between line departments and various governmental and non-governmental training agencies may be difficult to achieve.

WALMIs as Training Institutes

Even after more than 20 years of existence, the WALMIs have not been able to emerge as significant knowledge institutions even for irrigation departments of respective states, leave alone the water resources sector as a whole. As the report of the Small Study Group (SSG, 1999) states: "Overall WALMI has been a great opportunity lost. WALMI has a long way to go before it becomes much of an institution, leave alone an institution of excellence."

The top political and administrative leadership at state level has not taken much initiative to find out why WALMIs have not delivered despite the fact that they were all born with silver spoons in their mouth. The Government of Gujarat was the first to worry about this issue. As a result, in October 1998, it appointed a small study group to study the working of the Gujarat WALMI. The mandate of the study was to assess the performance of WALMI, Gujarat, and to understand the reasons that account for the gap between its performance and potential and finally, to recommend to the government a course of action to transform WALMI into a high performing institution. The study group submitted its report to the Gujarat government in March 1999.

WALMIs are subject to limitations. The report points out that WALMI remains a mediocre institution because of the following reasons:

- Its vision is limited being a captive institution of the irrigation department.
- No comprehensive view of water resources sectors.
- Approach and staff narrowly oriented towards agriculture engineering and agriculture extension – hardly any competence in social sciences, behavioural sciences, public systems, and management organization theory.

Further, during discussions with various officials of the WALMIs, other problems emerged which include:

- Poor attendance in the training programmes.
- Faculty is largely drawn from the irrigation department (and to some extent from agriculture department) on deputation. This often results in short tenures. Further, postings at the training institutes are considered inferior to other postings and are largely, unwanted. Hence, there is an accompanying lack of motivated staff in the training institutes.

It is quite clear that the WALMIs and IMTIs in the country need major reorientation and capacity building if they are to become effective instruments of PIM propagation as well as PIM training. (An insider's personal view about capacity building of WALMIs is given in Sinha, 2001, "Education, Training and Other Capacity Building Measures in Water Sector for 21st Century", National Seminar, 1–2 March, 2001, Technical Papers, UPWALMI).

Measures for Building Capacity for the Training Institutions

There have been some initiatives from the government to identify shortcomings in the current training programmes and the corrective actions that are required. The Gujarat government appointed the small study group for training in PIM with Mr Anil Shah as its chairman. The study group concentrated on the training needs of Gujarat state and reported in November 1999 recommending: (a) to give priority to training the field staff, (b) training should be in two modules: (i) conceptual understanding of why PIM, the process of promoting WUAs and changing role of field staff from implementers to facilitators, and (ii) issues in working of WUAs and the actual role of field staff; and (c) of the 4,000 field staff, 50 per cent may be trained in next three years through the WALMI and three existing NGOs.

A training and awareness building strategy specifically aimed at propagating PIM needs to be worked out for each state of India. Some measures for building capacity including for training institutions are suggested below:

Involvement with State Policy Decision-Making

Training is often viewed as an isolated, one-time activity with little impact on or relevance to the state's decision-making system. This perception needs to be altered and an awareness generated about the relevance of training in the policy making process. This could be achieved through exposure workshops of senior management officials as well as awareness camps for creating awareness about the relevance of training.

There has to supporting policy change in the central and state governments backing a comprehensive, need-based, demand-driven training programme. It should be promoted on the basis of detailed analysis of training needs in a state, based on projects or scale of irrigation, and careful identification of the trainees. The process could be initiated with the identification of priority states. These include those states that have passed new legislation for PIM and there is need to identify training programmes that have to be conducted before, during and after the enactment of the law following the example of Andhra

Pradesh. For areas where PIM has been under implementation for some time, the training needs and packages would require to be different. Secondly, identification of the trainees has to be rigorous and need-based, supported by evaluation of the impact of training through examining the post-training activities of the trainee.

Evaluation of Training Programmes

There should be mechanism designed to evaluate PIM training both in terms of impact of a particular training programme, and in terms of the impact of the overall PIM training and orientation efforts in a particular area or the country as a whole.

TOT Programmes

Conducting more ToT (Training of Trainers) programmes based on needs analysis. Expert groups should be set up for development of curriculum and methodology. This process should also be participatory, especially incorporating the feedback from past trainees and from persons who have been course coordinators. Curriculum and methodology should be developed for each different category of trainees through PRA techniques with the assistance of consultants and local NGOs.

Physical Equipment and Infrastructure

Training institutions should be equipped with sufficient infrastructure and training materials, especially audio-visuals aids, etc.

Exposure Visits

This is an important activity for all levels of trainees. Exposure visits to other areas for interaction with counterparts is considered an effective way of exchange of ideas and information.

Networking

While this idea is brought up at various forums, there is little progress in reality. During the meeting of the Committee for Training on Participatory Irrigation Management constituted by Ministry of Water Resources (MoWR) in 1999 (which unfortunately did not finalize its report or recommendations), the idea for creating a network for institutions promoting PIM in the country was mooted. The SPWD (Society for Promotion of Watershed Development) concept of a 'training grid' as has been considered for watershed development was also discussed. However, this had not achieved success due to lack of clarity on the role of the coordination agency (SPWD), or the incentives or disincentives for various institutions to become a part of such a network. This threat faces any proposed network for PIM training institution as well. Hence, initiatives need to begin with a reasonable consensus about the need for a network, the value addition for each participant and the incentives/disincentives in being participants to the network.

Clientele Group

The training programmes need to gradually be made more demand-oriented. However, for quite sometime most of the training would have to continue to be government or donor-driven as training would be a major instrument of propogating PIM amongst those who have not realized the importance of PIM or those who need help with the operational details related to PIM.

Trainee Groups

The training imparted should be functionally relevant and this could be ensured through appropriate trainee groups, with similar needs, past experience and expected follow-up activity, rather than clubbing trainees from diverse backgrounds. However, some horizontally integrated courses would also be required particularly where attitudes are to be changed.

Some critical aspects of training that make a difference to the quality of training need to be emphasized. These are:

- Training is not a one-time input, but a process of continued interaction.
- Training programme should be oriented towards the needs of the client group and the objectives of the particular training programme.
- Networking between different institutes for exchange of ideas and other resources.
- Financial support should be in-built in the system for each activity. Support needs to be provided not only for the training component but also for field support during project implementation.
- Standardized training material should be prepared with maximum consultation and then adapted for the specific purpose of each particular course.

Recommendations

Broad View of Training of PIM

Training has to be seen not only as a means to impart knowledge and skills or to bring about awareness and attitudinal change, but as a means of propagation of PIM and speeding up reforms in the water sector.

Resources for Promotion of PIM

The Government of India and the state government as well as donor agencies would need to liberally provide resources for various types of awareness building and training courses related to PIM. The Government of India should share training costs with state governments or NGOs on 90:10 sharing basis and also fund WALMIs, etc., on a 100 per cent basis for national or regional programmes of PIM training.

Finalization of Training Modules

PIM awareness and training strategies need to be prepared separately for each state. This should be followed by preparation of a perspective plan for PIM training for each state. Training modules for different training objectives, different categories of trainees, and for areas at different levels or stages of implementation of PIM, would need to be developed.

Development of Training Material

There is need for a documentation centre/clearing house of training material produced all over the country and abroad. The variety of training courses and corresponding training material required for PIM is likely to be vast.

Creation of a Network of Training Institutes

A network of various institutes providing PIM-related training could be set up as a centralized source of information about forthcoming training programmes, and for evolving a common database for feedback and upgradation of the training programmes.

Creation of a Network of Training and Implementing Agencies

Networking between training institutes and implementing agencies which would need to use the training facilities would be useful in ensuring that the training is useful and relevant to the client group.

Creation of a Network of Funding Agencies

Networking between the central government, state governments and important agencies like the World Bank, Ford Foundation, NABARD, etc., could further the training and orientation efforts so as to propagate PIM. This could lead to the development of comprehensive, state-wise plans and provision of funds and resources for training and identification of the trainees and their needs as per the states' overall objectives.

Training and Orientation is too Important to be left only to the Training Institutions

Policy makers, PIM implementers, WUA chairpersons NGOs, trainers all need to be jointly involved along with trainers at training institutions in planning and imparting PIM training. Their training skills would need to be enhanced and nurtured.

Need for Clubbing National, State and Regional Training with Local Training

From the point of view of sharing of experiences, national or multi-state training would be desirable, however, state or local level training would also be necessary to go into the details of PIM processes in particular regions or projects.

Annual Training Needs Assessment for Each State followed by Annual Training Plan

Keeping in view the objectives of the training, categories of trainees, state/level of acceptance and spread of PIM, etc., and the state perspective plan for PIM training, each state should conduct once a year a training needs assessment specific to the state. Similarly, the training facilities and resources available to the state should be assessed. This should be followed by a detailed Annual PIM Training Plan being formulated for each state. This plan should then be implemented efficiently.

Careful Planning of Each Course

Each individual course needs to be well-planned, not based on easily available guest faculty or available training material, but on the objectives of the training, category of trainees, expectations from the course, etc. Course coordinator's role is also vital.

Assessing Impact of Training

Not only should each training programme be evaluated, but the impact of the entire training programme in each state should be assessed once in six months.

Conclusion: Suggested Strategies for PIM Training

To recapitulate and sum up, the proposed PIM training strategy is being summarized below:

As regards policies and strategies for PIM training, the central government needs to prepare a brief policy/strategy statement for PIM training exhorting the state governments, water professionals, training institutes and other related people to give priority to PIM-related orientation and training and suggesting modalities for such efforts. The central government would also need to provide technical and financial support to various states for conducting PIM training. There is need to constitute a National Support Group on PIM to facilitate the central/state governments and other agencies involved in PIM training. Similarly, the government needs to sponsor the creation of a National Documentation Centre/Information Clearing House on training material and other documents related to PIM. Numerous national and regional level workshops on strategies and policies for PIM training need to be organized along with some national level training courses to enable inter-state interactions. Similarly, there is need for organizing researchers conferences on PIM which would, amongst other things, generate training material on PIM and provide feedback for policy initiatives and improved implementational strategies for PIM. Government should also facilitate the creation of a network of WALMIs and other training institutes across the country which are involved in PIM training. Networking between training facilities and agencies which can provide funds and resources for training as also with PIM implementers would also need to be evolved.

The Government of India also needs to facilitate the creation of model training manuals (which each state could then adopt to suit its own specific needs) and earmark funds for PIM training in various existing Government of India schemes whereby training and capacity building funds could be provided to various state governments, training institutes and NGOs for performing the role of a National Support Group and of a National Documentation Centre. For instance, the state governments could be provided 80 per cent assistance for conducting a specific number of PIM trainings, for appointing a state level PIM Training Coordinator and for preparing PIM training material. The National Support Group and the National Documentation Centre could be provided 100 per cent assistance for PIM training courses and other related work including preparing standard PIM training material and suggesting strategies for more effective PIM training.

At the state level, both the Perspective Plan on PIM Training Capacity Building and an annual PIM training plan would need to be prepared, following a training needs assessment for each state which would encompass not merely the annual WALMI plans but all aspects of PIM training.

An agency (WALMI, an NGO, or a special cell in a government department) would need to be identified to act as the state level support group and documentation centre for PIM training and orientation. The state governments would need to set apart earmarked funds for PIM training.

As has been indicated elsewhere, on many occasions (see, for example, Joshi and Hooja, eds), by this author, training for PIM is too important to be left only to trainers in places like WALMIs. This is not to decry the useful role of WALMIs, but to point out that multidisciplinary teams of those knowledgeable about social interaction, irrigation, agriculture, groundwater, rural development, extension services, training, administrative coordination and the like need to collaborate with government functionaries, farmers and NGOs who are intimately involved in implementation of PIM for imparting training in PIM. Thus, the multidisciplinary mobile PIM propagation teams being used for implementing PIM programmes, and the government staff, chairpersons of WUAs and community organizers involved in PIM projects, should be jointly used along with the specialist trainers in training institutions to impart PIM training and orientation. The state level PIM cell responsible for policy making and implementation of PIM should directly coordinate such training.

A multi-agency/multidisciplinary state level PIM Training Committee should be set up in each state having direct linkage with the state level PIM cell overseeing policy making and implementation in the field. This committee should help prepare and review the Annual State PIM Training Plan, suggest activities to be undertaken, suggest aspects on which training manuals and model training modules should be developed, obtain feedback about training conducted, evaluate the impact of the training courses and suggest modifications, if required, in the approaches/strategies being followed, as also refinements in the subsequent years training plan. This committee should also be able to suggest as to how to attract funds from various sources for PIM training. It should also have links with all concerned state government departments, training institutes (specially those related to agriculture/irrigation and CAD/rural development sectors), NGOs working on PIM, some of the more active WUAs, irrigation projects where PIM has started picking up, and also with the National Support Group and National Level Documentation Centre for Training on PIM.

State level PIM training and orientation manuals would need to be prepared with due attention being paid to different requirements of different regions of the state and to those WUAs which have just being created, as well as older WUAs facing second generation problems.

Formal training would need to be coupled with non-formal PIM orientation programmes and appropriate use of mass media channels. Extensive use of mass media should be made. In addition to the central government generating and providing mass media packages, at the state level also video and audio cassettes, TV and radio programmes, newspaper articles, pamphlets, leaflets, posters need to be prepared and disseminated on a continuing basis. Schools and colleges and especially Planning Forums in colleges and the National Service Scheme could also be used to make, not only students, but also all people, aware about PIM – its need, the problems in its implementation, as well as the likely benefits. Government agencies' staff, especially in rural areas, which are not directly assigned PIM-related responsibilities, would also need to be convinced and motivated about the need for them to take a supportive approach to the propagation of PIM.

There is need to ensure speedy universalization of PIM in all irrigation systems and, therefore, PIM training and orientation needs to receive major attention so as to help in achieving this.

References

GoI, 1996. Report of the Working Group on Participatory Irrigation Management Programme for the IX Five Year Plan. Government of India. Ministry of Water Resources. Command Area Development Wing.

Groenfeldt, D., 1998. *Handbook on Participatory Irrigation Management,* EDI, World Bank.

Groenfeldt, D. and M. Svendson, 2000. *Case Studies-PIM.* World Bank Institute.

Gupta, D. and L.P. Srivastava, 1999. Status of Participatory Irrigation Management in India: A Documentary Critique. ISS Manuscript Report 13, Institute of Social Science, New Delhi.

Hooja, Rakesh, 1995. Multidisciplinary Management of Irrigation Schemes and CAD Agencies, Occasional Paper No 2, HCM RIPA, Jaipur.

——. 2001. Multidisciplinary and Participatory Water Management for Irrigation Command Areas, Working Paper/Monograph No. 2, India-NPIM, New Delhi.

——. 2002. A Strategy for Training for PIM in India, Working Paper, Monograph No 7, India NPIM, Jaipur.

——. 2003. "Revisiting Participatory Irrigation Management", *Indian Journal of Public Administration,* Vol. 49, No. 3, July-September, 2003.

——. 2006. *The Management of Water for Agriculture: Essays on Irrigation, Watersheds, and Drainage* Rawat, Jaipur.

Hooja, Rakesh, Anjali Bhatia and Ganesh Pangare, 2001, Training for Participatory Irrigation Management in India Present Status and Need: A Policy Aid Document, Working Paper/Monograph No. 4, IndiaNPIM, New Delhi.

Hooja, Rakesh, Ganesh Pangare and K.V. Raju (eds), 2002. *Users in Water Management: The Andhra Model and its Replicability in India* Rawat Publications, Jaipur.

IndiaNPIM, 2000. Attitudinal and Behavioural Change for PIM: *A* Workshop Report.

——. 2001. Report of the International Training of Trainers Programme on PIM: A Way Forward.

IRDAS, 1996. *Participatory Irrigation Management: A Handbook for Farmers and Field Functionaries:* See Sithapathi Rao et al., 1999.

Joshi, L. K. and R. Hooja (eds), 2000. *Participatory Irrigation Management. Paradigm for the 21st Century* (2 volumes), Rawat Publishers, New Delhi.

Maloney, C. and K.V. Raju, 1994. *Managing Irrigation Together,* Sage Publications, New Delhi.

Meinzen Dick R., 1997. "Farmers Participation in Irrigation: 20 Years of Experiences and Lessons for the Future", *Irrigation and Drainage Systems,* Vol.II.

NSPDART, 1998. Proceedings of the Workshop on Attitude and Behaviour Change in Participatory Processes, 24th-28th August, 1998, Ministry of Rural Areas and Employment, GoI, National Society for Promotion of Development Administration, Research and Training, LBSNAA, Mussoorie.

Oza, A., 1997. "Training as a Priority for Participatory Irrigation Management", National Conference on PIM, 20–22 January, 1997, New Delhi.

Rao, Sithapathi, et al., 1999. *PIM:* A *Handbook for Farmers and Field Functionaries,* IRDAS and WALAMTARI, Hyderabad.

Shah, Anil, 1999. "Capacity Building for Participatory Irrigation Management". Paper presented in the plenary session of National Conference on Participatory Irrigation Management at Hyderabad, 19–23 January, 1999.

Sinha, P.K., 2001. "Education, Training and Other Capacity Building Measures in Water Sector for 21st Century". National Seminar on Land and Water Management Issues for 21st Century, 1–2 March, 2001. Technical Papers. UPWALMI, Lucknow.

Sivamohan, M.V.K. and C.Scott (eds), 1994. *India: Irrigation Management Partnerships,* Booklinks, Hyderabad.

SSG, Government of Gujarat, 1999. Report of the Small Study Group Appointed by the Government of Gujarat to Evolve a Plan for Restructuring the Water and Land Management Institute, Gujarat. Small Study Group, Government of Gujarat.

Uphoff, N., M.J. Esman and A. Krishna, 1998. *Reasons for Success: Learning from Instructive Experiences in Rural Development,* Vistaar Publications, New Delhi.

Annexure I

Indicative Lists of Topics for Training Workshops Categorized as per Various Groups That Need to be Trained (these lists have been taken from Rakesh Hooja, Anjali Bhatia and Ganesh Pangare, Training for Participatory Irrigation Management in India Present Status and Needs, Working Paper/Monograph No. 4, IndiaNPIM India)

1A. Politicians

Training objective: The objective of having orientation programmes for the political leadership is to acquaint them with the developments in the field of PIM in various countries and to equip them with information on the process of irrigation reforms and the political implications thereof.

Knowledge

1. Problems in the present water management
    - Existing irrigation management practices.
    - Analysis of irrigation coverage, efficiency, head and tall end problem, inequity, frequency and reliability of water supply.
    - Financial aspects of the present system.
    - Details on cost effectiveness in O&M – total expenditure and assessment of water fees and recoveries and the effect of O&M budgeting.
2. Introduction to PIM
    - Experiences of other countries in PIM.
    - The essential features of PIM.
    - Legal and policy issues in PIM.
    - Expected outcomes from PIM.
3. The implication of PIM
    - Role of Irrigation Department after reform.
    - Role of community organizers/NGOs.
    - Gender issues in PIM.

Skills

1. Steps in PIM
    - Methodology, approach and implementation strategy for PIM.
    - Planning and monitoring and evaluation tools and processes.

Attitudinal Issues

1. Mental block
2. Apprehensions.
3. Political implications.

1B. Senior Management

Training objectives: For the Irrigation Department, training aims to initiate a process of attitudinal change towards farmers, and for a movement from complete authority over management to joint management of the irrigation systems and to appreciate the role of the farmer association. For other departments (Agriculture, Rural Development, district administration, etc.), the objective could be an orientation to PIM, and how they could aid the process.

For Irrigation Department

Knowledge

1. Introduction to PIM
    - Experiences of other countries in PIM.
    - The essential features of PIM.
    - Legal and Policy issues in PIM.
2. The implication of PIM
    - Role of Irrigation Department after reform.
    - Role of community organizers/NGOs.
    - Gender issues in PIM.
3. Practical details of the legal back-up
    - Irrigation Act, Canal Rules, Command Area Development Act, etc.
    - Turnover process, signing MoUs and its implication.

Skills

1. Planning for PIM
    - Legal and policy decisions and back-up.
2. Steps in PIM
    - Methodology, approach and implementation strategy for PIM.
    - Planning, monitoring and evaluation tools and processes.
3. Management issues
    - Models of WUAs and farmers' organizations at minor, distributory branch level and main canal level.

- Functions, rights and responsibilities of farmers' organizations at each level.
- Formation and operation of WUAs.

4. Participatory tools and issues
   - PRA and tools for participatory planning and implementation.
   - Climate building for PIM.
   - Conflict resolution.
   - Breaking hierarchy barriers.

Attitudinal Issues (Adapted from NSPDART, 1998)

1. Mental block
   - Mistrust in capacity of people.
   - Lack of confidence.
   - Fear of accountability.
2. Apprehensions
   - Income loss.
   - Loss of power.
   - Enhanced bargaining position of the farmer.
   - Altered social, status.
3. Political implications
   - Deprivation of contract or support.
   - Anxiety arising from uncertainty.
   - Compulsions to spend on O&M.

1C. Middle Management

Training objective: Training to impart knowledge and skills for implementing reform. The training needs to explain the purpose and the inevitability of the reforms, the changes to be expected. It should focus on removing the fears and problems associated with uncertainty in the face of change.

Knowledge

1. Problems in the present water management
   - Existing irrigation management practices.
   - Analysis of irrigation coverage, efficiency, head and tail end problem, insecurity, frequency and reliability of water supply.
   - Financial aspect of the present system.

- Details on cost effectiveness in O&M - total expenditure and assessment of water fees and recoveries and effect on O&M budgeting.
- The inevitability of reform.

2. Introduction to PIM
   - Experiences of other countries in PIM.
   - The essential features of PIM.
   - Legal and policy issues in PIM.
   - Forms of organizations and WUAs.
3. The implications of PIM
   - Role of Irrigation Department after reform.
   - Role of community organizations and joint management.
   - Role of community organizers/NGOs.
   - Gender issues in PIM.
4. Planning for PIM
   - Legal and policy decisions and back-up.

Skills

1. Aspects of joint management
   - Joint inspection, fixing water quotas, evolving volumetric rates, rehabilitation of irrigation network as per users' views, hydraulic tests of the system before handing over, etc.
2. Practical details of the legal back-up
   - Irrigation Act, Canal Rules, Command Area Development Act, etc.
   - Turnover process, signing MOUs and its implications.
3. Participatory tools and issues
   - PRA and tools for participatory planning and implementation.
   - Climate building for PIM.
   - Conflict resolution.
   - Breaking hierarchy barriers.

Attitudinal Issues

1. Mental block
   - Mistrust in capacity of people.
   - Lack of confidence.
   - Fear of accountability.

2. Apprehensions
   - Income loss.
   - Loss of power.
   - Enhanced bargaining position of the farmer.
   - Altered social status.
3. Political implications
   - Deprivation of contract or support.
   - Anxiety arising from uncertainty.

1D. Section Officers/Field Staff

1. Introduction to PIM
   - Experiences of other countries in PIM.
   - The essential features of PIM.
   - Legal and policy issues in PIM.
2. The implication of PIM
   - Rote of Irrigation Department after reform with emphasis on the role of the field staff.
   - Role of community organizers/NGOs.
   - Gender issues in PIM.
3. Forms of organization
   - Responsibilities and duties at various levels.

Skills

1. Water User Association
   - Formation of WUA – its rights and responsibilities.
   - Registration of WUAs, conducting meetings, joint inspections.
   - Record keeping and reporting.
   - Conflict resolution.
2. Technical issues in joint management
   - Hydraulic tests.
   - System operation and rotational water supplies.
   - Water deliveries to minors, water allocation principles, water-measuring devices, control structures – locations, nature, conditions, accuracy and maintenance policy.
3. Legal issues in PIM
   - Canal Rules, Command Area Development Act, etc.
   - Turnover process, signing MOUs and its implication.

4. Monitoring and evaluation for supervisory capability for activities carried out by the WUAs
    - Distribution of water.
    - Rules for water distribution.
    - Scheduling of irrigation.
    - Water accounting.
    - Annual financial budget and water budget.
    - Book-keeping and auditing the expenditure.
    - Maintenance of the system.

Attitudinal Issues

1. Mental block
    - Mistrust in capacity of people.
    - Lack of confidence.
    - Fear of accountability.
    - Participatory techniques.
    - Communication with farmers – how to approach farmers, how to talk with them, motivation, etc.
2. Apprehensions
    - Income loss.
    - Loss of power.
    - Enhanced bargaining position of the farmer.
    - Altered social status.
3. Political implications
    - Deprivation of contract or support.
    - Anxiety arising from uncertainty.

1E. Farmers

Knowledge

1. Water User Associations
    - Formation of WUAs – their rights and responsibilities and functions.
    - Functions and responsibilities of the Irrigation Department.
    - Functions of office bearers, executive committee, general body of the organizations at minor, distributory, branch level and main canal level.

- Registration of WUAs.
- Procedures for conducting meetings and decision-making of WUAs.
- Record-keeping and reporting.
- Conflict resolution.
- Fixing water fees for different crops to meet management costs of WUAs.

2. Legal issues in PIM
   - Irrigation Act and Canal Rules, Command Area Development Act, etc.
   - Turnover processing MoUs and its implication.
   - By-laws of WUAs, MoU between Irrigation Department and WUAs.

Skills

1. Technical issues in joint management
   - Existing practices of O&M by the Irrigation Department.
   - Joint inspection for rehabilitation.
   - Hydraulic tests.
   - Preparation of annual water budget.
   - Water deliveries to minors, water allocation principles, water measuring devices, control structures – locations, nature, conditions, accuracy and maintenance policy.
   - Environmental aspects.
   - System operation and rotational water supplies.
   - System maintenance: Maintenance of repairs of canals, field channel and drain maintenance.
2. Activities carried out by the WUAs
   - Distribution of water.
   - Rules for water distribution.
   - Scheduling of irrigation.
   - Water accounting and water budgets.
3. Accounting and financial management
   - Annual financial budget.
   - Book-keeping, balance-sheet, profit and loss accounts.
   - Auditing the expenditure.
   - Maintenance of the system.

Attitudinal Issues

- Leadership.
- Self-organization-group functioning.

IF. NGOs

1. Organizing training programmes.
2. Training needs assessment.
3. Participatory tools: Participatory development of training material.
4. Overview of PIM in Indian states and other countries.

16 Training for, and Expectations from, District Planners

Rakesh Hooja

Decentralized Planning: Objectives and Expectations from District Planners

With the passing of the 73rd Constitution Amendment Act, the legislatures of various states in India have been empowered to devolve powers and responsibilities, subject to such conditions as the legislature may specify, regarding the preparation of plans for economic development and social justice, upon panchayat bodies at the district, intermediate, and village levels. The 74th Constitution Amendment Act provides for the setting up of a District Planning Committee at the district level to consolidate the plans prepared by the panchayats and the municipalities in the district and to prepare a draft district development plan for the district as a whole. Many states have constituted such DPCs. Thus, district planning, which has been talked about and tried out in various ways to a lesser or larger extent for the last few decades, is now getting better institutionalized.

This has imparted an urgency to the need for better understanding of issues such as the relationship between national and state level plans and the district plans, planning structures at state and especially district

The views of the author are purely personal and academic. In the writing of this paper I have made use of many of my own earlier writings. I have also benefited from reactions of trainees at numerous training courses on district and decentralized planning held at HCM RIPA, Jaipur, and IGPRS, Jaipur, and from comments by readers of my earlier published works which are listed as part of the references and particularly my 1998 occasional paper published by HCM RIPA, Jaipur, on "District Planning Practice and Theory with Special Reference to the 'How To' Aspects."

levels; funding arrangements; planning functions more appropriate for each level; methodologies of spatial and areal planning and for planning for infrastructure development, provision of services and production and income generation using resources optimally and how district planners can integrate these with techniques for participative planning; training of state and district level personnel; the various experiments and experiences over time in different parts of the country at district, block or micro-area planning; the various government reports and related literature on the issues; and the like.

There is also a need to figure out what sort of exposure, orientation, and training needs to be provided to concerned functionaries, and even to people's representatives at the district and lower levels, i.e., to the district planners, so that the objectives of decentralized planning can be achieved. Such objectives include:

(a) increased people's participation;
(b) Improved quality of development efforts and improved management of programmes;
(c) the provision of resources and programmes for each area and for different groups inhabiting the area on the basis of an assessment of the specific area's problems, resources and potentialities,
(d) spatial planning (considering the need for relaxation of uniform norms related to distance or population thresholds) for provision of services and facilities in specific areas;
(e) use of locational theory and rural growth centre or central place planning and centrality scoring techniques;
(f) greater feeling of involvement in the planning effort on the part of both lower level functionaries and the local people including elected Panchayati Raj representatives;
(g) strengthening of local government bodies,
(h) locally optimal arrangements for each cluster of villages, or people within a village, to meet their own perceptions of their needs rather than through uniform standards prescribed in a uniform manner for the entire country or state as a whole;
(i) better consideration of available local level resources or of the lack of and need for the same, and of local problems than would be possible through planning at higher levels;
(j) greater mobilization of resources at the local level;
(k) evolution of participatory mechanisms to promote local level leadership, habits of self-help, motivation and willingness to undertake local plan formulation and implementation;

(l) creating a psychology for development and change at local levels;
(m) reduction in regional disparities;
(n) meeting of basic needs of the people in a better manner which could help to bring into the mainstream peripheral groups, the poor and the deprived;
(o) better partnership may be achieved between the people and development agencies;
(p) small mini-projects may be individually planned for using project approach-based analysis at the local or district level which may not be possible at higher levels where only generalized guidelines can be framed for particular types of small schemes;
(q) successful marriage of project planning and participatory planning may prove easier at levels closer to the grassroots;
(r) local social or physical barriers not always apparent on maps can only be considered while planning locally which is not possible during state or higher level plan exercises;
(s) better spatial convergence and sequencing of interrelated activities and optimization and prioritization of investments may be enabled;
(t) integrated and comprehensive multi-sector planning may prove easier at lower levels, while at higher levels mono-sector planning or sectorally segmented planning subsequently compiled into an overall plan, as is being done at present, may have to be resorted to; and
(u) greater integration between developmental needs and priorities of smaller areas (micro-regions) and of different socio-economic groups with regional sub-national, state and national level policies and goals may be possible.

The above list of possible benefits from decentralized planning must be kept in mind while determining what role is expected to be played by district planners all over the country. However, it is not always easy to provide orientation to district or lower level functionaries and politicians who are jointly expected to undertake district planning which could (i) give them the proper philosophical background for the entire efforts; (ii) provide some idea of the background of the evolution of thinking and concepts of district and decentralized planning in India; (iii) make available to them the results of, and methodologies used for, the various types of district and block level planning tried out in various parts of the country; (iv) inform them about the legal and administrative measures that exist and are relevant for district planning; (v) explain the state level planning structures and procedures to them so that their district plans can be dovetailed with the state plans; (vi) teach techniques to invoke people's participation in planning; and (vii) teach them some basics of planning as well project planning techniques which could enable them to use their knowledge of the area, its resources, problems as well as local needs and aspirations and local socio-political groups, to enable them to prepare local plans which fit into the multi-level planning system in a manner that furthers the country's developmental needs. Many at the state level could also profit from such orientation.

It should, however, be clarified that there we are not thinking of district planning as only the planning of governmental programmes, but as something much broader encompassing the planning for both governmental and private activities for the local area and its development so as to lead to the achievement of national, state level and local area goals in an integrated manner. What is needed is a two-way approach, the process of planning from below lending realism and concreteness of content and being sensitive to regional variations, with the downward movement of planning from the above setting broad macro priorities, providing coherency, and ensuring flow of national and regional resources and funds to various local areas as well as to national and state sponsored programmes. Thus, planning has to be done in a multi-level framework to ensure maximum results. At all but the highest and lowest levels, planning impulses would emanate not only within the level itself but also from the higher and lower levels.

As Abdul Aziz and P.V. Shenoy in *Journal of Rural Development* (1997) suggest, decentralized planning should be (i) people's need and local resource based, (ii) people-directed, (iii) its focus should be on developing backward sub-regions and weaker sections, (iv) project implementation and monitoring should be cost-effective, and (v) the development targeted should be sustainable using an integrated area development framework.

As far back as over 25 years ago, this author (Hooja, 1978) had raised the issue whether district planning should be physical (involving land use, communications, services and utilities); economic (involving production and distribution, overall productivity etc.); administrative (involving creation of structures, procedures and rules, fixing targets and norms etc.); fiscal (arranging for and providing funds) or socio-political. Hooja (1986) had added the question whether the district plan should be more spatial and temporal, or client-based, or sectoral, in character. Perhaps, all these aspects need to be part of the district plan and, therefore, the expectations from the district planners are quite high.

Who Are the District Planners Who Need to Be Trained?

In order that district and decentralized planning may succeed, it is necessary that the key actors involved in the process need to be trained as well as oriented to the needs and methodology of decentralized planning and be inculcated with the planning skills necessary. The knowledge required would pertain to the district planning process, tools and techniques for regional planning, as well as participatory techniques. The skills to be imparted would be those required by the planner to undertake the analysis and detailing of the plan as well as specialized skills relating to the management and development of resources or related to specific sectoral aspects of planning.

The target groups for such training would be:

1. Panchayat officials at the district level and the Chief Executive Officer, Zila Parishad.
2. BDO and other line officers at the block level.
3. Elected non-officials of Zila Parishad Panchayat Samiti/Mandal Panchayat including Zila Pramukh and Pradhan of Panchayat Samiti.
4. Members of the District Planning Committee and officers of the district planning cell which services the District Planning Committee.
5. District level officers (or DLOs; heads of district offices of various departments).
6. Assistants dealing with planning in the district offices.
7. Officers at the state level, both in state planning department and in other administrative departments dealing with planning.
8. Officers in the intermediate region level organizations like offices of the Command Area Development Commissioner, Tribal Development Commissioner, Desert Development Commissioner and Divisional Commissioners.

Of the above, those in categories 1 to 6 are the ones who would be directly involved in decentralized planning and collectively comprise the district planners.

Decentralized Project Planning: Analytical Skills and Techniques

Now to turn to the question regarding what skills and knowledge are likely to prove relevant for decentralized and district planning. What is required is:

(a) Knowledge of the area's needs, potentials, resources and resource gaps.
(b) Knowledge of state and national level goals, plans, schemes and resource flows.

(c) Responsiveness to people's needs and knowledge of their aspirations.
(d) Knowledge of participatory planning and local mobilization techniques.
(e) Knowledge of how the government administrative system and the existing market system works in the regions/area.
(f) Knowledge about local political and administrative pulls and pressures.
(g) Planning and project planning expertise.
(h) Area and spatial planning knowledge and concepts.
(i) Some knowledge of various disciplines and technical subjects having a bearing on development (i.e., basic knowledge regarding agriculture, animal husbandry, civil engineering, rural industries, health and education management, and similar subjects).
(j) Ability to combine the above and prepare integrated and comprehensive plans based on a broad vision.

Such knowledge would not be available with any one single individual even at the highest policy level in the country. However, teams of local administrators, people's representatives, etc., could be built up gradually to develop a feel and understanding for each of the above points. For that, at least initially, attempts should be made to impart training not only to district and block level planners but also to state level planners in:

1. Identifying locally felt needs (as well as aspirations, which may match neither the needs nor the available resources) and mobilizing the local populace to ensure people's participation and participatory planning.
2. Project/scheme identification.
3. The project approach and basics of project planning.
4. Area planning and concepts like growth centre planning.
5. Integrating and compiling different aspects of plan proposals and proposals regarding various schemes/projects into a coherent district or local area plan.
6. Interacting with state government planning cells and planning departments and various state government departments and their district level staff.
7. Interacting with the large-sized panchayat bodies that have come into existence as a result of the recent constitutional amendments.
8. National and state level planning goals.

9. Sources of, and ways to gain access to, data available at national and state levels as well as locally which could prove useful for decentralized planning.
10. Nowadays, some knowledge in the use of computers could also be imparted as their use could make planning exercises that much easier.

For identification of the local needs and aspirations, it is techniques like problem tree analysis, or problem-matrix analysis on the one hand and rapid rural appraisal (RRA) and participatory rural appraisal (PRA) on the other, which need to be taught. Of course, as regards motivation of the populace, there is no simple formula or technique that could be taught.

As regards project identification, it could be suggested to the potential district and decentralized planners that project/scheme ideas can come to them from either analytical or non-analytical sources like the following:

Analytical Sources	*Non-analytical Sources*
1. Resource analysis of areas and households	1. Political directions
2. Needs analysis	2. Political pressures
3. Demands analysis	3. Declared government policies and objectives
4. Market analysis	4. Formal (and even informal) interaction amongst officers or between officials and non-officials
5. Rapid Rural Appraisal (RRA)	5. Guidelines of aid giving agencies/national programmes, etc.
6. Social mapping/cultural inventories	6. Replication of existing project ideas
7. Diagnostic and strategy exercises	7. Feedback from failed projects
8. Brainstorming	8. Touring of the area
9. Surveys of literature	9. Common sense administrative or political experience
10. Project/identification missions or groups	10. Bargaining between sanctioning and implementing agencies/departments
11. The censuses related to population, agriculture, animal husbandry, industry, etc., conducted at regular intervals	11. Casual reading of newspapers, magazines, books
	12 Meetings of villagers and panchayat bodies or community-based organizations
	13. Citizens' petitions and applications

Curtis and Watson (1987) have suggested that analytical sources of project ideas can be further divided into the sub-categories of administrative search and intellectual search. Some possible methods of the two types of search are given below:

Administrative Search	*Intellectual (Academic) Search*
Consult populations (surveys, local committees, discussions, villagers meetings)	Analyze economy
Consult local leaders and other key informants formally or informally (even in a seminar)	Analyze society
Consult government departments through routine meetings and special working groups	Special problem-oriented analytical studies
Consult research organizations/consultants through planning studies	Diagnostic and strategy exercises

Just as for purposes of decentralized planning the project identification needs to be kept simple, similarly project planning also need not entail full and detailed project analysis with Net Present Value (NPV), Internal Rate of Return (IRR) and cost-benefit ratios in detail not being required for each and every project appraisal.

In fact, for many small projects, even a rough use of the project approach with a rough comparison of costs and benefits may prove adequate and would also be an improvement over the scheme budget exercises presently most often done in government. Not every project needs to have exact values assigned to the costs, benefits and rates of returns and in some cases mere quantification, and in others even identification, may be enough.

Roberts Chambers (1992) has indicated the following criteria for simple project selection: cost-effectiveness, decision matrices, priority ranking, check-listing, and preparation of lists of costs and benefits.

Of course, the project approach needs to be properly understood at the district and lower levels, both among administrators and panchayat leaders, not only for project formulation purposes, but also for project implementation since it would help avoidance of blind application of norms worked out by some other agency without trying to see if any special local conditions exist that would lead to unintended latent impacts of implementation which had not been anticipated by the project formulator.

Similarly, if the project approach is understood at the local planning level, then better sensitivity analysis is possible since instead of abstract generalized eventualities like percentage cost on time overrun and its impact on cost and benefit flows being considered at state or regional level, at the local level locally specific likely eventualities can be better identified and, quantified for sensitivity analysis with respect to each such specific eventuality.

Local planners mistakenly think of project life as only covering the period up to benefit, delivery or completion of construction, and have to be reminded that the period in which the impact of a project is being felt has to be considered part of project life for pre-project appraisal purposes and that intangible benefits and costs both have to be considered just as possible negative impacts of projects have been.

It also needs to be explained to local planners as to how project analysis needs to include technical appraisal, institutional-organizational-managerial-appraisal, commercial appraisal, financial appraisal, economic sustainability appraisal (with its sub-categories of social appraisal and environmental appraisal) and what this writer likes to refer to as acceptability appraisal (involving acceptability on the part of the beneficiaries, the non-beneficiaries in the area, and the lower, middle and senior level implementers as well as concerned officials and non-officials including people's representatives) since in case acceptability is not forthcoming then either the project objectives may need to be modified (the second best may be better than the optimal or the 'best') or special acceptability-including mechanisms may need to be built into the project at a cost. Only after the above can the decisions about accepting/rejecting projects, or regarding ranking of projects be undertaken.

The training should also emphasize that a lot of sources for funds and projects may be available outside government (from banks, various trusts and autonomous bodies, etc.,) or if within the government not through routine state government budgets which are partly devolved upon panchayats but are available upon special application being made for them. Thus, panchayat bodies need to know about sources of such funds, guidelines for applying for them and ways in which to prepare implementable and sanctionable projects for such sanctioning. In today's era of economic liberalization and with the post-Fifth Pay Commission scenario, normal flow of government funds to PR may not be large and may, in fact, reduce overtime as state governments face a resource crunch. Hence, such tapping of other sources by panchayat bodies, as also tapping of user charges, may have to be learnt by PR officials and non-officials who undertake district planning.

Both for training regarding planning and training for actually doing things (implementing), it is case studies, examples, demonstrations, films and audio-visual aids as well as discussions rather than lectures which should be used for both the lower level government functionaries and elected persons in panchayats. Concepts need to be simplified with use of examples that are meaningful in the rural milieu in which they live.

All of the above have to be done in the local language and without use of the academic/semi-academic jargon. This writer has experience of training sessions with both elected panchayat representatives and officials of district and lower levels where the basic concepts were quickly understood and appreciated by them.

Most district and block level functionaries have never really thought in terms of locational and area planning or of growth centre concepts. However, once exposed to basic area-based concepts, most are quick to understand issues of both geographic and social distance and of physical and social barriers as also how to fit their projects/schemes into a framework of spatial planning that would prove most beneficial for the area they are to plan for and implement in. They also start appreciating how sectoral plans and growth/service centre plans can each lead to modifications in each other so that an integrated area development plan catering to sectoral needs and central place based planning can evolve. Use of methodological devices like Gutmans Scalogram for growth centres and for facilities provided at such centres are also easily understood by them. Experiences of the Government of India-Ford Foundation Pilot Project on Rural Growth Centres in the late 1960s and early 1970s may, however, caution planners that the growth centre approach has to be integrated with other approaches and cannot be the sole criteria for preparing plans.

Now to turn to what is expected from the district planners as that would determine how they need to be trained and oriented to develop capabilities for fulfilling district planning tasks.

Previous Thinking About the Role of District Planner

As regards preparing holistic district plans, many writers have set forth their views over the last few decades and numerous model district plans have also been prepared. However, this writer feels that if Gadgil's views from the 1960s, V.K.R.V. Rao's and those of the Asoka Mehta Committee on Panchayati Raj Institutions (PRIs) from the 1970s and those of the Hanumantha Rao (Group) Report of 1984 and of the 2001 Report of the Task Force on PRIs of the Planning Commission as well as the Working Group Report on Decentralized Planning and PRIs for Tenth Five-Year Plan published in the same year are put across to potential planners at the district or block levels, then many of the significant issues on district planning would get properly discussed.

Gadgil (1966) had suggested that each district be divided into mandi areas each of which would have a market centre as its nucleus.

He suggested (as this reader has understood his Kale Memorial Lecture of 1966) that the district planning exercise starts with the preparation of a physico-geographic plan of socio-economic overheads so as to direct the activities of producers and consumers. This would involve the provision of basic services and amenities to be spread throughout the area. The next aspect to be considered is the conservation, proper exploitation and development of natural resources. Then one needs to plan for production through a system of incentives and disincentives for individual workers, managers and entrepreneurs and the use of encouragement, regulation and prohibition. Also required is planning for unemployment involving the choice of the type and volume of projects which provide employment. The plan would also have to be dovetailed. This would involve questions of balances and availabilities, of priorities and of financial resources available – all to be considered within the framework of national objectives, policies and plans. Also to be considered would be the questions regarding the need for setting up new organizations, or of re-allocating functions amongst various existing institutions. Finally, according to Gadgil, the district planner would have to ensure coordination, synchronization and proportionality of the various parts of the plan.

According to V.K.R.V. Rao (1973), the district planner (which in today's post-Constitutional Amendment era would mean the District Planning Committee and the officers assisting it) has to work at two levels: the district and the economic area. (The summary that follows reflects the way this author has understood Rao's views.) He has to look to speedy economic growth, integrated and effective utilization of resources (both human and natural), increase in employment, increase in social services and social consumption, redressal of regional imbalances, improving the lot of socially and economically backward sections of the population, and speedy abolition of poverty. While details of plans for conservation of natural resources and for production, etc., need to be worked out at the economic area level, areawise and sectoral financial allocation, distribution of employment-oriented schemes and solving of organizational problems are best done at the district level with coordination and synchronization efforts being done at both levels and the overall integration with state and natural plans being done at the district level. The district planner must identify his district's resources and the extent of their utilization, the nature and extent of infrastructural development required, the district's socio-cultural profile, the nature and extent of the existing social infrastructure and the production generating infrastructure and facilities, the consumption requirements, existing social stratification, the position of the deprived, wage levels, unemployment and underemployment and the prevailing income distribution. He has also to learn to anticipate local reactions.

The district plan should not be a mere collection of various department or sub-departments' proposals, nor a mere spelling out of targets and financial allocations, but a much more comprehensive document, which, keeping in mind financial constraints, spells out logical relations between sectoral and department plans and between various economic areas in a district, and which determines the chronological order in which schemes are to be started and implemented. It is to be based on calculations of demand and supply where the needs for equipment, trained personnel, buildings, raw material, skilled and unskilled labour, etc., have been checked against available supply and an attempt is made to improve the internal organization of the implementing agencies.

The planner, according to V.K.R.V. Rao, must combine knowledge of local and district conditions with that of plan formulation techniques. He has to be able to anticipate crisis situations so as to avoid emergencies and crash programmes and to replace them by consistent and routinized efforts. Given the knowledge of central and state projects in the district, and the corresponding inflows of outlays, as well as of local natural resources, production, land uses, credit supply, infrastructure and social service facilities, etc., the district planner should give priority to the development of socio-economic overheads and to resource development rather than to the social services that local pressures demand. V.K.R.V. Rao was obviously thinking of experts or officials as "the planner" but in today's context "the planner" would be both the elected representatives and officials in the District Planning Committee (DPC) and the official District Planning Cell providing back up to the DPC.

Some recommendations made by the Asoka Mehta Committee on PRIs in 1978 are as follows (summary adapted by this author from Anil Dutta Mishra, 1998):

1. With the district as the strategic level for economic planning, the Zila Parishad should be made responsible for planning at the district level. The appreciation of the total resources, the credit availability and the necessary strategy formulation covering several blocks would be feasible at the district level. An elected Zila Parishad would also provide the much-needed correctives to the

techno-economic plans. The production and employment programmes prepared at the block level will fit into the totality of the plan.

2. A professionally qualified team should be stationed at the district level for preparation of district plans. While formulating the plans, the expertise of the district level staff should take into account a cross-section of all shades of public opinion relevant to the district.
3. The state government would have to provide continuous assistance in the process of district planning. It would have to ensure that the national objectives relating to weaker sections are pursued by the PRIs. It will also have to provide the financial and physical parameters as well as technical expertise to the technical group. It should also ensure equitable allocation of resources and fixation of long range priorities.
4. The district plan prepared by the technical group would be placed before the "committee of the whole" of the Zila Parishad where the MPs, MLAs and MLCs are also members.
5. The state government should provide necessary machinery for examining the district plans to enable formulation of the state plans. It should also hold a dialogue with the Zila Parishad in this regard.
6. The district planning should take care of urban-rural continuum. The district plan should also analyze data on growth points and growth centres in order to provide for necessary economic flows.
7. Intensive exploitation of new opportunities of resources earmarked for the weaker sections should be a part of the plan process itself. The District Social Justice Committee will be of considerable help in this regard.
8. The ongoing exercise of district planning should also take into account the formulation of sound projects and short-term action plans covering areas of specific endowments, poverty belts and specific target groups.
9. In order to avoid the problem of non-implementation and non-absorption of the many "delivery systems", which are already functioning, the several implementational components of all the local-level projects should be analyzed in advance and greater attention should be paid towards synchronization and orchestration of the activities of the project-level functionaries of different disciplines. Coherent activity analysis, standardized micro-project plans, including flow-charts of goods, services and

functionaries, will also have to be prepared so that the Mandal Panchayat can play an effective role in administrative coordination and institutional supervision.

10. To begin with, the Mandal Panchayats may be limited to implementation and promotional roles, but they would have a key role in supplying the necessary information about the various schemes and suggest the potential areas of development as well as their requirements to the Zila Parishad. They would have to play this role on a continuous basis and not merely by holding a meeting to consider the draft plan or sending their comments on it to the Zila Parishad. The planning unit at the district level should take note of the views articulated by the Mandal Panchayats from time to time.
11. The total credit inflow for agricultural development is expected to rise significantly in the years to come. The PRIs should, therefore, pay greater attention to institutional finance rather than concentrating on budgetary sources as in the past. This would be possible only if the PRIs pay due attention to ensuring greater responsiveness in project implementation by ascertaining the views of the beneficiaries since those require considerable people's participation like the Revised Minimum Needs Programme.
12. The PRIs should not only be regarded as a forum for obtaining the views of people's representatives but, in due course, they should become capable of planning for themselves within the resources available to them.

The Planning Commission had constituted a Working Group on District Planning under Dr Hanumantha Rao whose recommendations made in 1984 were accepted by the Government of India as part of the Seventh Plan.

The functions of the district planning body, as suggested by the Working Group, are: (a) crystallization of local needs and objectives within the broad framework of national and state level objectives, (b) taking stock of the natural and human endowments of the district and the regions within the district as well as the level and pattern of development attained so far, (c) listing and mapping of amenities at the village, block and district levels, (d) formulation of district plans in their socio-economic, temporal and spatial dimensions along with their linkages with the rest of the economy, (e) formulating of policies, programmes and priorities relevant for the district, (f) coordination and implementation of the district plan, and (g) monitoring and review of implementation of the district plan and programmes with due regard to their linkages and dependencies.

The Working Group suggested the following steps for the planning exercise: (i) formulation of the major objectives of district planning; (ii) compilation of data; (iii) bringing out the profile of the district in relation to the basic objectives; (iv) formulating the main strategy and thrust, (v) analyzing existing programmes and projects regarding (a) modifications of ongoing schemes/projects, (b) removal of inter-block disparities, (c) assessment of unemployment/underemployment and proposals regarding manpower planning/budgeting, (d) inclusion of new projects and plans, (e) interlinkages between various projects/programmes, (f) organization and management to eliminate gaps in implementation, and (g) the relationship and links between the district plan and the state development plan; (vi) assessment of resources for allocation to various programmes/projects, and (vii) preparing a statement of physical and financial components of the plan.

For each local level scheme, the minimum details required are: (a) description of the scheme and its significance to the area, (b) location, (c) raw material and inputs requirement and linkages, (d) volume and value of likely resultant output, (e) number of beneficiaries, (f) likely employment generation, and (g) (for some select schemes only) simple cost-benefit calculation.

The district planner would also have to dovetail in an integrated manner, resources available from: (a) State Plan for particular projects, (b) State Plan for schemes of general nature not tied to specific projects, (c) local bodies, (d) from credit institutions, and (e) raised by voluntary agencies and other local sources.

The Working Group also emphasized manpower planning, spatial planning, implementational coordination, plan integration and public participation.

This is what the Planning Commission's Task Force on PRIs, which submitted its report in December 2001, has to say:

To facilitate the preparation of the plans at the district level, a core planning team comprising experts from various disciplines needs to be formed for each district which could help in the preparation of plans keeping in view the physical and natural resource endowments of the area, availability of funds and the priorities of the people. In addition, experts could be hired on a consultancy basis if expertise is required in a specific area. In Kerala, a Voluntary Technical Corps (VTC) has been created consisting of about 10,000 experts to vet and re-work projects prepared by the panchayats. These include retired persons with technical expertise, bank personnel and officials of government departments. Similarly, in other states, voluntary groups and institutions need to be identified for providing services, training and support for effective implementation of programmes at the local level. The Kerala model for people's campaign for decentralized planning to empower the local bodies to prepare their plans in a transparent and participatory manner could be replicated in other states. The details of Kerala model are given in Box 1.

The report of the Working Group on Decentralized Planning and PRIs for the Tenth Five-Year Plan 2002–2007, which came out at about the same time in 2001 as the above mentioned Task Force report, states that "while preparing draft development plan, the DPC should keep in view the matters of common interest between panchayats and the municipalities including special planning, sharing of water, other physical and natural resources, the integrated development of infrastructure, environment conservation, and the extent and type of

Box 1 ***People's Planning Campaign in Kerala***

The People's Planning Campaign has succeeded in providing a concrete methodology for participatory planning for local level development. The roots of the methodology can be traced back to an experiment carried out in Kalliassery Panchayat of Kannur District in the early 90s. In 1996, it was modified and adapted for large-scale application. The salient features of this methodology are described below, stage-by-stage:

1. *Needs Identification:* Through a meeting of Gram Sabha, i.e., the ward or the electoral constituency of a village panchayat member, the felt needs of the community are identified. There is a period of environment creation to mobilize maximum participation in the Gram Sabha. Statistics reveal that about 10–12 per cent of the rural population has participated in the Gram Sabhas held as part of the People's Planning Campaign. The Gram Sabha meetings are held in a semi-structured manner with plenary sessions and sub-group sessions dealing with specific developmental issues. The decisions are minuted and forwarded to the panchayats. Each Gram Sabha is chaired by the elected member and has an official as its coordinator.
2. *Situation Analysis:* Based on the demands emanating from the first special Gram Sabha and based on developmental data, both primary and secondary exhaustive development reports have been prepared and printed in the case of every PRI in the state. These reports describe the status in each sector of development with reference to available data, analyze the problems and point out the

Cont'd... Box 1

Cont'd... Box 1

direction for further development. This is a one-time exercise and the reports will be revised before the next five-year plan.

3. *Strategy Setting:* Based on the Gram Sabha feedback and the development report, a one-day seminar is held at the PRI level in which participation of experts, elected members, representatives nominated by Gram Sabhas, practitioners from among the public is ensured. The development seminars suggest the broad priorities and general strategies of development projects to be taken up for a particular year.
4. *Projectization:* The ideas thrown up by the above three stages are translated in the form of projects by Task Forces at the PRI level. For each PRI, there are about 12 Task Forces dealing with different sectors of development. Each Task Force is headed by an elected member and is convened by the concerned government official. The Vice Chairman of the Task Force is normally a non-government expert in the sector. The projects are prepared in the suggested format outlining the objectives, describing the benefits, explaining the funding and detailing the mode of execution and phasing of the project.
5. *Plan Finalization:* From among the projects, based on the allocation communicated, the concerned PRI finalizes its plan for the year and this plan is submitted to the DPCs through the Expert Committees. The panchayat is free to take up any project, irrespective of its cost, subject of course to the resources actually available and within the sectoral limits.
6. *Plan Vetting:* The Expert Committee at the block or the district level vets the projects for their technical viability and conformity with the mandatory government guidelines on planning and costing and forwards them to the DPC. They cannot change priorities of projects; they can only ask for rectification.
7. *Plan Approval:* The DPC gives formal approval to the plans after which the PRI can start implementation. It is to be noted that the DPC also cannot change the priority of a PRI. It can only ensure that government guidelines are followed. Administrative approval for implementation is given project-wise by the PRI. Every PRI has unlimited powers of administrative sanction subject only to the limits of its financial resources.

The campaign is facilitated by about 650 Key Resource Persons at the state level, about 10,000 District Resource Persons and about 100,000 Local Resource Persons (100 per Village Panchayat) – all of them trained in the basics.

resources available in the district". The Working Group Report adds that "the important aspect of decentralized planning is identifying ingredients of (a) a strategy of rural development, (b) determination of spatial and temporal references of activities and their coordination, (c) infrastructure for essential services, and (d) social institutional framework". Further, "another important aspect of the rural development strategy and decentralized planning is to maintain coordination not only among different sets of functionaries but also among different sections of the rural economy".

The Working Group thereupon admits that unfortunately, in many parts of the country, rural communities are not yet fully equipped to handle the task of planning as envisaged in the 74th Amendment Act and accordingly it suggests that training programmes for Panchayati Raj-related functionaries should concentrate on providing basic skills of planning to the rural population.

At this stage, it would prove interesting to note what the Working Group on Decentralized Planning and Panchayati Raj Institutions for the Tenth Five-Year Plan (2002–2007) had to say about training.

The scope of training should, the Working Group report suggested, include within its fold the following:

1. Duties and responsibilities, and power and authority.
2. Financial management, resource mobilization, budgeting, accounting, auditing, etc.
3. Social issues – reproductive health, child development, environmental issues, human rights, etc.
4. Constitution, concerned Acts, rules and regulations, development schemes, etc.
5. Training content should also include how to work in a group, building *esprit de corps,* developing leadership skills, decision-making acumen, motivation and morale building, etc.
6. Self-governance, social justice and ethics in public affairs.
7. Training can be organized under the following heads for panchayats and municipalities:
   (a) Participatory Poverty Assessment
   (b) Participatory Vulnerability Mapping
   (c) Participatory Resource Planning
   (d) Participatory Assessment and Action Related to Education, Health and Infrastructure
   (e) Participatory Heritage Mapping

8. Training content should aim at linking training interventions to development programmes.
9. Emerging areas like natural disaster management, micro-level planning, etc., should be included in training programmes.
10. Gender sensitization,

The Working Group also emphasizes that a sound approach to training must focus on the significance of preparing people for proper planning for socio-economic development in the light of the area in which they live. The training approach should keep in mind the impact of specific customs, traditions and conventions of the people whom it intends to train. The Working Group further cautions that training cannot be a one-time effort but has to be a continuous process, an idea that this writer thoroughly endorses and has long propagated.

Towards the Future: An Organizational Model

It is my belief that the current practice of planning in isolation of individual sectoral programmes and projects would have to be discarded as far as planning at the district level is concerned. District planning has to be a single wholistic operation wherein different activities (including activities in the private sector) are harmonized into an integrated area plan.

The 74th Amendment Act, 1992, has provided for a district planning committee to consolidate the panchayat (rural) and municipal (urban) plans of the district. About 80 per cent of its membership has to be from panchayat and municipal bodies. As per the 2001 report of the Task Force on PRIs, eleven states and two union territories had constituted DPCs and in some states either a Minister or the District Collector heads the DPC while the Zila Pramukh or Chairman, District Panchayat does so in others.

However, in addition to the feedback that elected representatives of local bodies can provide and the detailed discussions that can be held in their forums, district planning would also need detailed analysis and studies and inputs from experts and government servants. Further, due to the overlap of functions, there is need for a body with functionaries from the state and district levels to work with the panchayat/municipality non-officials to minimize the differences and to reduce the strains between the state and district levels. In this context and keeping in view the fact that the new post-Constitution Amendment panchayat bodies like Zila Parishad and Panchayat Samiti are prone to be large and somewhat unwieldy (perhaps functioning and behaving like mini-legislative assemblies) and that the same may be the case with the District Planning Committee which may become more of a deliberating body than a functional body undertaking plan and project formulational exercises, a recommendation of the NDC Committee on Micro Level Planning and Involvement of People at Grass Roots Level (Chimanbhai) Patel Committee 1993) that the District Rural Development Agency (DRDA) and the District Planning Board (DPB) be merged into District Planning and Development Board and that the Zila Parishad continue to exist as a separate agency, becomes significant because the Zila Parishads would definitely be too large to themselves undertake a meaningful planning exercise. The Chimanbhai Committee had also emphasized training and making available central assistance for providing district planning staff at district and block levels. In fact, what would be required would be compact and competent planning teams in each district and block. Hence, I feel that, in addition to the constitutional body as prescribed in the 74th Amendment Act, we should have a District Planning Council to smoothen the process of multi-level planning and give better results. That many states had found such an arrangement convenient in the pre-Constitutional Amendment era is bourne out by the remarks of Patnayak and Mishra (2003) that there was tendency to have a three-tier planning machinery at the district level consisting of a deliberative and decision-making body, a smaller executive committee of this body, and a district planning cell.

The District Planning Council could be the apex body at the district level with a Cabinet Minister not belonging to the district as chairman and consisting of both official and non-official (elected) members. Of course, having the Divisional Commissioner or District Collector as the chairman may also be considered as an alternative. The composition of this council may vary from state to state, but an illustrative possible model has been worked out as follows (this model for District Planning Council could be compared meaningfully with Sunderam's suggestions about the composition of District Planning Committees in *Journal of Rural Development*, 1997):

Minister	Chairman
Divisional Commissioner	Co-Chairman
Collector	Vice Chairman
Zila Pramukh or Chairman District Level Panchayat	Vice Chairman
MPs (all) and MLAs (3)	Members
Nominees from Members of Zila Parishad/Panchayat Samitis (3)	Members

Two Pradhans (3 if total Pradhans in district are more than 8)	Members
Five main district level officers	Members
Chairman, Urban Improvement Trust/Municipal Council (2)	
Representative of Commissioner, Command Area Development/Tribal Area Development/Desert Development Commissioner	Members
Lead Bank Officer	Member
Chief Executive Officer of Zila Parishad	Member
Representative of State Planning Department	Member
Nominated planning experts	Members
Additional Collector, Development and Project Director, DRDA	Member-Secretary
Chief Planning Officer	Co-Secretary

A smaller District Planning Executive Committee could be the main executive body at the district level responsible for formulation of the plan and the monitoring of its implementation subject to guidance and supervision by the District Planning Council as well as ultimate overall supervision by the constitutionally created District Planning Committee. The Collector would be the chairman of this Executive Committee. The other members may include Zila Pramukh, two district level officers, two planning experts, two non-official members of the District Planning Council, Lead Bank Officer, Additional Collector, Development in charge of the DRDA, and Chief Planning Officer.

A multidisciplinary district planning cell, headed by the Chief Planning Officer, would assist the Collector and District Planning Executive Committee in plan formulation and monitoring of its implementation. The Collector would need to be vested with sufficient coordinational authority to ensure integrated plans can be prepared with the help of departmental officers available at the district level.

In the scheme being suggested above, this author feels that the District Planning Committee and the PRIs like Zila Parishad and Panchayat Samiti and even Gram Panchayat would lay more emphasis on participatory planning and socio-political considerations, while the District Planning Council, its Executive Committee and the District Planning Cell would lean more towards analysis and towards the technical, the economic and the administrative-managerial while planning. The District Planning Committees and PRIs would be more responsive to planning messages from the grassroots and to reconciliation of the competing interests pushing for alternative courses of action, while the District Planning Council and its executive committee and the district planning cell would be more attuned to analyzing the merits and demerits or costs and benefits of alternatives as also to the planning impulses emanating from national or regional objectives and guidelines set forth by state government and its district level set-up (or Government of India through its centrally sponsored schemes). The difference between the two would be more of degree than of the absolute because the District Planning Committee and PRIs can also be sensitive to central or regional policies and also go into detailed planning exercises, while the District Planning Council and its Executive Committee can be equally concerned about ideas coming up from the grassroots and participative planning as well as accommodating various socio-political interests while undertaking planning. Naturally, in a democracy, the constitutionally recognized District Planning Committee, four-fifths of whose members are elected representatives, would have to reconcile and bring about a balance between the recommendations thrown up by the two types of approaches discussed in this paragraph.

In addition to the District Planning Committee and District Planning Councils, at the state level also the State Planning Department should set up a District Planning Facilitation Cell and many other departments may have to follow suit since the departments at the state level and their officers at various levels would have to play a significant advisory role in the district planning process.

The district planners would also have to sensitize themselves to, and yet keep themselves removed from and above, the differing perceptions about the needs and objectives of their area and its people that the members and Chairman of the Gram Sabha, Panchayat Samiti and Zila Parishads as also members of the State Legislature have. This can lead to inter-level conflicts. In fact, since in the post-Constitution Amendment Panchayati Raj, direct elections to various levels have been provided for, instead of the earlier practice of indirect elections, the Chairman, Gram Panchayat and members on behalf of the Gram Panchayat in the Panchayat Samiti no more being the same person, could have very different objectives and interests. Similar could be the position between the Chairman, Panchayat Samiti and the Panchayat Samiti representative in the Zila Parishad who would also, in the new dispensation, cease to be the same person. Similarly, even amongst administrators, the perceptions about appropriate goals and objectives are likely to differ from department to department and level to level.

Thus, many conflicts of interest exist which the planner would have to sort out while preparing his proposals. Hence, the district planner would need to develop great inter-personal dealing skills. It is interesting to recall that in their postscript on "methodological rigour versus practical considerations in planning and its decentralization" in Hooja and Yerram Raju (1993), the editors had recorded that "in his repeated interaction with young Indian Administrative Service officers freshly being introduced to the field, one of us found that on the subject of decentralized planning, compromises with political and administrative expediency were preferred by them to methodological rigour in plan preparation. The reasons ascribed for such an approach were:

(a) devolution of financial resources were not on a set pattern or were too meagre to pursue the micro plan goals;
(b) political pressures go beyond any logical framework;
(c) not all the tools and techniques are available at the district level; and
(d) lack of training in applicable methodologies for all the district level functionaries who have to prepare the sectoral plans and integrate them into a district plan.

Such problems exist even today, but it is hoped that the type of training and orientation described in this paper could help in overcoming many, if not all, of them.

Thus, the reality in decentralized planning under the new Panchayati Raj would prove to be very different from what many district and block level functionaries and panchayat leaders as well as scholar activists interested in Panchayati Raj have been expecting and hoping for. It does not imply merely the delegation of powers to sanction certain types of government works within certain limits to lower level bodies. Nor is it likely to mean that state and central governments would merely pass on some of the resources raised by them to panchayat bodies to spend as they like, thereby enabling panchayat leaders to distribute more largesse.

Instead, as had been indicated above throughout this paper, the nature of planning functions changes from level to level. Accordingly, a table of level-wise planning functions, originally prepared by Kuklinsky and modified twice by this paper writer (the last time for a Bibliography on Multi-Level and District Planning brought out in 1995 by Madhya Pradesh Institute of Social Science Research as a monograph), is being reproduced here:

Types of Planning in Multi-Level Framework (in the Indian Context)

1. National Planning	(a) Global or macro-level planning (b) Inter-sectoral planning (c) Inter-regional planning (d) Planning for special target groups and special areas (e) Integrating with State Plans (f) Planning to facilitate and catalyze private activity
2. Regional Planning: (done at state level) (a) Inter-local planning	1. Macro planning for region 2. Inter-sectoral planning for region 3. Functional-spatial-equity integration
(b) Local planning	1. Macro planning for local areas 2. Inter-sectoral planning for local area 3. Spatial planning 4. Planning for the provision of services and facilities 5. Planning for special target groups and area 6. Planning to catalyze and facilitate private activity
(c) Planning region-specific details of national programmes (d) Integrating with national plans and micro-level plans	
3. Micro-Level Planning (done at district level) (a) Inter-local planning	1. Macro planning for district 2. Inter-sectoral planning for district 3. Functional-spatial-equity integration 4. Spatial planning 5. Planning for the provision of services and facilities 6. Planning for special target groups and areas 7. Participative planning
(b) Local planning for needs of localities (cluster of villages, or a block, or even a single village) (c) Planning details of national and state programmes for the district (d) Integrating with State Plans	

Source: This table has been further adapted and modified from Rakesh Hooja, "District and Regional Planning: Why and How" in Hoshiar Singh and D.P. Singh (eds), *Indian Administration: Current Issues and Problems (1990)*, where it had been originally adapted from A.R. Kuklinsky, "Some Basic Issues in Regional Planning" in R.P. Mishra, D.V. Urs and V.K. Nataraj (eds), *Regional Planning and National Development (1978)*. It is being reproduced from the author's monograph published by MPISSR, Ujjain (1995).

Thus, a good local plan would be one which would be partly sanctioned at the local level and partly at the state or intermediate levels and partly left to private agencies and individuals to undertake after an integrated view of various activities desirable for the local area has been taken.

It is to be hoped that, after proper orientation and training, the district and block level functionaries and elected panchayat leaders who jointly would function as the district planners shall bring about not only better planning aimed at the prioritization of goals and at such resource mobilization and use which is closer to the optimal than is being achieved at present, but would also enable multi-level interaction in the planning process which is based on greater knowledge, understanding and trust than at present.

Accordingly, the various states that are now busy working out how to ensure the conditions necessary to facilitate decentralized and multi-level planning as well as how to solve the operational problems involved in the renewed endeavour at decentralized planning that has been reinforced by the amendments to the Constitution and the subsequent changes each of the states has effected in their panchayat and municipal legislations, would do well to remember that decentralized planning is not going to be easy and that a long drawn out and steady, in fact perhaps slow and steady, effort would be required to achieve the results of genuine decentralized district planning.

Policy makers in the states and at the national level would also do well to remember what FAO's Social and Economic Report No. 52 had pointed out way back in 1985 that there are certain pre-requisites in whose absence decentralized planning may not succeed. These include political and official willingness to operate multi-level planning, appropriate politico-administrative structures with clearly distinguished roles for the participating partners, clear definition of function sharing between various levels, provision of adequate financing at all levels to match the functions to be performed along with rational allocation criteria for such finances, the power and authority at lower levels to mobilize funds to augment transfers from higher levels, the autonomy to plan for the decentralized sector in line with national and state priorities and objectives, a properly equipped planning machinery with adequate capabilities to plan, programme, analyze and translate projects into action, and adequate powers and authorities at sub-national and district levels as well as the freedom to function within reasonable limits of control. To these pre-requisites we may add the suitable orientation and training of both the elected representatives and officials, especially at the district and Panchayat Samiti (block) levels, to provide them with the capabilities, knowledge, skills, attitude, etc., to enable them to carry out the district planning exercises properly.

References

Arora, R.K. and Rakesh Hooja (eds). 1994. *Administration of Rural Development,* Arihant, Jaipur.

Aziz, Abdul. 1994. *Decentralized Planning, The Karnataka Experiment,* Sage, New Delhi.

Bendavid, Val A. and P. Waller (ed.). 1975. *Action Oriented Approaches to Regional Development Planning,* Praeger, New York.

Cernea, Michael (ed.). 1991. *Putting People First,* Oxford University Press.

Chambers, R. 1978. "Project Selection for Poverty Focussed Rural Development", *World Development,* Vol. 6.

——. 1992. Rural Appraisal: Rapid Relaxed and Participatory. Discussion Paper 3, IDS, Sussex.

Curtis, D. and J.R. Watson. 1987. "Planning That Non Planners Can Do", *Journal of Rural Development.*

F.A.O. 1985. Towards Improved Multi-Level Planning for Agriculture and Rural Development, F.A.O. Economic and Social Development Paper No. 52.

Fisher, H. Benjamin. 1979. "Growth Centre Planning in India", in R.P. Misra and K.V. Sunderam(eds), *Rural Area Development,* Sterling, New Delhi.

Gadgil, DR .1966. *District Development Planning,* Gokhale Institute of Politics and Economics, Poona.

Hanumantha Rao, C.H. 1989. "Decentralized Planning: Overview of Experience and Prospects", *Economic and Political Weekly,* 25, February, Vol. 24, No.8.

Hooja, Meenakshi and Rakesh Hooja 1998. "Panchayati Raj in Rajasthan Policy Issues and Concerns", in *IJPA,* Vol. 44, No. 3.

——. 2001. "Institutions of Self-Governance or Agencies for Development: Panchayati Raj in India", in *South Asian Journal of Socio-Political Studies,* Vol. 2, No. 1, January-June 2001.

Hooja, Rakesh 1973. "District as a Planning Unit: Style and Locus", in *Indian Journal of Public Administration (IJPA),* Vol. 19, No.2.

——. 1974. "District Planning Approaches", in *Journal* of *LBS National Academy of Administration,* Vol. 19, Summer 1974.

——. 1975. "District and Regional Planning: Some Aspects with Regard to India", in *Journal of LBS National Academy of Administration,* Vol. 20, Spring 1975.

——. 1978. "District Planning: Some Assumption and Implications", in Ramesh K. Arora et al. (eds), *The Indian Administrative System,* Associated Delhi.

——. 1980(a). "Project Approach and Development Administration in India", in *Prashasnika,* Vol. 9.

——. 1980(b). "Planning for Rural Development by Field Staff", in *IJPA,* Vol. 26.

——. 1981. "Project Formulation for Rural Development Administration – A Rajasthan Viewpoint", in *Administrative Change,* Vol. 9.

——. 1983. "Project Formulation and Planning: Special Problems of Rural Projects And Some Examples of Rajasthan Responses", in *Prashasnika,* Vol. 12.

——. 1986. District Planning: Concept Setting and State Level Applications, Aalekh, Jaipur.

——. 1987. *Administrative Interventions In Rural Development,* Rawat, Jaipur.

——. 1991. "District and Regional Planning Why and How", in Hoshiar Singh and D.P. Singh(eds), *Indian Administration: Current Issues and Problems,* Aalekh, Jaipur.

——. 1994(a). "Decentralized Planning and the Hanumantha Rao Report", in Asha Kaushik (ed.), *Democratic Concerns: The Indian Experience,* Aalekh, Jaipur.

——. 1994(b). "Three Disparate Books on Panchayati Raj: Past and Present", *Indian Book Chronicle, Vol.* 19, No.8

——. 1994(c). "Issues in Preparing Manpower for Effective Decentralized Planning", in *Political Economy Journal of India,* Vol. 3, No. 2.

——. 1995. *Bibliography on Multi-Level and District Planning,* Madhya Pradesh Institute of Social Science Research, Ujjain.

——. 1997. "Training of Panchayat Raj Functionaries: Some Issues", *Journal of Rural Development,* Vol. 16, No. 4.

——. 2004. Book review of V. Vyasulu (ed.), *Panchayats, Democracy and Development* (2003), *South Asian Journal of Socio-Politico Studies,* July-December 2004.

Hooja, R. and Meenakshi Hooja. 2005. *Panchayati Raj in Rajasthan: Continuity and Change,* HCM RIPA, Jaipur.

Hooja, R. and P.C. Mathur (eds). 1991. *District and Decentralized Planning,* Rawat, Jaipur.

Hooja, R. and B. Yerram Raju (eds). 1993. *Decentralized Planning in Multi-Level Framework,* Rawat, Jaipur.

Inamdar, N.R. 1989. *Development Administration,* Rawat, Jaipur

Inamdar, N.R. and K.V. Kshire. 1986. *District Planning in India,* Oxford and I.B.H., New Delhi.

Institute of Social Sciences. 2000. *The Status of Panchayati Raj in the States and Union Territories of India,* Concept, New Delhi.

Jacob, George (ed). 1967. *Readings in Panchayati Raj,* NICD, Hyderabad.

Jain, R.B.(ed.). 1981. *Panchayati Raj,* IIPA, New Delhi.

Joshi, B.M. 1989. "Evolution and Practice of Decentralized Planning in India", in *IJPA,* Vol. 35, No. 1.

Kamath, A.R. 1973. *Selected Writings and Speeches of D.R. Gadgil on Planning and Development,* Orient Longman.

Mathew, George. 1994. *Panchayati Raj: From Legislation to Movement,* Concept, Delhi.

Mathur, Kuldeep. 1980. "Promise and Prospect of Local Planning", in *IJPA,* Vol. 26, No.3.

——. (ed.). 1996. *Development Policy and Administration,* Sage, New Delhi.

Mathur, M.V. and Iqbal Narain (eds). 1969. *Panchayati Raj Planning and Democracy,* Asia Publishing House, Bombay.

Mathur, P.C. 1990. *The Political Dynamics of Panchayati Raj,* Konark, New Delhi.

Mathur, P.C and Rakesh Hooja. 1996. *Projects, Planning and Development Administration,* Rawat, Jaipur.

Mishra, A.D. 1998. *Decentralized Planning: A Study of Objectives and Operational Framework,* Uppal Publishing House, New Delhi.

Mishra, R.P. (ed.). 1992. *Regional Planning Concepts, Techniques, Policies, Case Studies,* Concept, New Delhi.

Mishra, R.P. and R.N. Achyuta. 1990. *Micro Level Rural Planning* Concept, New Delhi.

Mishra, R.P. and K.V. Sunderam. 1980. *Multi-Level Planning and Integrated Rural Development,* Heritage, New Delhi.

Mishra, R.P., D.V. Urs and V.K. Nataraj (eds). 1978. *Regional* Planning and *National Development,* Vikas, New Delhi.

Mishra, Sweta. 1994. *Democratic Decentralization in India,* Mittal Publications, New Delhi.

Mukherjee, Amitabh. 1991. *Methodology and Database for Decentralized Planning,* Heritage, Delhi.

——. (ed.). 1995. *Participatory Rural Appraisal Methods And Applications in Rural Planning,* Vikas, New Delhi.

Mundle, S. 1977. *District Planning in India,* IIPA, New Delhi.

Patnayak, Rama and A.D. Mishra. 2003. "Decentralized Planning in India: A Conceptual Framework", in S.N. Mishra, A.D. Mishra and Sweta Mishra (eds), *Public Governance and Decentralization,* Mittal, New Delhi.

Planning Commission. 1969. *Guidelines for the Formulation of District Plans,* New Delhi.

Prasad, Kamta (ed.). 1984. *Planning and its Implementation, IPA,* New Delhi.

——. 1985. *Planning At The Grass Roots,* Sterling, New Delhi.

Raghavaiah, V. 1967. "District Planning and Administration: The Case for a Unified and Integrated Approach", in *IJPA,* Vol. 23, No.4

Rajeev Gandhi Foundation. 2000. *Panchayati Raj in India: Status Report 1999,* RGF, New Delhi.

Rao, V.K.R.V. 1973. "District Planning Concept", in V.L.S. Prakasa Rao et. al., Working Paper on District Planning Officers Programme, Institute of Social and Economic Change, Bangalore (also published in *The Times of India).*

Rao, V.M. 1989. "Decentralized Planning: Priority Issues", in *Economic and Political Weekly.*

Reddy, G. Ram (ed.). 1977. *Patterns of Panchayati Raj in India,* Macmillan.

Reddy, Y. Venugopal. 1979. *Multi Level Planning in India,* Vikas, New Delhi.

Report of the Team for the Study of Community Projects and National Extension Service (Chairman: Balwantrai Mehta), 1958, Government of India.

Report of Committee on Panchayati Raj Institutions (Chairman: Asok Mehta) 1978, Government of India.

Report of Planning Commission's Working Group on District Planning (Chairman: C.H. Hanumantha Rao), 1984, Government of India.

Report of Planning Commission's Working Group on Block Level Planning (Chairman: M.L. Dantwala), 1978, Government of India.

Report of the National Development Council Committee on Micro Level Planning and Involvement of People at the Grassroots Level (Chairman: Chimanbhai Patel), 1993, Government of India.

Report of the Working Group on Decentralized Planning and Panchayati Raj Institutions for the Tenth Five-Year Plan (2002–2007), November 2001, Planning Commission, Government of India.

Report of the Task Force on Panchayati Raj Institutions (PRIs), December 2001, Planning Commission, Government of India.

Roy, Prodipto and B.P. Patil. 1977. *Manual for Block Level Planning,* Macmillan, New Delhi.

Sen, L.K. 1972(a). *Integrated Area Development,* Department of Personnel, Government of India.

——. (ed.). 1972(b). *Readings in Micro Level Planning and Rural Growth Centres,* NICD, Hyderabad.

Sharma, Sudesh, K. 1976. *Panchayati Raj in India,* Trimurti, New Delhi.

Singh, S.S. and S. Mishra. 1993. *Legislative Framework of Panchayati Raj in India,* Intellectual Publishing House, New Delhi.

Smith, Peter (ed.). 1987. *Project Identification in Developing Countries,* Institute of Development Policy and Management, University of Manchester.

Sundram, K.V. 1979. "District Planning: The Case of Maharashtra", *IJPA,* Vol. 25, No. 1.

Thaha, M. 1993. *Status of Micro Level Planning in India,* Daya, Delhi.

Yugandhar, B.N. and A. Mukherjee (eds). 1991. *Readings in Decentralized Planning,* Concept, New Delhi.

Special Number on Multi-Level Planning, *IJPA,* 1973, Vol. 19, No. 3.

Special Number, on District Planning, *Journal of L.B.S. National Academy of Administration,* 1975, Vol. 20, No. 1.

Special Number on Decentralization, *IJPA,* 1978, Vol. 24, No. 3.

Special Number on Panchayati Raj, *Journal of Rural Development, 1991,* Vol. 10, No. 5.

Special Number on Decentralized Planning, *The Administrator.* 1991, Vol. 36, No. 3.

Special Number on Panchayati Raj, *Journal of Rural Development,* 1997, Vol. 16, No. 4.

17 Role of State ATIs and SIRDs in Training for Better District Planning*

Rakesh Hooja

A recent national-level workshop on 'Strengthening State Training Institutions' saw this writer being asked to make a presentation on the institutional arrangements of training organizations, particularly state Administrative Training Institutions (ATIs) and State Institutes of Rural Development (SIRDs), to meet the needs of more effective district planning. I interpreted the theme assigned to mean that I should share my reflections on what is the role that training organizations like state ATIs and SIRDs can play in various states for multi-level training for more effective district planning within a multi-level planning-cum-implementation framework.

---

* This article is based on a presentation made on February 15, 2008, by the author at an ASCI-UNDP National Workshop on Strengthening State Training Institutions at Administrative Staff College of India, Hyderabad. It has built upon ideas from the author's earlier articles: (1) "Training for, and Expectations from District Planners" ASTI *Journal of Training and Development, Vol. 6,* No. 2, July-December 2005, (2) "Capacity Building for Rajasthan's Panchayat Representatives and Functionaries What the Training Effort Should Cover" (Occasional Paper 7), HCM RIPA, Jaipur, 2006, (3) "Reflections Occasional by New Guidelines for District Planning by Panchayati Raj Institutions", Training Reprint 4/2007, HCM RIPA, Jaipur, 2007, copies of all three articles having been circulated at the ASCI-UNDP National Workshop on Strengthening State Training Institutions. The article is written keeping in mind states where ATIs and SIRDs are separate institutions though much of what has been discussed would also apply to states where a single institution doubles as state ATI and SIRD, and even to Kerala where KILA is separate from both the state ATI and the SIRD and KILA is responsible for much of the training related to district planning.

Rural Development and Panchayati Raj Departments of State Governments and, as their creations, the SIRDs, view the district plan as a plan of and by Panchayati Raj Institutions (PRIs) (with a slight nod towards planning by urban local bodies ULBs – mind you not an urban development plan or a rural development plan but a PRI plan or ULB plan) with some integration of the above plan with some elements of the State Plan. Despite guidelines specifically saying that it should be avoided, plans coming up from the three tiers tend to be wish lists of the three levels of PRIs with block-level sectoral government officers and district-level sectoral officers (or DLOs) scrutinizing plans with reference to departmental norms, to the financial resources available for various schemes, and to technical parameters. The DLOs are also to prepare sectoral vision documents at the district level which merge into a district vision and which hopefully fits in with what has been proposed in a bottom-up approach by PRIs. The District Planning Committee (DPC) is to integrate the PRI plans and ULB plans for the district and to send them up to the Rural Development and Panchayati Raj Department. At the district level, a Chief Planning Officer/District Planning Officer (CPO/DPO) is to integrate the block plan, and get it approved from Zila Parishad and DPC before it is sent to Rural Development and Panchayati Raj Department.

These district plans totally lack in convergence of local body (PRI/ULB) activities with those of state government at regional or divisional, district and sub-district levels, and with those of private sector entities, NGOs and community-based organizations. Even convergence between schemes of various government departments may not be achieved. They also lack in an operational or implementational component of the plan for the district to ensure convergence of various schemes of government, of PRIs, of ULBs etc., for proper coordination and phasing of implementation and better service delivery.

The District Plan, which is the point of contact and integration of bottom-up participatory planning and top-down national and state level planning impulses and inputs, needs to be more comprehensive to succeed as a whole, as well as from the point of view of its human development components.

The District Plan has to be owned up to not only by PRIs and ULBs, or by the Rural Development and Panchayati Raj Department. It has to be owned up to by all state government departments and by all DLOs; only then can it succeed.

To be more comprehensive the District Plan has to include District Drought Proofing and Disaster Mitigation Plan, District Natural Resources and Inventory Plan, District Manpower and Employment (including Self-Employment) Plan, District Livelihoods and Food Security Plan, District Livestock and Agriculture Plan, and District Mining and Industry (including Artisan Activity) Plan. It has to be integrated with the District Annual Credit or Institutional Finance and Banking Plan, and with a village-wise Infrastructure and Facilities Mapping Plan. It also has to make use of a growth centre approach and spatial or geographic planning as well as techno-economic and project planning along with participatory planning.

PPP ventures and raising of resources locally, in addition to those flowing down from state and central governments, also have to form part of the plan.

Thus, a strong feeling has emerged that while the Rural Development and Panchayati Raj Department could continue to coordinate the planning of PRI activities in the district, a District Planning Division of the State Plan Department, which already coordinates the State Plan and the achievement of Millennium Development Goals (MDGs) and human development goals within the state, should also coordinate comprehensive district planning.

Databases at district, regional and state levels focusing on district and block data need to be built up and the CPO's office or cell at the district level strengthened with technical support groups of functionaries from DLO offices etc. being attached to it.

What does this mean for training?

State Government Secretaries/Principal Secretaries and Heads of Departments (HoDs) need to be oriented about the needs of district planning. All State Planning Departments and Directorates of Economics and Statistics staff need to be trained in district planning related aspects. The CPO or DPO is normally an office of State Planning Department/State Statistics and Economics Service (earlier Rajasthan Administrative Service officers were also tried in this post) and thus training of Plan Department Economics and Statistics Service personnel would include CPOs. Regional Joint Directors of various functional or sectoral departments need to be trained for district planning as do all district level officers and their sectoral staff at sub-district levels.

Collectors require major orientation in district planning.

Of course, PRI/ULB staff needs repeated trainings, both for the elected representatives and the functionaries of the local bodies.

Local experts need to be developed at village, block and district levels to help in preparation of local plans.

MLAs/MPs/State Ministers also need to be oriented about importance and relevant aspects of district planning.

Most of the functionaries of PRIs/ULBs as well as the DLOs, many sub-district sectoral officers and those in various departments at the headquarters level and in the State Secretariat, belong to the 30–40–50 services that exist in each state. Thus, we need to tackle them at the induction training stage which is meant to equip them for the first ten years of their service career, by exposing them to district planning and implementation issues during the common foundation courses managed by state ATIs and in institutional for various state services professional courses for each state service managed by state ATI and/or the concerned departments/training institutions in the state.

As regards specific district planning-related training, the PRI officers and non-officials (functionaries and representatives) come within the ambit of SIRDs for training on running and operating Panchayati Raj, on district planning, and on various schemes of the State Rural Development and Panchayati Raj Department. In fact, in a way, SIRD can be seen as the departmental training institute of the State Rural Development and Panchayati Raj Department though it has links with NIRD and the Union Ministry of Rural Development and Panchayats.

In-service training (both compulsory and voluntary) of government officers of all state services has been the mandate of the state ATIs with various departmental training institutes supplementing the work of the state ATI. Thus, it is the state ATI, through its main or satellite campuses in various districts of the state, that has to ensure that training courses or orientation workshops for Principal Secretaries/Secretaries of State Departments, for Heads of Departments, for DLOs etc., on various aspects of district planning, human development planning, planning for achieving MDGs etc. are organized in sufficient numbers. Normally, the State Finance Department, State Plan Department and services like Rajasthan Administrative Service, Rajasthan Accounts Service and Rajasthan Economic and Statistics Service, do not have their separate departmental training institutions and are linked to the state ATI for all their training needs. For some other departments, the state ATI, as the apex training institute at the state level, can guide the various departmental training institutes in organizing district planning-related training.

A practice in some states of Director, ATI being a member of the governing body or executive committee or academic committee of each and every departmental state level training institute is worth emulating elsewhere for effective coordination. It also facilitates cross-fertilization of innovative ideas from one training institute and another.

The state ATI also supports the various departmental training institutes through faculty development programmes, ToTs, coordinating Training Needs Analysis (TNA), preparation of training modules, fixing of common norms etc. State ATIs also undertake some training and orientation for NGO staff.

For elected representatives and functionaries of municipal ULBs, the state ATI is already involved in such training. Though this requires significant stepping up and some sort of a cascade type approach, as is already being followed in the case of personnel and representatives of PRIs by some SIRDs, needs to be emulated by state ATIs. Urban poverty renewal, service delivery and economic accounting reform in municipalities are already part of the mandate of ATIs many of which have HUDCO Professorial Chairs and Centres for Urban Development within their fold.

Many ATIs have Disaster Management Centres, so disaster risk mitigation and convergence of disaster management and development activities in District Disaster Management Plans are already the subject matter of ATIs, which also prepare jointly with district authorities the District Disaster Management Plans and are even involved in preparation of the State Disaster Management Plan.

Many ATIs are also already involved in rural development, natural resources management, women and child, health, education etc. related training. E-governance and computer training is also a focus or strength of state ATIs.

In fact, state ATIs with their various functional centres are well equipped for interdisciplinary and multidisciplinary training with a very broad coverage in various sectors which can prove to be a major asset for district planning.

Some ATIs also have a Centre for Good Governance attached to them (Hyderabad is an exception) which concentrate on good governance at both district and state levels. These often cover public policy, public systems management, PPPs, financial management, access to information, convergence in implementation, citizen-centric delivery, etc., providing advice to state governments, undertaking capacity building measures, conducting studies, etc.

Intensive and saturation training of all Class I, II, III and IV functionaries in a district by state ATIs, as has been tried out in many states, with people from different functional departments attending the same short course conducted locally, helps in better implementation and service delivery at the district level.

Orientation training for MLAs/MPs if at all organized is done by ATIs. Even panchayat/municipal representatives and officials are called from time to time for programmes at ATIs.

The state ATI's coordinating role could be further strengthened, if the number of functional centres that form part of, or are attached to it, could be supplemented by a Centre for Capacity Building in Multi-level Planning having two sub-centres – one for district level planning and the other for state level planning – since the two are interrelated.

As regards the development of local experts in planning (may be retired personnel) at village etc. level, this task could be that of either the SIRD or of the state ATI. Both can use distance education or conventional training approaches and can make use of posters, comics, workbooks, etc., as both have developed competencies in the same. SIRDs tend to primarily focus on participatory aspects of planning while state ATIs tend to be more interdisciplinary using a mix of approaches.

State ATIs are more comprehensive in terms of capabilities of documentation, the variety of publications in their libraries, and their ability to work as clearing houses of knowledge and information.

As regards coordination of all the training/capacity building aspects, the state ATIs, as the apex training institute and intimately linked to the training department of state government, can coordinate all training, including pedagogy, aspects. On district planning, the State Planning Department as nodal department could coordinate the TNAs for district planning with the state ATI and other departments and training institutions just as presently the State Disaster Management Department and ATIs interact with all departments regarding TNA etc. for disaster management.

State ATIs also serve as think tanks for various government departments and for the state government as a whole. Thus, they can also make suggestions for improved practices to be followed for district planning and implementation, and even suggest modifications in guidelines for district planning and for state level planning.

Drafting of state's training policy is within the domain of ATIs.

State ATIs also have an all-India network of similar institutes in the form of Association of State Training Institutions (ASTI) to exchange ideas on various aspects of good governance, policy and administrative reform, planning and implementation, and training and capacity building.

Thus, while SIRDs have an important role to play particularly in training of representatives and functionaries of PRIs in planning at the district level, overall coordination of and much of the actual training for comprehensive district planning within a multi-level planning framework has to be the responsibility of the state ATI in each state.

18 Role of, and Expectations from, State ATIs and Disaster Management Centres in the Sphere of Disaster Management*

Rakesh Hooja

Mr Kanda, Mr Dhar Chakrabarti, representatives of central ministries and state governments and fellow heads and faculty members of state ATIs (Administrative Training Institutes).

I wonder why I have been accorded the privilege of delivering today's special address at this annual training conference on disaster management. Is it merely because with the passing of years I have achieved the Chief Secretary's scale and status, or is it because having spent almost three years heading one of the older, better established, state ATIs – HCM Rajasthan State Institute of Public Administration (HCM RIPA), Jaipur, now 50 years old, and acting as Director of all its centres including the Centre for Disaster Management or CDM (and having attended both the earlier annual training conferences on disaster management at NIDM). I may be expected to have some relevant and useful ideas to share on disaster management and capacity building through state ATIs.

I believe the latter is the case and accordingly in the next few minutes I shall try to set forth a perspective from the viewpoint of the state level on the expectations and role of state ATIs and their Centres of Disaster Management. I also intend to hint at some of the constraints. I

---

*Text of special address delivered at inaugural session of the 3rd Annual Training Conference at National Institute of Disaster Management (NIDM), New Delhi, on 28 January 2008.

hope, what I say would prove applicable not only to HCM RIPA, Jaipur, but equally to other state ATIs also (especially those having Disaster Management Centres attached to them) and they would find much of what I say familiar to them.

Expectations from state ATIs are in the following spheres:

1. Planning for and conducting capacity building and training programmes on various aspects of disaster management for government servants, representatives of NGOs, local bodies and community-based organizations.
2. Orientation efforts for elected representatives of local bodies, for grassroots functionaries like gram sewaks, anganwadi workers, patwaris etc., NGOs, school and college students and teachers, NSS (ATIs also often run centres for NSS organizers' training), scouts and guides, NCC, Nehru Yuvak Kendras, the media, etc.
3. Preparation of training modules and training material on disaster management and their validation before use.
4. Preparation and dissemination of IEC material – posters, comic books, booklets, monographs, cinema slides, etc., on various disasters and on aspects of disaster management.
5. Integrating aspects on disaster management with regular training courses both at the induction level and at in-service level for State Services and Subordinate Services officers (since many ATIs have more than one campus in their state, such trainings are conducted both at district and state levels).
6. As the apex training institute in the state, organizing Training of Trainers (ToT) courses, so that the various training institutes of individual state government departments and NGOs can in turn conduct training courses on disaster management at their own level.
7. Organizing state level and national level seminars, workshops and symposiums to discuss and debate various aspects of disaster management.
8. Some ATIs are also recognized to deliver ICS (Incident Command System)-related trainings on disaster management.

The above are expectations from state ATIs in their basic sphere or role of training. But state ATIs and their Centres for Disaster Management (CDMs) are expected to do much more.

The recently promulgated Rajasthan Government's State Policy for Disaster Management and Prevention has not only declared HCM RIPA as the nodal agency for capacity building and training on disaster management at various levels, but has also laid down that HCM RIPA is to provide institutional and management-related support, back-up and advice to the State Disaster Management and Relief Department. This involves the preparation of State, Divisional and District Disaster Management Plans, validating guidelines as also knowledge and technologies regarding their possible use in disaster management, collection of documentation and knowledge regarding disaster management to be provided when required to government departments and other institutions, collecting information about disasters in the state and elsewhere and about the relief and rehabilitation efforts following each disaster and acting as a clearing house for such information, studying impacts of disasters and of climate change and global warming and of steps taken to tackle them, etc.

As in the case of NIDM vis-à-vis central government, the state ATIs and its CDMs are expected to work as the think tank on disaster management for the state government.

In fact, our ATI and CDM have initially worked out the structure of a desirable district disaster management plan, and then worked with the State Government Disaster Management Department and the various collectors and the district administrations in a series of workshops to get district disaster management plans prepared for each district; and now each year one or two rounds of workshops of groups of districts are organized by HCM RIPA to update each district's disaster management plan. Similarly, the state ATI and its CDM have prepared over 150 village disaster management plans to be used not only if a disaster strikes the particular village, but also as models so that similar village disaster management plans can now be prepared by NGOs or district administration for other villages. Similarly, model community-based disaster management plans are being prepared.

Now, the ATIs and their CDMs are acting as the lead agency along with State Government Disaster Management Department for preparing Rajasthan's State Disaster Management Plan whose work has just commenced.

HCM RIPA has also provided inputs to the State Disaster Management Department in the preparation of (1) Drought Management Manual, (2) Flood Manual, (3) Earthquake Manual, (4) Rajasthan State Disaster Management Guidelines, (5) Aapada Prabhandan Evam Sahayta Nirdeshika, a compendium of instructions, and (6) the State Disaster Management Policy, all since published by the state government. This is part of liasoning with state government to assist it in preparing its disaster prevention mitigation, preparation, rescue and relief, and long-term rehabilitation and reconstruction strategies and policies. In fact, the Director, HCM RIPA has been made a permanent standing invitee to all meetings of Rajasthan State Disaster Management Authority and its committee, headed by the Chief Secretary.

State ATIs and their CDMs are being expected to take up research and consultancy services, to help networking amongst NGOs and between NGOs and government agencies, to help prepare manpower and equipment inventory databases, to document best practices and to work as clearing houses of information, to suggest changes in acts and rules as well as guidelines (including the means to ensure better enforcement) and in the duties regarding disaster management assigned to various government functionaries at various levels, and to help state government to develop a technologically competent and dedicated cadre for disaster management.

In a way, the state government wants the Centre for Disaster Management in the state ATI to act as a sort of executive or line department of the State Government Secretariat Department of Disaster Management and Relief which (not having its own field department) otherwise operates through the Collector and district administration and with the help of other Secretariat and executive departments.

But, is a state ATI or its CDM geared for performing such functions? I think, the answer has to be in the form of a 'no'. State ATIs function as training and capacity building bodies. As a number of other centres (on Good Governance, Management, Urban/Rural Development, Gender Studies, General Administration, etc.) are also attached to the ATIs, they do bring an interdisciplinary flavour to their disaster management capacity building which is one of their strengths along with their core competency in the field of training. But, even for training, when the ATIs call nodal officers of all state government departments and public sector entities for the annual Training Needs Assessment (TNA) prior to finalizing the forthcoming year's training calendar, the departments either send their nodal officer for training or any officer nominated on an ad hoc basis. Such officers may provide feedback about general type of trainings required but are seldom the department's nodal officer for disaster management and therefore cannot discuss special requirements of training in the disaster management sector. Perhaps, now, for preparing the State Disaster Management Plan, the state ATI and its CDM would be able to interact with disaster management-related nodal officers of various departments which would also enable a proper disaster management-related TNA to be conducted.

ATIs have IAS, State Administrative Service and State Accounts Service personnel on deputation, also persons from State College Education Service or universities again on deputation, and regularly selected academicians on their faculty (though many state governments discourage this last category, and prefer ATIs take retired persons on contractual basis on Rs 10,000 per month as visiting professors). While each of these categories either already possesses or easily develops training-related skills (and for training even guest faculty is available to deliver specific lectures), only the first category, i.e., IAS, State Administrative Service, and to some extent State Accounts Service, have the necessary field experience to provide the policy, managerial and institutional back-up to the State Disaster Management Department. And, these officers are all subject to transfer after some time. The other categories of academics can develop expertise in training and in various technical aspects of disaster management, but seldom develop an understanding of the working procedures and systems of government such that they can help in framing policies or in changing administrative structures and procedures.

State governments are rarely willing to provide separate funding for disaster management staff or programmes and activities related to disaster management unless it is from the CRF – and CRF funding gets concentrated on relief work to the exclusion of other activities like training in any year when a significant disaster strikes.

In any case, out of 400-plus training courses per year, that we conduct in HCM RIPA, the government training budget is sufficient for less than 300 courses which are to cover all sectors and not just disaster management. (At HCM RIPA, we have categorized our training into 14 broad categories and disaster management is only one of them. Similarly, we cater to the needs of about 75 to 80 state level departments and public sector entities and State Disaster Management Department is only one of them; and we also cater to needs of the local bodies at the district level and in addition to those of some central ministries.) I have to attract funds from central ministers, bodies like UNICEF or international NGOs for over 100 courses a year and out of this normally it is only for 10 to 15 courses that I am able to attract funding in the sphere of disaster management. Even for workshops either sponsors have to be found or we jointly conduct a workshop with an NGO with both of us sharing the costs. And I am lucky because my institute is a government department with three registered societies working jointly which gives me much flexibility, as does the fact that, in addition to being Director of HCM RIPA, I am Additional Chief Secretary to Government (earlier Principal Secretary to Government, for Training. The non-training work regarding disaster management indicated above also needs funds and resources.

As regards IEC material, until last year, when NDMA provided some support through the State Government Disaster Management Department, I had to rely on UNICEF and NGOs like Save the Children for funds to print such material. For workshop reports/monographs on disaster management, I have used savings from training related to urban development, to training on planning and Millennium Development Goals (MDGs) and training for medical officers, which is not fair to those sectors since those savings should preferably have been used in those very sectors.

State governments generally hold the view that staff, office equipment and facilities and funds for programmes/activities related to specialized activities of disaster management (and even for the various activities from other specialized centres in other sectors) should come of the central government, in this case Disaster Management Division of the Ministry of Home Affairs (MHA), National Institute of Disaster Management (NIDM) and Natural Disaster Management Authority (NDMA), and that state governments should only partly fund the overall development of training infrastructure and general training courses and preparation of training modules material for such general courses.

This year, the problems of state ATIs and the CDMs have been further compounded since the MHA's centrally sponsored scheme – NDMP – is being revamped and MHA/NIDM have not been able to transfer any funds to the ATIs asking them to go ahead with expenditure and to await reimbursement once the scheme is revised. In some ATIs, the disaster management staff has not even received salaries nor any funds for activities as a consequence. But I believe a solution is expected shortly.

NIDM normally funds and organizes a five-day training course at each ATI/CDM each year. This should now be increased to two programmes a year at each ATI – one of four days' duration and the second of three days. These would catalyze and encourage the ATIs to do more in the sphere of disaster management.

The Training Division of Department of Personnel and Training, Government of India, runs Faculty Development Programme for general training skills in government training institutes (for preparing Master Trainers and Recognized Users) and even funds the preparation of training modules by the state ATIs. Something similar needs to be anchored by NIDM and Disaster Management Division of MHA for disaster management-related capacity building, i.e., funding ATIs to prepare training modules and funding faculty development activities in disaster management. Training modules and training material prepared by NIDM should be shared with ATIs and their Disaster Management Centres along with funding to adapt the modules for local conditions in each state and to validate them before use in actual training.

I could go on about the problem of ATIs and CDMs. But let me instead briefly mention three general points regarding disaster management before I end.

However, before that a word about ASTI or Association of State Training Institutions in India. I would like to bring out an ASTI publication on "Role and Expectations from CDMs and State ATIs in the Sphere of Disaster Management" and would like representatives of ASTI and CDMs to send in notes or articles containing their views for inclusion in the proposed publication. (This has since been published.)

Now, for my concluding remarks on three aspects of disaster management that I consider significant:

(a) There is a tendency of state government and people to plan for disasters which have already occurred in a region in the recent past, perhaps because they are more comfortable dealing with and working out responses to types of disasters which had occurred and were responded to within living memory. But, there is no guarantee that a particular type of disaster may not strike an area for the first time. Thus, preparedness planning for any area should be across a very wide range of possible disasters and not just limited to the commonly occurring disasters in the region.

(b) If the possible leakage points (due to either inefficiencies or to malafides and corruption) in disaster management implementation were to be identified during the planning stage – then plugging such leakage points may prove easier at the implementation stage.

(c) For disaster management we need the right (relevant and practical) knowledge and the right people with the right skills and attitudes, with the right equipment, and the right systems and structures in place with well-defined roles for different categories of individuals (in government, in NGOs, in community-based organizations) at the right place when a disaster occurs. That is what the ATIs, CDMs or DMCs, NIDM, etc., together need to strive towards.

19 Creating City Managers

A Capacity Building Initiative

Rakesh Hooja

As the United Nations Population Fund's *The State of World Population 2007 Report on Unleashing the Potential of Urban Growth* indicates that in 2008, for the first time in history, more than half of the world's population will be living in urban areas. The population of towns and cities in developing countries is henceforth likely to double within the space of a single generation. Today's towns and cities are struggling to meet current needs. It will be an even greater challenge to meet future requirements which would be on a very much larger scale.

The challenge of managing the growing towns and cities not only throws up problems of urban poverty, environmental pollution and keeping cities clean, disorganized urban sprawl, provision of services, sustainable growth, industrialization and the like but also offers opportunities to come up with innovative solutions through planned, and organized pre-emptive and proactive action involving the use of fast evolving technology, partnerships with the citizens and citizen groups, and effective administration. The potential benefits of urbanization can far outweigh the disadvantages in this era of speedily urbanization, globalization and technical as well as social change.

The expectations of citizens are fast increasing as they all now look forward to world class urban facilities and services. Our city dwellers need to be facilitated in becoming globally competitive in all professions, in all walks of life. Accordingly, governments and policy makers have started paying greater attention to issues of urban and city management and development. The 74th Constitutional Amendment looks to strengthening municipal bodies in the country. Simultaneously, the structures and processes of governmental organizations involved in developing and managing urban areas are being reviewed to make them capable of better delivery.

All this calls for city managers with new orientations and capabilities to successfully meet the emerging urban challenges.

In the Indian system, it is primarily officials in municipal bodies who perform the city management functions. Thus, creating effective city managers involves overhauling their induction training.

Recently, an opportunity for this occurred in Rajasthan, when the government decided to recruit about 60 persons through the State Public Service Commission to the Rajasthan Municipal Service for postings as executive officers in municipal bodies. Earlier, such functionaries were either placed on jobs without training or provided some knowledge of municipal laws or rules at the time of relatively less structured induction training.

This time, the State Government Local Self-Government/Local Bodies Department and the Harish Chandra Mathur Rajasthan State Institute of Public Administration (HCM RIPA), Jaipur, decided to collaborate on designing a tailor-made course for the future city managers with HCM RIPA to conduct the course.

HCM RIPA's suggestion that the induction training should be a comprehensive package to equip the trainees for the first ten years of their service life in the municipalities in a manner similar to what is being done for various other state-level services like Rajasthan Administrative Service (RAS) was accepted by the Local Bodies Department.

Then started a discussion on the appropriate duration of the induction training. HCM RIPA suggested that there be a Foundation Course (FC) of 15 weeks' duration followed by an Institutional-Professional Course (I-PC) of either six months' duration as is being arranged for most of the Rajasthan State Services or of one year as is being arranged for the RAS and Rajasthan Accounts Service, with the I-PC to include attachments with state level and district agencies as well as actual on-the-job field training in municipalities, along with the regular classroom training. The Local Bodies Department, while desiring more and more to be included in the training, did not want the training period to be too long or they were keen (having about 90 vacancies in their 187 urban local bodies of the state) that the selected and trained officers take up regular assignments as early as possible. It was pointed out that there is a limit to the receptivity of trainees and accordingly the number of learning hours each day could not be increased beyond a point. Eventually, discussions led to a mutual agreement that there would be an eight-week FC and a nine-and-a half-week I-PC, with the on-the-job training being dispensed with during the I-PC and substituted by a one-and-a-half-week 'learning visit' in groups to a well-administered city outside Rajasthan. This decision was taken when tentative course contents for the FC and I P-C had been worked out and were being discussed in a course validation workshop. It was also agreed that the induction training would be residential with the trainees having to compulsorily stay in the HCM RIPA hostel to involve themselves in group activities on weekends and before and after class on working days.

Since the training is aimed at all-round development of the selected officers, co-curricular and extra curricular activities (sports, physical exercises, cultural and literacy activities, quizzes, bringing out a magazine, shramdaan, social and environmental activities, public speaking, book review writing, syndicate group work, writing of term paper etc.) were made a part of both FC and I-PC. There may be many occasions when the need for public speaking on the part of municipal officials may arise. Cities organize many state, national or international level sports, literary, or cultural events and municipal bodies are involved in their management. Hence, municipal officers should not only learn how to manage them but also have some idea of the activities *per se*. Thus, not only were such co-curricular and extra-curricular activities made an integral and compulsory part of the training course, but participation in them is to be evaluated and marked. Of course, such activities also enrich campus life during the training and develop the individual trainee's creative expression and overall personality.

The Foundation Course

The FC aims to introduce the officer-trainees to various aspects of the state administration and the social, political, administrative, cultural and economic environment in which they would be required to work. It will attempt to inculcate appropriate attitudes and values for a government municipal servant. And it also aims at developing an *esprit de corps* among officers of Rajasthan Municipal Service, a perception that they are partners in the wider enterprise of public service for the development of the people and the state of Rajasthan.

The major objectives of the FC are:

- developing basic values and attitudes and motivation needed for responsive and citizen-friendly administration;
- developing awareness of the challenges and opportunities in public service;

- acquaintance with the basic tools and techniques of administration and management; and
- an all-round development of the personality – intellectual, moral and physical.

At the end of the course, the officer-trainee should *inter alia* be able to:

- understand the concepts and context of good and effective administration;
- imbibe and internalize the relevant parts of the Constitution of India and its philosophy;
- be equipped to introduce innovation in responsive administration in their areas of work;
- appreciate main provisions of Right to Information Act and the structure and importance of Citizen Charters and undertake their implementation;
- understand nature of and issues about the national and regional economies;
- be aware about nuances of implementation of programmes and schemes of rural and urban development;
- apply basic skills for effective management in government organizations and municipal bodies;
- adopt appropriate individual and organizational behaviour;
- describe the working of Panchayati Raj and urban bodies, development issues with reference to 73rd and 74th Constitutional Amendment and welfare administration;
- examine and appreciate various policies of the state government;
- apply main provisions of the service, financial and accounts rules in their work;
- run their offices in an efficient manner;
- adopt salient features of sound financial management in government organizations;
- understand the importance of various progressive and regulatory laws and rules;
- undertake disaster management activities expected from municipal bodies;
- learn to coordinate with various government agencies at the district level;
- apply basic computer skills for e-governance; and

- function as a positive, motivated, result-oriented administrator sympathetic to the needs of the people and society.

The subject matter syllabus of the FC is as follows:

Paper I: Administrative Environment

(a) Basic knowledge of the Constitution of India: Preamble, Fundamental Duties, Fundamental Rights, Directive Principles of State Policy, Centre-State Relations, Distribution of Powers
(b) Good Governance
(c) Brief Introduction to Human Rights, Consumers Protection Act, Special Provisions for Minorities and Weaker Sections
(d) Offences related to Public Servants
(e) Parliamentary/Assembly Work: Parliament Questions, Assembly Questions, Cut Motions, Call Attention Motions, Parliamentary/Assembly Committees
(f) Administrative Ethics and Work Culture
(g) Integrity, Social Commitment and Objectivity in Public Services
(h) Citizen and Administration (including RTI Act, Citizen's Charters, Handling of Public Grievances)
(i) Recent Socio-economic Trends affecting Government Organizations

Paper II: Economic Environment and Financial Management

(i) Economic Environment

(a) Planning in Rajasthan: Plan Formulation, Concept of Decentralized Planning, Essential Features of Planning in Rajasthan, Plan Financing and Achievements of Planning in the State, Social Sector and Infrastructure Development
(b) Constraints on Economic Growth of Rajasthan: Geographical, Financial, Administrative, and Centre-State Relationship
(c) Development Potential in Rajasthan; Problems and Prospects of Tourism in Rajasthan: Minerals, Animal Husbandry, Handicrafts, Exports
(d) Development Vision of Rajasthan
(e) Issues related with VAT, Service Tax and Income Tax.
(f) Droughts: Causes, Impacts, Solutions, Drought-Proofing Measures

(g) Water: Availability in Rajasthan, Sectoral Use, Present Policy, Strategies for Efficient Use of Water in Various Sectors, Watersheds and Water Harvesting in Urban Areas

(ii) Financial Management

(a) Basics of accounts rules (GF and AR, PWF and AR) (with special reference to municipal working and rules of procurement of goods and services, including consultancies)

(b) Overview of Budgeting, Municipal Budgeting, State Finance Commissions

(c) Overview of Audit and Compliance of Audit Paras, Legislative Scrutiny through PAC, PUC

Paper III: Management, Organizational Behaviour and Office Procedure

(i) Management

(a) Basic concepts of Management in Government Working

(b) Overview of Project Concept, Project Features, Aspects of Project Appraisal and Project Formulation in Project Management

(c) Preparation of Proposals of Developmental Projects

(d) Presentation Skills

(ii) Organizational Behaviour

(a) Communication Skills

(b) Employee Motivation, Administrative Leadership and Team Building

(c) Supervision Skills and Monitoring Techniques

(d) Stress Management

(e) Time Management

(f) Conflict Resolution

(iii) Office Management

(a) Rajasthan Service Rules (basic principles)

(b) CCA Rules (basic principles)

(c) Office Procedure

(d) Conducting Meetings: Preparation of Agenda, Meeting Proceedings and Drafting Minutes

(e) Record Management in Government: Record Keeping and Documentation
(f) Office Allegiance, Office Environment and Economy-Austerity Measures
(g) Etiquettes and Manners as Expected from a Civil Servant (OLQ or Officer-Like Qualities)
(h) Use of Files for Quick and Quality Decision-Making

Paper IV: Development and Welfare Administration

(a) Overview of Development Administration; Linkage with Regulatory Administration
(b) Participatory Approaches in Development
(c) Role of NGOs in Development
(d) Cooperative Movement: Achievements and Limitations
(e) Gender Concerns in Development: Urban and Rural
(f) Social Welfare Programmes for Women, Children, Senior Citizens, Disabled Persons, SCs, STs and Other Weaker Sections
(g) Overview of Local Self-Government and Panchayati Raj: Its History and the Institutional Framework for Rural and Urban Development in the State; 73rd and 74th Constitutional Amendments
(h) Issues related to Integrating Rural and Urban Development
(i) Introduction to Issues of Urban Planning and Management
(j) Land-Water Management in Rajasthan

Paper V: Progressive, Developmental and Regulatory Activities (including Acts/Rules)

(a) Prevention of Corruption Act
(b) Rajasthan Famine Code and the Guidelines Issued by the Government of Rajasthan
(c) Missions and Major Policies of the State
(d) Management of Corporations and Boards
(e) Disaster Management (three-day capsule with special reference to role of municipalities in disaster management)
(f) Laws relating to Protection of Environment

(g) Rajasthan Soil and Water Conservation Act
(h) Laws relating to Consumer Protection

Paper VI: Information Technology

(a) Computer Familiarization
(b) E-Governance including various applications as implemented in the Government of Rajasthan
(c) Report Writing using Word Processing
(d) Presentations using Power Point
(e) Internet and Email
(f) Demonstration of Various Applications related to Municipal Working

Note: Paper VI would lead into topics related to E-Governance in Urban Local Bodies (ULBs) which form part of Paper I of the Institutional-Professional Course.

Lectures, panel discussions and participative training methodologies like role play are all being used during the training. It is hoped to distribute significant quantity of readings and other training material to the trainees.

For subject streams, assessment will be both concurrent and all through fill the end of course examinations. Continuous assessment will be through individual and group assignments, exercises, quizzes, and hands-on computer work, etc., and will have a weightage in the total assessment for the subject.

The marks allotted to the subjects are as follows:

Subjects	*Paper*	*Marks*
Administrative Environment	I	100
Economic Environment and Financial Management	II	100
Management and OB, Officer Procedure	III	100
Development and Welfare Administration	IV	100
Progressive, Development and Regulatory Activities	V	100
Information Technology	VI	100
Total		600

Note: For Paper VI, no separate exam would be conducted but practical computer tests would be conducted from time to time.

The following co-curricular and extra-curricular activities will be evaluated:

Activities	*Assessment Criteria*
Syndicate Group Report Writing Project	100
Term Paper	100
Other Activities (Sports, Cultural, Literary, Public Speaking, Extempore Speaking, Book Review, etc., and general assessment)	100
Total	300

There would be an overall or general assessment of each trainee on the basis of personal conduct, discipline and sincerity. Detailed guidelines for preparation and presentation of syndicate group reports, term papers and book reviews have been prepared and made known to the trainees.

Trainees will be required to obtain at least 45 per cent marks in each subject and activity in order to pass the examination. Those who fail to pass their examination would have their probation extended till the time as they pass the examination.

Systematic feedback would be obtained from the trainees to enable mid-course corrections and modifications in teaching methods and even in course content.

The trainees have been divided into Counsellor Groups of eight trainees each for academic and personal guidance. This system would continue throughout both the Foundation Course and the Institutional-Professional Course.

Institutional-Professional Course

The Institutional-Professional Training Programme is intended to achieve the following objectives:

The participants should be able to:

1. appreciate the global urbanization trends, national trends and trends of urbanization in Rajasthan and various national level programmes launched for urban development, housing and poverty alleviation;
2. understand the national and state administrative structure for urban governance and important legislation covering urban governance at national, state and city levels and the processes and procedures at the district level and in local bodies;

3. learn to work with elected ward members and mayors;
4. understand the concept and modes of effective e-governance and the various e-governance initiatives taken up in the urban development sector in the state;
5. understand the planning and implementation processes at institutions concerned with urban management and describe the procedure for preparation of city development plans, regional plans and urban master plans;
6. appreciate the concept, nature and magnitude of urban poverty and Rajasthan's strategy for urban poverty reduction and various schemes for housing for the poor;
7. undertake innovative schemes of resource mobilization for municipal bodies, pooled financing, and to implement the concept of user charges;
8. understand the concept of municipal budgeting, gender budgeting, and accounting reforms for ULBs, and public-private partnership in ULBs;
9. undertake service delivery to overcome the challenges of water and sewerage, urban transport, sanitation and solid waste management and appreciate the importance of fire services and street light maintenance, cleaning of streets and public places, etc.;
10. understand and be able to apply the concept of project planning and management as well as change management including preparation of HRD plan for municipalities;
11. be able to supervise integrated town development and integrated city management; and
12. act as effective city managers.

The subject matter for Institutional-Professional Course is as follows:

Paper I: Urbanization Trends and Urban Governance

Urbanization Trends

(a) Trends of Urbanization in Rajasthan
State Level Programmes
- Shahari Jan Sahbhagi Yojana
- Heritage Conservation Plan
- Jan Sathi Rojgar Yojana
- Jaipur Agenda Action Group (JAAG)
- State Urban Agenda for Rajasthan (SUARAJ)

(b) Urbanization in India, Urban Policy in India
National Level Programmes
   (i) JNNURM
   (ii) IHSDP
   (iii) Urban Infrastructure Development Schemes for Small and Medium Towns (UIDSSMT)

(c) Urbanization-Global Trends.

Urban Governance

(i) The Administrative Structure
   - National
   - State
   - Local

(ii) Decentralization and Municipalities:
74th Constitution Amendment Act and its Implementation in Rajasthan

(iii) Essentials of Municipal Administration

(iv) Organizational Structure of Department of Urban Governance, Government of Rajasthan, and Directorate of Local Bodies, and Important Legislations concerning Urban Sector in Rajasthan
   - The Rajasthan Municipalities Act, 1959 and Draft New Act
   - The Rajasthan Urban Improvement Trust Act, 1959
   - The Rajasthan Housing Board Act, 1970
   - The Rajasthan Urban Improvement Trust (Disposal of Urban Land) Rules, 1974
   - The Rajasthan Urban Areas (Sub-Division, Reconstitution and Improvement of Plots) Rules, 1975
   - The Jaipur Development Authority Act, 1982
   - District Planning Committee, Metropolitan Plan Committee as per 74th Constitutional Amendment
   - Relevant Sections of Land Revenue Act
   - Conversion of Agricultural Land for Residential Purposes: Section 90B of Land Revenue Act
   - National Building Act

(v) JNNURM Reform Agenda

(vi) E-Governance in ULBs
   (i) Birth and Death Certificate
   (ii) GIS
   (iii) Property Tax

(iv) Building Plan Approval
(v) E-Procurement
(vi) License and SWM
(vi) Accounting System
(vii) Personnel Information System

Paper II: Urban Planning and Urban Poverty

Urban Planning

(i) Basic Concepts for Understanding the Planning and Implementation Processes at Institutions Concerned with Urban Management
(ii) Rent Control Act
(iii) Procedure for Preparation of

- City Development Plans (CDPs)
- Regional Plans
- Master Plans

Urban Poverty

Concept, Nature and Magnitude of Urban Poverty
Current Situation – Health, Education, Slum Population, Demographic Profile
Housing for Poor Programmes

- IHSDP
- BSUP
- Rajasthan Draft Urban Housing and Habitat Policy
- Rajasthan Strategy for Urban Poverty Reduction
- Rajasthan Mission on Urban Poverty SJSRY (Swarna Jayanti Shahari Rozgar Yojna) in Rajasthan
- Visits to Slum Projects

Paper III: Urban Finance, Urban Infrastructure and Service Delivery

Urban Finance

(i) Innovative Resource Mobilization and Infrastructure Financing for Urban Local Bodies with Specific Reference to Rajasthan

- Pooled Financing
- Financing Urban Infrastructure – Accessing Debt Market
- Municipal Credit Rating

(ii) User Charges
(iii) Municipal Accounting Reforms
(iv) Municipal Budgeting
(v) Finance Rules and PWF and AR Rules applicable to Municipalities in Rajasthan
(vi) Public-Private Partnerships and Urban Local Bodies
(vii) Gender Budgeting in ULBs
(viii) Property Tax Reforms
(ix) Land and land-based instruments for resource mobilization

Urban Infrastructure and Service Delivery

1. Water and Sewerage
    - Challenges and priority of water and sanitation, and institutional framework within India and abroad with specific reference to needs of Rajasthan
    - Field visit
2. Urban Transport
    (a) Transport Planning Process
    - Planning and Design of Urban Roads
    - Transport and Traffic Problems in Urban Areas
    - Mass Transportation System (MRTS/BRTS/LRT/Mono Rail/PTS Improvements)

    (b) Maintenance of Roads
3. Sanitation and Solid Waste Management
    - Solid Waste Management in India: Critical Issues, Good Practices And Implementation Plans
    - Panel Discussion: Solid Waste Management Strategies For Implementation
    - Achieving Citywide Universal Sanitation: Challenges and Strategies
    - Visits
4. Fire Services
5. Street Lighting, especially maintenance of streetlights

Paper IV: Project Planning, Change Management and HRD

Project Planning and Management

- Preparation of Detailed Project Report (DPR)
- Overview of Procurement Process
- Contract Management

- National/International Good Practices
- Participatory Planning for Service Delivery to the Poor

Change Management

1. Organizational Change: Meaning, Implications, Importance
2. Facets of Organizational Change: Structural, Procedural, Behavioural
3. Catalysts to Change: Change Agents
4. Obstacles to Change, especially in Government Systems

Organizational Development and HRD

1. Organizational Development: Meaning and Importance
2. Human Resource Management and Human Resource Development
3. Enhancing Effectiveness of HRD system in Urban Administration
4. Preparing an HRD Plan for a Municipality

The probationers will also in addition have to submit a project report for which marks will be awarded. Each counsellor group would prepare a project report.

Each of the four papers and the project work shall each carry 100 marks.

There will also be dinner talks with experts addressing the trainees on urban issues approximately one per week.

At least one computer session per week will be arranged either from 9.00 to 10.00 or 5.00 to 6.00. Computer sessions may club two counsellors groups for each session.

One day (four sessions) will be reserved for a 'Seminar on Jaipur City and its Problems', where experts and practitioners involved in implementation would make presentations and interact with the trainees through panel discussions. It is expected that most issues in tackling urban problems, as are found in the cities and towns of Rajasthan, would get highlighted during this training seminar on Jaipur.

The I-PC will culminate with a one-and-a-half week 'learning visit' in groups to some of the better managed cities outside Rajasthan so that the trainees can observe the best practices followed there and get an exposure about how municipal bodies and state governments are jointly undertaking the administration of urban areas in various parts of the country. This would, it is hoped, hold them in good stead when they take up regular assignments in the various municipalities of Rajasthan following the examinations of the institutional-professional course which shall be held immediately after the 'learning visit'.

There is an appreciation that 18 weeks of concentrated training may not be sufficient to immediately convert ordinary graduates or post-graduates, selected by the Rajasthan Public Service Commission, into hot-shot, super-efficient, city managers. However, an attempt has been made to use the available 18 weeks of training in the most fruitful manner. For this HCM RIPA faculty visited some state Administrative Training Institutions (ATIs) in other states as well as institutes like Administrative Staff College of India (ASCI), Hyderabad, to pick up hints for developing the course contents and training modules. Available experience within HCM RIPA and its Centre of Urban Development of conducting short courses on urban issues, including those organized in collaboration with HUDCO's Human Settlements Management Institute (HSMI) and National Institute of Urban Affairs (NIUA), and of conducting studies on Rajasthan's housing and urban policy, as also of training modules prepared at HCM RIPA and used for short orientation courses for elected municipal counsellors were tapped and made use of. Relevant reports and literature on urban issues and municipal and city administration were browsed through. There were repeated interactions with the Directorate of Local Bodies and the Secretariat Local Bodies Department. Once the draft course contents was ready, a validation workshop was convened by Director, HCM RIPA, where serving and retired officers of IAS, RAS, Rajasthan Accounts Service, Rajasthan Municipal Service, and academics, discussed the course contents in detail, including the training methodology most suitable for each component or session of the proposed training, as also specific resource persons who would be most suitable on each specific theme.

Thus, great effort has been made to try and ensure that the training is comprehensive and relevant as well as practical in terms of the knowledge and skills required by municipal city managers, yet is also such as entails the cultivation of appropriate attitudes and organizational behaviour amongst the trainees.

In fact, if there had not been administrative compulsions of keeping the training short to ensure that the probationers get posted in municipalities by early 2009, we would have preferred a foundation course of at least 10 weeks rather than the present eight weeks' one, an institutional-professional course of at least 15 weeks rather that the present nine-and-a-half weeks and at least five weeks of district and field training involving attachments in the Collectorate, in Urban Improvement Trusts and City Development Authorities, with District Level Officers related to activities like water and electricity supply, road construction, the police etc., and a two-day visit in groups to the state-level Department of Local Bodies. After all, the intention is that the induction training equips them for the various sorts of assignments during the first ten years of their service careers.

The course has been conducted recently. Its fruits or impacts would really be known over the next few years as the persons trained go about their jobs as city managers in various municipalities of the state. However, it is hoped that this initiative would prove a useful beginning for improved efforts at induction training, and that gradually a large core of professionally competent city managers shall build up in the state. Reading about this effort may also provide ideas to others states for similar capacity building efforts for creating city managers.

Section V
Aspects and Components of Training

20 Identification of Training Needs vis-à-vis Mission, Goals and Strategies*

V.P. Mathur and Tanjul Saxena

Indian industry is at a threshold where the discussion on whether training as an HRM activity is important or not has ceased to exist. Nevertheless, there is no denying the fact that in case of economic deterioration of a company, training and development are the first frills to be cut. Are training and development really frills adding to the aesthetic beauty of a company? Is this function in no way contributing to company goals that it could be equated with contributions of marketing function, or finance function, or export, or import or for that matter even personnel function? Is training an indulgence of rich and aspiration of poor companies? These are the questions that portray a *mannequinne persona* for training and development activities, because of the intangibility of the benefits that it provides.

Partly the charges are true also, because most training is either 'technical' to comply with immediate, short-term deficiencies or very person-focused, behavioural, far-fetched from organizational mission, goals and strategies. And training providers are neither answerable nor accountable for showing measurable results. As a consequence, training has come to establish itself as an expense-incurring activity with no returns.

Training that is unrelated and unserving to mission, goals and strategies needs abstract inputs and long gestation period for expected

* While this article pertains to training in companies, many of the techniques can be adopted for government.

change to result and this adds to the questioning of the worth of training function in organization.

The "Ought To Be" Training Function Profile

A more pragmatic, strategy-integrated, goal-oriented and mission-fulfilling training activity can only justify the practice of this function as truly necessary for the organization. No function can be effective unless it is objective-driven. Objectives should be need-based. Many concepts in HRM have evolved over a period of time, attracting a lot of attention, discussions, deliberations, and hype; but these have fizzled over time, mainly because they did not fit into the need system of indigenous industry. The need system is hierarchical. Training till now is catering to lower order needs of personal growth, but it does not address synchronized needs of the organization and employees together in an orchestrated manner. The time has come when training should take more mature form, addressing the integrated corporate and personal mission, goals and strategies.

Training Mission in Perspective

A training need assessment programme for developing individualized mission, goals and strategies, congruent to organization mission, goals and strategies, should be the first clause in a training mission.

Every company envisions a mission for itself. This mission is realized by directed goals, which are in turn a function of realistic identified strategies to be designed and implemented by 'people' in the organization. The corporate mission, goals and strategies of the company cannot be achieved unless these are in synergy with employees' mission, goals and strategies. And, to achieve this synergy at every stage of determining, designing, defending, coping, learning to handle exceptions, aligning and realigning of personal mission, goals and strategies, training intervention is needed. All training interventions must be need-based, identifying the present status, the desired status, the gaps and must aim to fill these gaps.

Training Function Environment

Since we are envisaging a much mature and responsible role for the training department in terms of identification of needs with respect to mission, goals and strategies, it is necessary to ponder over the present status of organizational and individual mission, goals and strategies. Even an informal question (What is your mission?) survey of the brightest of the brains will reveal pathetic profiles of unidentified personal mission. Things are brighter at the corporate end. At least some companies, if not too many, do have a mission statement, many have goals, both short-term and long-term, and almost all have strategies. Hold on! Nothing to celebrate about, because the irony is – strategies are relevant only for identified goals and goals should necessarily be a function of mission. That means the starting point is wrong. Though serious malacies, these are often overlooked, rather not even recognized, because education of these is not imbibed in the system. It is only lately, say, not more than two decades ago, that the concepts like vision, mission, etc., were added to management education. And management education has only recently been accepted openly without any reservations by the Indian corporate culture.

This has made the task of trainers more difficult because they have not only to initiate new learning but also delearning and lateral learning. The trainer fraternity has to work not only at individual level but also has to educate the Board of Directors or the CEO or corporate grade managers for writing down a realistic mission, achievable goals and workable competitive strategies. Practically, since many of us do not appreciate thinking by writing, we subordinate the importance of written down mission, goals and strategies to more short-term quick return or tangible gratification.

The Integrative Approach

The concepts, viz., mission, goal and strategy need to be defined for better comprehension.

Mission: A mission is a narrative statement that helps an organization to link its activities to the needs of society and legitimize its existence.

Goal: Goals are closed-ended attributes that are precise and expressed in specific terms.

Strategy: Strategies are means to end goals in the context.

A company where the exercise of writing mission for the company and the employees occurs simultaneously at the time of the inception of the company, it certainly stands to gain against the competition. In view of the served background, there are not really many companies who can boast of this competitive advantage. Even if the company has been in existence for a number of years, it is never too late to have a mission. Such companies need to take a little different approach from those writing mission statement at the time of inception.

Another important consideration is that over the time goals and strategies change but mission being more value system-oriented seldom, if ever, changes. The changes in goals and strategies can be both positive or negative, for growth or towards decline in view of changes in the environment, added resources, increased information and lines of activities etc. So, a periodic review of corporate goals and strategies as well as proper alignment of personal mission, goals and strategies is another area that needs constant working by the Training Department.

For training function to be substantially serving, the training life cycle must be superimposed on one-to-one basis upon that of company life cycle in stages of introduction and growth and should show higher or increased activity (precedence to company life cycle) during maturity and decline stages of the company. The Training Department is the link-pin between the two entities – the organization and the employees. The onus is on the Training Department to diagnose organizational and individual's parameters separately first and then to map them one over another.

Proposed Strategy

Understandably, the Training Department must take roles starting from identifying training needs through designing training inputs, career management, conducting training up to evaluation of training efforts. The salient dimensions in this context are:

- Individual dimension.
- Organizational/corporate dimension.
- Integral dimension.

A detailed suggestive training policy for all the three dimensions is discussed below:

Individual Dimension

Need Area 1

Do employees have a mission? Is it written down?

- *Probable training intervention:* Training for crystallizing a mission/self-actualization concept in life, and also to put mission into words on paper in pencil (skill for writing objectively).
- *Objective served:* To get each employee to write down objectively, a crystallized mission/self-concept in life.
- *Action plan for identification of needs:* The selection process should incorporate the description of personal mission, either in

the application form or it should be assessed during the interview, categorically. Later, it should be transferred to Human Resource Information System. If no clear mission emerges, use/design a self-assessment and aspiration test/questionnaire incorporating instrumental and terminal life values.

- *Uses in ultimate training programme:* The inputs from above may be utilized to help the employee appreciate and accept the importance of mission. It may serve as a trigger for training employees through simulation exercises, writing an objective personal mission, validating it against the principles of mission and focusing their career and life on the mission.
- *Follow-up:* Through formalizing personal mission statement, if not objectively laid down, can become the initial planning point for exploring further needs of training.

Need Area 2

Do employees have long- and short-term goals and strategies fulfilling the mission both at personal and professional platforms? Have they written down chalked strategies to reach goals?

- *Probable training intervention:* Training for identification of possible realistic goals to fulfil mission. Training for chalking out goal-directed strategies.
- *Objective served:* To help employees determine realistic goals and directed strategies to attain their mission in life.
- *Action plan for identification of needs:* Pre-training exercise to identify existing level of skills for writing realistic goals and strategies. Training in understanding the concepts of goal and strategy and techniques like brainstorming, Pareto analysis, fish-bone analysis, etc. (for all, without any need identification process). Personal interview with HR executive or immediate mentor/guide (superior).
- *Uses in ultimate training programme:* Present level of skills will determine the starting point for designing training for objective to be served. Different skills imparted will help employees broaden their horizon of thinking and ability to analyze.
- *Follow-up:* Same as for need area 1.

Need Area 3

Other behavioural areas like SWOT analysis, learning, delearning, handling compromises, adjustments, aligning with growing success, etc.

- *Probable training intervention:* Training to do self-SWOT, for learning and delearning, to handle compromises, adjustments, and to align with growing success.
- *Objective served:* As gesture of personal care and development orientation of the company.
- *Action plan for identification of needs:* Sociometric techniques and attitude survey questionnaire. Personal interview of the employee/his (her) mentor by HR executive. Introspection and assessment exercises.
- *Uses in ultimate training programme:* To substantiate overall orientation to professional and personal life. Benchmarking for future/desired behavioural profile.
- *Follow-up:* Continuous gauging/scanning mechanism by way of performance, records, personal interactions and observations by peer group, boss and subordinates.

Organizational/Corporate Dimension

Need Area 1

Does the company have a mission? Is it realistic?

- *Probable training intervention:* Train the part of management entrusted for writing a mission statement. Training for writing realistic mission.
- *Objective served:* To set a mission for the company incorporating interests of all concerned, e.g., shareholders, customers, society, employees, economy and polity of the country.
- *Action plan for identification of needs:* Identify skills required to write a mission. Gauge existing level of skills through personal discussion and interviews (since it is mostly the CEO/BOD level responsible for writing the mission, brief sessions on concept, process and inputs about various tools used, like focus group discussion, brainstorming, etc., could be without even assessing existing status of skills).
- *Follow-up:* After the training, a management game/customized exercise(s) could be conducted providing inputs/information for a hypothetical company. A simulation exercise for writing the mission and recording of proceedings shall indicate deficiencies in the training.

Need Area 2

Does the company have goals serving the mission? Are strategies operational and goal-directed or are they too conservative or aspirational?

- *Probable training intervention:* Training for aligning goals to mission, and also for making realistic strategies to align with achievable goals.
- *Objective served:* To aspire goals serving the mission and to design realistic and operational strategies to achieve goals.
- *Action plan for identification* of *needs:* Structured assessment of existing level of competencies for deciding goals and strategies. Management simulation exercises to judge POSDCORB abilities. Past performance records.
- *Uses in ultimate training programme:* Result of training needs identification to be utilized for designing training inputs for formulating goals and strategies.
- *Follow-up:* Personal interview/group discussion.

Need Area 3

Is the company competent to proactively and reactively adapt to changes in mission, goals and strategies in view of environmental changes?

- *Probable training intervention:* Impact training for adapting to changes.
- *Objective served:* Prepare organization as a whole to absorb and adjust to changes without much negative effects.
- *Action plan for identification of needs:* Continuous diagnostic survey of environment and organization culture.
- *Uses in ultimate training programme:* Preparing proactively and being equipped for reactive steps for changes. Planning future skills and roles.
- *Follow-up:* Periodic organizational culture surveys.

Need Area 4

Has the company done its SWOT analysis?

- *Probable training intervention:* Training for performing company *SWOT*.
- *Objective served:* To become more realistially aware and pursue this awareness as competitive advantage.
- *Action plan for identification of needs:* General orientation to corporate grade on *exodus operandi* for performing SWOT.
- *Follow-up:* Periodic surprise test activities with simulated situation. Follow-up by revision of SWOT analysis of company at a pre-determined period.

Integral Dimension

Need Area 1

Do individual mission, goals and strategies integrate well with corporate mission, goals and strategies?

- *Probable training intervention:* Training for aligning personal mission, goals and strategies to that of the organization's.
- *Objective served:* Achieving synergy by superimposing personal mission, goals and strategies of employees upon those of the organization.
- *Action plan for identification of needs:* (a) General training: explaining importance of synergy and interdependency of employees and organization. (b) Specific training: comparison of employees' personal and organization's mission, goals and strategies.
- *Uses in ultimate training programme:* Identified gaps to be used for designing training programme for aligning employees' and organization's mission, goals and strategies.
- *Follow-up:* Periodic review of organizational and employees' goals and strategies independently and in relation to each other.

Need Area 2

Does the company policies facilitate achieving personal mission, goals and practice/implement identified strategies?

- *Probable training intervention:* Either align employees to company policies, or company policies could be flexed or improved or changed for good. Train employees to work out alternatives.
- *Objective served:* Organizational policies to emerge as a facilitating platform for individual development, for example, increasing level of emotional intelligence.
- *Action plan for identification of needs:* HR Department to carry out diagnostic study of company policies. Any personal deviations from performance norms/standards/expectations to be seen in company policies perspective too.
- *Uses in ultimate training programme:* Designing training for policy makers to incorporate possible changes without creating much turbulence in related areas.
- *Follow-up:* Periodic review of company policies.

Need Area 3

Cases of heavy digression from company policies leading to employee separation.

- *Probable training intervention:* Delearning and preparing for fresh alignment with new company and its mission, goals and strategies.
- *Objective served:* Ethical obligations of organization to care for employees beyond premises.
- *Action plan for identification of needs:* Counselling the employee.
- *Uses in ultimate training programme:* Training for delearning and preparing for fresh alignment with new company's revalidated, as the case may be, mission, goals and strategies.
- *Follow-up:* Follow-up for response even literally till settled in next employment.

Need Area 4

Is the company practising MBO? Is the concept of MBO diluted by practising it in ascending manner, starting from bottom to top?

- *Probable training intervention:* Shape up the company to inculcate MBO that would offer premises for integrating employees and company mission, goals and strategies. Train for a blend of top to bottom and bottom to top MBO integrating mission, goals and strategies of all. Training for an upward shift in conservative cases of company's goals and strategies in view of higher aggregate of individual's goals and strategies.
- *Objective served:* Crystallizing objectives of company in tandem with individual goals, initiated at planning platform.
- *Action plan for identification of needs:* The top management to decide on objective planning method.
- *Uses in ultimate training programme:* Designing training for policy makers as well as for all employees on concept and practices and benefits of MBO.
- *Follow-up:* Periodic review of the practice of MBO.

The Indian corporate world, whether in the public or the private sector, has achieved global connectivity and is now at a threshold of being fully exposed to foreign investors and markets. It is also a time for our indigenous professionals to contribute towards learning, and developing multi-locational organizations in cross-cultural settings. The new millennium will provide people more choices and alternatives, and training cannot remain merely an activity to generate awareness. It has to incubate with proactive strategies in monitoring, coaching and career planning to increase retention and reduce turnover in a bullish environment.

The frames of reference of training have to be linked with cognitive and behavioural learning at the theoretical as well as empirical level.

Any management strategy to succeed needs team effort, decentralized, agile and empathetic leadership. Each action has to make significant efforts to manifest the latent power of each individual in the organization. Let the transformation be a natural process with effective hiring, performance management and training systems, linking rewards to performance and ensuring that 'exit management' is human to employees.

21 Designing a Training Programme

Some Important Issues

Girish K. Srivastava

In a fast-changing organizational world, the role of a trainer and the skill of designing a training programme is very important. For conducting an efficient and effective training function, a sound design of training programme is required. It is a powerful tool both for developing trainer himself and for enriching the learning opportunities the trainer creates for others. In the absence of a proper designed training programme, training goals cannot be achieved. For effective design, both the aspects, i.e., the trainer's predicted outcome and the desired outcome for the learner should be achieved (Binstead, 1980). In designing a training programme, a number of issues should be kept in mind but in this paper we have discussed only those issues which are related to learning theories. Theories about how people (individuals) learn (Burgoyne and Stuart, 1977 and Jones, 1979) are the key factors in designing a training programme. There is no single coherent body of learning theory, which can be successfully translated into practice for the whole spectrum of the training activity. So, a combination of several theories mainly behaviouristic (stimulus-response approach), humanistic (highly value-oriented and philosophical) and cognitive (learning by block based on perception and problem solving) are being used for training activity in actual practice. One should provide proper weightage to various aspects of these learning theories at proper places while designing a training programme. Following are some important issues which may be considered while designing an effective and efficient training programme:

Need-based Programme

As per the humanistic approach, significant learning takes place when the learners are motivated during a training programme. They can be motivated by discussing useful and interesting topics which are helpful in their jobs. For this purpose, learner's needs should be assessed in advance and these should be given proper weightage in training programme. Thus, a training programme must have details of the aims and objectives of the training.

Practical Input

Significant learning is acquired through doing rather than talking. In case of industrial training, we are concerned about organizational performance which can be achieved by effective application of training. So, one should also provide practical input in designing a training programme.

Learning Environment

It includes healthy, physical, psychological, and sociological elements. Proper freedom should be given (Freire, 1972) to the learners to choose their own direction and the trainer should act as a facilitator. Field visits will also help them in providing work-learning environment. In this way, various elements should also be taken into account while designing a training programme.

Participative Approach

According to Roger (1986), learning is facilitated when the learner participates responsibly in the entire learning process. The use of participative method must be also considered in training programme. For this purpose, other training methods, viz., workshop, group discussions, etc., should be given proper place in training design.

Use of Audio-visual Aids

People learn through the senses. Experiments show that people's recalling rate is 70–85 per cent through sight. Visual aids appeal to the eye, which helps people learn. They create interest, help towards easier understanding, save time during instruction and provide variety, which lend it a lasting impression. For this purpose, one should provide proper place for the use of variety of visual aids, viz., video films, interactive video, slides, transparencies, etc., while designing a training programme.

Action-Learning Approach

It is true that people learn from others' job experiences. In this respect, action-learning approach of Revans (1983) can also be adopted in designing of training programme. This approach also helps in solving real-life problems.

Outdoor Management Development (OMD) Approach

The OMD British approach also helps in learning for development. In this regard, author's experience of UK is worth mentioning. In this approach, the outdoor environment is used as a vehicle to speed and increase learning. It provides a context in which learning is facilitated and reinforced. It is also a good technique where experience becomes a resource for learning. In this approach, the trainer has to play a crucial role. He has to encourage the learners to reflect on their experiences, to develop generalization and explanatory concept and to commit themselves to trying new behaviours. This approach can be used for development of leadership abilities, experience of team building, a workshop of communication skills, dealing with change and uncertainty and self-development through personal audit (e.g., confidence). Thus, this approach could also be included in the long-duration training courses.

Case Studies and Other Exercises

People learn more from real-life experiences rather than through listening or talking about them. For this purpose, case studies and other exercises, e.g., management games, role-plays, group exercises, etc., should be included in designing a training programme. Case studies are often used in interpersonal industrial relations such as disciplinary cases and grievance handling. Providing exercises and case studies in a training programme also improve learning, thinking, problem solving, gaining confidence in decision-making and developing analytical skills.

Factors Developing Cognitive Growth

Factors like curiosity, exploration, creative thinking, discovery, etc., should be given proper weightage in designing a programme. These factors aid the cognitive growth of a learner, which helps them in understanding the organization's situation and making a sound personality.

New Ideas and Problem-Solving Sessions

New ideas, concepts, practices and new styles of management and administration should be communicated to the participants because they get in training institutes. Problem-solving sessions also affect their efficiency and working styles. For this purpose, a relevant senior person may be called from their working organization so that he may guide them and tell them the correct way of doing things, which perhaps may solve their problems.

Demonstrating or Modelling Behaviour

People learn more by watching demonstrative or modelling behaviour. For this purpose, learners should be shown alternative behaviour as in what to do and how to do it either through film or video input, or by the trainer or other learners. Such type of input stimulates the interest of learners because it shows correct/incorrect actions, procedures etc. Thus, some content of the programme should be covered by this method and provided proper place in designing a training programme.

Continuous Review and Evaluation Exercises

There should be continuous and deliberate review and evaluation sessions in a training programme. These sessions help the trainer in knowing the progress and performance of the programme. Evaluation leads to modification for improvement in designing for future programmes. Participants should also be asked to state formally their action plans to utilize their newly-developed abilities through this present training.

Resource Constraint

Time, money, material and equipment are the main resources of a training institute. Availability of these resources affects the design of training programme. One should plan about these resources in advance so that training programme can be launched in an effective manner. Proper spacing during various topics, use of various methodologies largely depends upon the availability of time and various resources.

Flexibility

One knows that people learn from various combinations of learning theories. Hence, scope should be provided to fit appropriate theories in designing a training programme. For this purpose, flexible approach of both participants and trainers should be kept in mind.

Web-Based Training

Martyn (1999) referred that web-based training is becoming one of the most important tools for trainers nowadays. The ability to deliver training and learning online to an individual's desk offers enormous flexibility to the organization as well as the employees, cost and time saving and the opportunity to keep pace with constant changes required for today's organizations to remain competitive.

In addition to the above issues, certain other practical issues should also be examined while designing a training programme. Will (1998) has explained the role of some basic information in this connection. This basic information can be gathered by asking various questions such as: Who is to be trained? Why are they to be trained? Where to train? When are they to be trained'? What course has been identified to meet the training requirement? What is/are the occupations(s) of the people who need to be trained? How long is the course? How much will the training cost? Apart from the answers to these questions, administrative support is also required. In designing a training programme, similar earlier training programme must also be evaluated regarding its effectiveness. The present programme should be modified so that its strengths are built upon and its weaknesses are eliminated as far as possible. In fact, the design of a training programme should be absorbing, insighting and enchanting to the participants.

References

Binstead, D. (1980). "Design for Learning in Management Training and Development: A View", *Journal of European Industrial Training,* Vol. 4, No.8.

Burgoyne, J.G. and Stuart, R. (1977). "Implicit Learning Theories as Determinants of the Effect of Management Development", *Personnel Review,* Vol. 6, No. 2.

Freire, Paulo (1972). *Pedagogy of the Oppressed,* Penguin.

Revans, R. (1983). *ABC of Action Learning,* Chartweb, Bratt Ltd., Kent (UK).

Rogers, A. (1986). *Teaching Adults,* Open University Press, England.

Sloman Martyn (1999). A *Handbook for Training Strategy,* Gower, UK.

Will Mike (1998), *Managing the Training Process,* Gower, UK.

22 Training Evaluation

Some Key Issues

T.K. Jain

Training in the modern technological era has become a dynamic concept which needs to be understood in that perspective. It may very well be asserted that organizations which do not respond to the dynamic changes that are seen in the changed environment may well fail to respond to the needs of organizations and people. Hence, organizations have to continually aspire to respond to the changes. These changes may be concerned with employees' behaviour or with the structural changes. One of the primary and effective means of bringing about change in an organization is training. Training is a system which caters to the need of skills and knowledge. These skills and knowledge are acquired to fulfil a specific purpose or goal.

Concept of Training

Training has been defined by various scholars and trainers alike. According to Edwin B. Flippo, "the act of increasing the skills of an employee for doing a particular job" can be termed as training.[1] Similarly, Lawrence Steinmitz has observed "Training is a process utilizing a systematic and organized procedure by which personnel learn technical knowledge and skills for a definite purpose."[2]

Likewise, William G. Torpey has defined training as "the process of developing skills, habits, knowledge and attitudes in employees for the purpose of increasing effectiveness of employees in their present government positions as well as preparing them for future government positions."[3]

From the above definitions it can asserted that training is basically concerned with the development of skills and knowledge in a particular art or discipline. Training is a conscious and concerted effort to enhance and improve a person's skill to impart knowledge to change his attitudes and values towards a particular direction. It is based on the assumption that all training is not necessary and beneficial. Training must be properly focused and must be directed towards the achievement of particular goals or objectives. Hence, identification of training needs is an important step towards identifying the techniques of training. The process of identifying training needs is a carefully thought-out programme that needs to be carried out with sensitivity because success of a training programme may be crucial for the survival of the organization.

Before going into the details of needs of training, it would be appropriate to look at the objectives of training. Training is imparted to people with certain defined objectives and goals. However, there is a vast difference in the identification of goals and objectives of different organizations. Hence, the defined objectives of a training programme should be assessed in the light of the goals of that organization. In 1944, the Asseton Committee stated the objectives of training in the following manner:[4]

(a) It endeavours to produce a civil servant whose precision and clarity in the transaction of business can be taken for granted.
(b) It helps attuning the civil servant to the task he is called upon to perform in a changing world. It, in other words, helps him to adjust his outlook and methods to the changing needs of new times.
(c) It saves the civil servant from becoming a robot-like mechanically perfect civil servant. He is made aware of his work and the service that he is required to render to his community.
(d) It not only enables an individual to perform his current work more efficiently but also makes him suitable for other duties. It develops in him capacity for higher work and greater responsibilities.
(e) It pays substantial regard to staff morale as the employees have to perform tasks of a routine character throughout their lives.

Likewise, Bhagwan and Bhushan have also identified the following objectives of training:[5]

(a) For the performance of certain peculiar activities pertaining to the government, training plays a significant part.
(b) Training helps the employees become people-oriented and inculcates in them respect and regard for general public.
(c) It broadens the vision and widens the outlook of the employees by explaining them national objectives and exhorting them to make substantial contribution towards their realization.

(d) It is vital to a career of service. It makes them fit for advancement which is assured to the employees when they join the government service at young age.
(e) It improves the tone and adds to the quality of organizations. Since it enhances the efficiency of the employees and develops their capacities, the efficiency and prestige of the department goes up.
(f) It fosters homogeneity of outlook and *esprit de corps* in the employees.

Identification of Training Needs

It is important for a training programmer to know exactly what is required from the training programme, as in accordance with the framework, tools, techniques, processes will be identified in designing and implementing efficient, effective, timely and productive training programmes for those who require it. Training needs will determine the nature of training programme. Before any training programme is formulated, certain factors must be taken into consideration so that evaluation of the programme in terms of techniques and skills can be properly considered.

A training programme is designed around three fundamental behavioural aspects, viz., organization, people and environment. As far as organizations are concerned, their survival rests on a certain minimum achievement of goals and objectives which are predefined to customers, owners, employees, etc. All these factors are continuously interacting with the organization whose objectives and goals have been formulated so as to benefit the members of the organization intermittently.

The second assumption that needs to be taken into consideration is the fact that these objectives can be achieved only through harnessing the abilities of people, releasing their potential and maximizing opportunities for their development. In other words, the objectives and goals can be effectively and efficiently achieved only if people within the organization possess adequate skills and abilities. Hence, a proper assessment of the abilities and skills of the employees must be considered before any training programme is formulated.

The third assumption is to assess the capability potential of the employees. The people who are engaged in the accomplishment of goals and objectives in the new perspective are capable of new learning. If the employees do not possess the required potential to adapt themselves to the new environment, the chances of training programme being a success will be doubtful.

The fourth assumption about people is concerned with the level of ability and the desire to learn. Training is all about learning. Learning basically involves people who make or break organization. The organization should be able to provide adequate opportunities and resources to help people learn through training new concepts and techniques of management. This assumption is also concerned with matching of achieving organizational goals on one the hand and providing attractive learning opportunities on the other. It basically requires that the programmes of training should be so designed so as to provide learning opportunities that are effective and efficient. The objective of training is to fulfil the individual needs of the employees and that of the organization as well.

The fifth assumption is concerned with the environment variable. In a dynamic situation, environment continues to put new pressures and demands upon the system even if it is for survival only. Because of liberalization, competition has become severe and public sector as well private sector have to compete with each other in order to stay as a viable entity. Hence, changes in the environment can no more be overlooked but need to be understood and adapted to. The need for training, therefore, becomes inevitable.

Once it is established that need for training is genuine, the question arises as to what type of training is required to meet the challenges discussed above. Another pertinent question that comes to mind is related to the effectiveness of the training programme or techniques for which it was conducted. First, we will have a close look at various types of training methods and then the question of evaluation will be looked into.

With regard to people working in the organization, their needs and aspirations must be properly evaluated. Specification of training needs means translating the needs of people into specific needs and achieving those aspirations by training programmes. The basic idea behind this evaluation is to make organization a learning organization. According to P. Senge, "where people continually expand their capacity to create results they truly desire, where new and expansive patterns are nurtured, where collective aspiration is set free, and where people are continually learning how to learn together"[6]

Factors Influencing Training Needs

Organizations are becoming complex in nature and their effectiveness depends on numerous factors. Complexity of organization is again a multifaceted implication being determined by various environmental factors. Hence, complexity of a given organization needs to be evaluated before determining its training needs. Some of the factors that increase complexity are being discussed keeping in view that all are not determinants of complexity for all organizations. Technology in the computer age is being upgraded frequently and hence is the most important factor in increasing the complexity of an organization, both structurally as well as behaviourally. According to Frances and Bee, "Technology is changing at an ever increasing rate. Today's state-of-the-art computer is tomorrow's junk. Robot assembly plants, laser printer, transplant and genetic surgery – wherever the workplace, whatever the task. There appears to be a technological solution for everything."[7]

The technological changes are influencing the basic settings of organizations. The changes are not only concerned with the structure or gadgets of an organization but also influence the behavioural aspects of the very people who are working in the organization. However, people do not usually change with the change in technology and environment. Change can be brought about in a smooth manner only through training techniques.

Another important factor that needs to be taken into consideration is concerned with social changes that are taking place in the new social environment. For most organizations, internal structures are bound to change in the computer age. People from different backgrounds and diverse nations will form the workforce of modern organizations. With increasing diversity in the culture, the organizations are bound to receive culture shock. Organizations with their existing format will not be in a position to absorb this culture shock. The change agents will be playing an important role in providing appropriate training to absorb culture shock.

The next factor that has influenced training needs is related to the new and sensitive role that the governments are being asked to play. This relates to controlling the business ethics activities on one hand and safeguarding the interests of consumers on the other. In the era of privatization and globalization, the governments are formulating legislations to facilitate business activity – both public and private – as well as safeguarding the consumer interests. Thus, managers and CEOs need to be acquainted with the new legislations that are being enacted from time to time.

Another important factor influencing the training needs is the emerging competitive market conditions. It may be asserted that both public and private sectors, even in monopolistic conditions, have to face competition. The pertinent questions are whether the new market situations will force the organizations to go in for training as they are going to face new marketing situations in the times to come? And, will the new emerging conditions give rise to pressure groups that have henceforth not been seen in the business world? Basically, organizations are going to face situations that are the result of competitive markets and development of consumerism. Many of the managers in public and private sectors could not possibly have been oriented towards these new situations. Hence, need of training is unavoidable.

The last factor is related to internal management of an organization. Internally, organizations are going to face new dilemmas and problems. Business needs are fulfilled by the human resources that exist within the framework of internal structure. Any strategic plan which does not take this fact into account is bound to face numerous problems. There will be a continuous pressure on the organization to improve performance. Human resources, like managers, workers, staff and others, have to be kept up-to-date in expertise and at the same time need to be motivated to perform better. This is a difficult task which cannot be handled by the staff of the organization. Experts called 'change agents' are required to fulfil the task. Training needs cannot be overlooked because it is an ongoing process. In addition, training is now considered a specialized function to be performed by the experts.

Techniques of Training

The object of this paper is not to discuss various techniques of training. Hence, training techniques are being shortlisted for the purpose of their identification and evaluation. However, we would like to throw light on some of the modern techniques of training. Some of the training techniques that are often used for re-education purposes are:

1. On-the-job-training
2. Demonstration
3. Job instruction training
4. Vestibule training
5. Apprenticeship
6. Coaching-understudy
7. Job rotation
8. Lectures and conferences
9. Syndicate
10. Simulation training

11. Role playing
12. In-basket exercise
13. Management game
14. Sensitivity training
15. Transactional analysis
16. Organization development

A detailed discussion of these techniques can be referred to many textbooks.[8] Here, we would like to discuss some of the training techniques that are considered by the experts as essential for improving the performance of organizations in competitive situations.

Diversity training is becoming extremely important for the organizations that are complex in nature. The workforce in these enterprises is diverse in nature. Diverse groups from different cultural and social backgrounds join one organization and thus submerging various cultures into one. The diverse workforce has to be trained so as to provide diversity training. According to Fred Luthans, one method of diverse training involves putting trainees into groups based on ethnic origin. Then, each group is asked to describe the others and listen to the way in which its own group is described.[9] Another method of diversity training has been stated in the following manner: "Another widely used approach is diversity board games, which require the participants to answer questions related to areas such as gender, race, cultural differences, age issues, sexual orientation, and disabilities. On the basis of the response, the games players are able to advance on the board or are forced to back up."[10]

The objective of these types of games is to acquaint the players in a non-threatening manner with legal rules and restrictions regarding how to manage members of the diverse groups. The third method of diverse training is concerned with participants' focus on cultural issues such as how to interact with personnel from other countries. It may be added that many of the training programmes related to diverse workforce also use other training programmes.[11]

Evaluating Training Programmes

It is extremely important to assess the results of any training programme. The participants must be made aware of the goals and objectives of the training programme and on completion of the training programme, they should be asked about the impact of the concerned training programme.

Evaluation of any programme is a difficult task and more so of a training programme. The first step towards evaluation of a training programme is to define the goals and objectives of the training programme. These should be stated in such a format so that they can be measured statistically. Also, both the trainer and the trainees must be well-acquainted with their roles in the training programme.

In the evaluation of any training programme, the first requirement is to collect valid and reliable data. The required data can be collected by using the following techniques[12]: (1) self-assessment answer sheets; (2) questions confronted by the trainees; (3) assessing the collected information and observation; and (4) final results based on earlier information plus the new data.

Each method of data collection has both advantages and disadvantages which need to be taken into consideration. The merits and demerits of each method are described as follows:

Self-Assessment Method

Merits

1. The cost factor is quite low.
2. Data can be easily collected.
3. Time consumption of both the trainer and trainee is negligible.
4. Outside interference is completely avoided.
5. Effective relationships develop between the trainer and the trainee.
6. Well-designed answer sheets can produce healthy results.

Demerits

1. Self-assessment is basically self-evaluation which can be based on biased responses. The assessment must have enough reliability so as to draw right conclusion in regard to individual assessment.
2. The responses given by the trainees can be based on misrepresentation or misinterpretation of the questions asked. Thus, self-assessment questions should be small and easy to understand. In addition, no information should be sought which will embarrass the trainees.
3. The information provided by the trainees cannot be evaluated in terms of their correctness. All the trainees do not prefer to give the required information, lest it may be used against them at any point of time.

All these problems can be easily solved. Self-assessment is basically adhered to by all the training managers. However, what is important to consider is to make effective use of this technique as the trainees provide valuable information which the trainer can use to formulate training strategy.

The second requirement for evaluating a training programme is concerned with evaluation when part of the training has been completed. The time factor must be decided before the programme is initiated and the evaluation criteria must be determined before the programme begins. The first evaluation will give adequate information to the trainers whether the programme is moving in the right direction or not. At the same time, trainees will be able to assess the value of the programme in terms of its usefulness. It is extremely important to realize whether the trainees have understood the need and importance of the training programme. At this stage, adequate data should be collected from the trainees to make proper evaluation of the training programme.

To collect data, interview and questionnaire methods can be most effective. Interviews can be conducted by seeking information face-to-face, by means of telephone, or by other strategies like group discussions etc. Each of these methods has its own merits and demerits.

Interview Method

Merits

1. Face-to-face interview ensures some response. If any response needs to be clarified, the trainer can do so instantly. Similarly, if the trainees want any clarification, the same can be done immediately. This helps in ensuring correct information.
2. As far as telephone interviews are concerned, though there is lack of personal touch, the trainee does not feel the pressure of the interviewer to give answers that suit the trainer. The trainee can answer all those questions that are complex in nature. These answers have far more validity as the responses are given without any pressure.

Demerits

1. The interview is a lengthy and costly process as it requires trained and skilled personnel to get results that are reliable.
2. Another important drawback is the possibility of the trainer becoming involved in the interview.
3. Data collected through interview method may be outdated and hence difficult to interpret.

Questionnaire Method

Questionnaires in one form or another do appear in all kinds of researches and surveys. Hence, it is extremely vital that the questionnaire is framed with utmost care so that it measures the variables in exactly the way it has been designed for. Once the initial design has been properly framed, a pre-test must be conducted to find out whether the questions mean the same thing to both the trainer and the trainee, and if found inappropriate, the questionnaire should be redesigned and a pilot survey should be conducted and if found inappropriate, the questionnaire should be redesigned again. The reliability and validity of the questionnaire should be properly evaluated before going in for full survey.

Regarding collection of data, it may be observed: "As with any method of data collection it is vital to plan how the data is to be collected. However, with this method, since it does not usually involve the design of some sort of formal survey instrument such as questionnaire, it is all too easy to leap straight in without a plan. This can lead to a considerable waste of time and even worse, the wrong data being collected – so the message is: Plan and design your desk research in the same way as you would any more formal survey."[13]

Thus, whatever technique or method we adopt, the validity and reliability of data must be determined. According to Frances and Bee,[14] the following three key aspects must be considered in any evaluation study. The first aspect is concerned with the internal validity of an evaluation study. Or, how well the study measures what we want or are aiming to find out. This usually involves the adequacy and appropriateness of the measuring tool, the instrument used. What needs to be considered is that whatever instruments we use for the purpose of collecting data, we must make sure that the terminology being used actually measures the variable that we intend to measure. Whether the instrument be interview or questionnaire, the terms must elicit the kind of information that is required.

The second aspect is concerned with the external validity. Or, in other words, with the extent that the findings can be applied beyond the group involved in the study. The conclusions should not be applicable to only that group which was the basis of collection of data. On the contrary, the collected data should have the reliability and validity to the extent that its conclusions are applicable to other similar situations.

The third aspect that needs to be considered is concerned with reliability. The reliability of an evaluation study is the extent to which the results can be replicated, i.e., if the study is repeated, the results would be the same. The obvious approach to deal with this issue is to repeat tests and observations. Also, techniques such as including the same questions but in different forms, using multiple observers, etc., can be helpful.

Another factor that needs to be considered in evaluating training programme is to conduct and determine reaction level of the trainees in respect of the training programme. The reaction criteria are to be determined in terms of open discussion between the trainers, the trainees, and the management. This will give ample opportunity to the management to ascertain whether or not the training programme is achieving the objectives for which it was organized. This evaluation should be conducted half way through the training period.

The reaction criteria tend to inform the trainers whether the training programme is achieving the goals as perceived by the trainers. In other words, the trainers come to know the level of happiness and satisfaction of the trainees in regard to the training programme. To ascertain and collect this kind of information, the trainees may be asked to fill a self-completed questionnaire in which they have to choose from a range of alternatives and answer some of the open-ended questions.

The self-fulfilled questionnaire seeks information in regard to entry briefing: whether the objectives of the training programme were achievable and how far have they been useful; whether the trainer's performance has been satisfactory; and the utility training methods. The mid-term evaluation clears the way for the trainers to reframe the training methodology and cater to the needs of the trainees.

Two fundamental problems need to be assessed in the evaluation process. The first is whether information sought should or should not be collected in the name of trainee. The evaluation as far as possible should be anonymous and give probably more accurate information than collected in the name of the participants. The second problem is concerned with the place where the questionnaire is filled up by the trainee. It is indeed desirable that the trainees provide information away from the course environment.

This mid-term evaluation can be very helpful in providing a lot of information that is reliable and valid. As a matter of fact, the cost of collecting such information is not only very low but it also helps trainers to redesign their training programmes accordingly. The approach of mid-term evaluation allows the trainer to make comparisons between different training programmes that were conducted in other organizations or by the trainer himself. However, reaction criteria of mid-term evaluation do generate an enormous amount of data for analysis. How much of this data is used by the trainer for readjusting the structure of the training programme depends on the management, participants and the trainer himself.

The final step in respect of evaluation of training programmes is to assess whether the basic objectives of the training programme have been achieved or not. In this, cost-effective and cost-benefit techniques need to be utilized to measure the performance. This assessment will demonstrate whether the expected learning, that was determined before the training programme was conducted, has taken place after the conclusion of the training programme or not.

Some of the scholars suggest that before going in for final evaluation, if feasible, one or two in-between evaluations can also be conducted. However, too many evaluation questionnaires can disrupt the training programme and also create doubts in the minds of trainees towards the effectiveness of the programme. Evaluation of the training programme should be undertaken only for the purpose of feedback and restructuring it.

The basic purpose of any training programme is to improve organizational performance, i.e., to assess whether the training programme has been able to achieve the changes that it desired. The final evaluation must take into consideration factors that might have affected the outcome, for example, competitor initiatives, general economic conditions, etc. Performance of an organization must be evaluative in terms of the whole unit and not its parts.

Hence, any evaluation of the training programme may not result in perfect achievement of the goals. We should identify the key factors and indicators that can influence the final results of the training programme. The assessment of these factors will help in the analysis of the needs of the concerned organization. In this respect, a comparative study should be undertaken with regard to the information collected before the training programme was initiated and after the training programme where changes need to be visualized and thereupon assessed. If possible, a comparative study can also be made of the similar training programme conducted in any other organization to analyze the differences in the final results. At the time of collecting the final data, proper monitoring should be assured. All the required data should be collected to make elaborate analysis.

In the final analysis, it can be stated that the final evaluation is the most important aspect in order to find and determine the effectiveness of the training programme. This assessment gives a clear picture of the impact of the training programme. As indicated earlier, clear-cut indicators of organizational performance determined prior to starting of the programme will make measurement of desired changes in terms of evaluation much easier.

Conclusion

The evaluation of any training programme has certain aims to fulfil. These are concerned with the determination of change in the organizational behaviour and also the change needed in the organizational structure. Hence, evaluation of any training programme must inform whether the training programme has been able to deliver the goals and objectives in terms of cost incurred and benefits achieved.

The analysis of information is the concluding part of any evaluation. The analysis of data should be summarized and then compared with the data of other training programmes of similar nature. On the basis of these comparisons, problems and strengths should be identified which would help the trainer in designing future programmes.

Notes

1. Edwin B. Flippo, *Personnel Management,* McGraw Hill, New York, 1984, p. 192.
2. Lawrence Steinmitz, "Age: Unrecognized Enigma of Executive Development", *Management of Personnel Quarterly,* Vol.VIII, 1968, p.73.
3. William G. Torpey, *Public Personnel Management,* 1959, p.154.
4. *Assheton Committee Report,* 1944, Para 15.
5. Vishnu Bhagwan and Vidya Bhushan, *Public Administration,* S. Chand & Company, New Delhi, 1998, pp. 393–94.
6. P. Senge, *The Fifth Discipline: The Art and Practice of the Learning Organisation,* Doubleday, New York, 1990.
7. Frances and Roland Bee, *Training Needs, Analysis and Evaluation,* University Press (India) Limited, New Delhi, 1994, p. 38.
8. L.M. Prasad., *Principles and Practice of Management,* S. Chand & Company, New Delhi, 2001, pp. 497–537.
9. Fred Luthans, *Organisational Behaviour,* McGraw Hill, New Delhi, 2002, p. 69.
10. L.M. Prasad, op. cit.
11. Tom Boydell and Malcolm Leary, *Identifying Training Needs,* University Press (India), New Delhi, 1996, p.65.
12. Ibid., p. 85.
13. Frances and Roland Bee, op. cit., p. 185.

23 Training through Distance Education

Gireesh Pradhan

There is no gainsaying the fact that training is a much-neglected input, especially for government servants. Regular training programmes form the cornerstone of an effective policy of human resource development (HRD). In India, both state and central governments recognize that the training component forms an important part of the overall HRD policy. This is reflected in the number of state/national training institutes that have been created. All these institutes are basically charged with the responsibility of providing training to government servants – both at induction/foundation and service levels. Besides these institutes, the government servants are also sent for training to other institutes of renown and excellence, both within and outside India. However, the aims of the HRD policy of the government have not been met in full, nor are they likely to meet in the future for certain obvious reasons.

Government servants form one of the largest segments of the white-collar workforce and the sheer numbers are such that neither the central government nor the state governments are in a position to meet the training needs in full. This is based on the presumption that all government employees need to be given some sort of a basic induction training input on joining service and then need to have further refresher/specialized training at regular intervals in their careers. At present, we are not even able to do full justice in terms of providing training to Group 'A' employees; the less said about the other categories the better.

The existing infrastructure is woefully short to handle such large numbers. There is also increasing pressure on the existing institutions involved in training government servants to provide specialized training in different areas and on different topics. Given the number of employees, on one hand, and the varied areas in which they require training, on the other, the conventional method of organizing training at physical locations, where trainees would assemble and participate, has certain limitations. However, the answer does not lie in erecting costly infrastructure to establish more institutes. An innovative method is now required that takes the maximum advantage of the emerging technology and is at, the same time, cost-effective.

Distance Learning through Information Technology

The emerging technology, which has been described as 'revolutionary', has been aptly named as Information Technology or IT. This has opened up a world of opportunities and it is believed that nothing will remain the same in the future. It will affect everyone and everything – from the way transactions take place in society to the way we organize and run our lives. In fact, it will also change the way we organize and run government. The new technology makes very good economic sense too. Not only would direct savings accrue but also the savings in time and energy would be phenomenal. The ramifications are so far reaching and deep that not many at present can visualize the full impact of the IT revolution. Harnessing this powerful technology to our own end of providing training to the maximum number of people will prove the greatest challenge for all of us who are working in various state and national training institutes. This technology will give a new meaning and dimension to 'distance learning'.

Distance learning or distance education is not a new concept. It has been around for a long period of time and anyone in the field of education/training is familiar with it. In the Indian context, the British rulers introduced the first modem postal system as early as the 19th century and by the beginning of the 20th century courses were being offered using the postal system. These courses which came to be known as 'correspondence courses' became extremely popular and are rightly regarded as the first step in modem distance learning or education. The logical path in the development of distance learning led to the establishment of the pioneering Indira Gandhi National Open University (IGNOU) at New Delhi in the year 1985. The establishment of this Open University signalled the coming of age of distance learning. This method was finally and formally recognized as a viable alternative to the conventional classroom system and quite appropriately so for country as vast, populous and diverse as India.

Internet: On-line Training

The spread of distance education over the past fifteen years has seen the use of diverse media to reach out to an ever-increasing number of students. The use of radio, followed by television, and now the use of the satellite, has given a completely new dimension to the field of distance education. The last couple of years have seen the introduction of online training programmes which are taking the maximum advantage of the most amazing aspect of the IT revolution that we spoke of earlier – the Internet. Courses are now being offered over the Internet, which are available anywhere, anytime and to anyone. The advantage of this medium is that it allows the use of audio, video, graphics, images and text. But, most importantly, it allows the programme to be interactive.

The method appears to be the answer to the complex problems that were discussed at the beginning. With more and more states going in for a statewide Internet facility, programmes could be made available to employees over both the Intranet as well as the Internet. The future lies in this and the faster we try and accept this the greater will be our advantage. It would also be possible through this medium to revise, store and disseminate materials far more rapidly than has been possible till now. All in all, it would also prove most cost-effective and reduce substantially the burden of creating costly infrastructure and other costs associated with conventional classroom training.

The best way is to proceed in such a manner so that we take the fullest advantage of both the concepts of distance learning and the new technology, is make available computer-based training (CBT) programmes/courses over the Internet/Intranet. Programmes and courses could be designed based on a wider area of subjects and topics. These ideally would be interactive and give trainees the freedom to sign up and do these programmes at their own pace and place. Thus, there would be the flexibility to choose programmes from a wide menu and with the knowledge that information available in the programme could be absorbed and studied at one's own place and any queries, doubts, etc., could be immediately and individually attended to.

To avoid the duplication of certain basic or universal training modules as well as to share and pool resources, it is possible that the state training institutes could divide the work of content creation and courseware amongst themselves. This could form a common pool that could be shared and disseminated to the largest numbers across the country. It is also possible that a central facility could be set up which would spearhead this effort and make available the CBTs to all those who are interested. It is now possible to make available all the content in different regional languages over the computer. Thus, making it relatively easy for the course content to be developed at one place and then have it launched in various languages. A task force needs to be immediately formed by the state training institutes and perhaps the ASTI could take the lead in this. The task force could have a rapid but focused look just at the issue of online training and present a report to the ASTI for its consideration.

Conclusion

The important point that must be grasped is that we have to begin using the new technology to further our interests and to suit our purpose. Secondly, under the present circumstances, this solution is a low-cost and effective one and relatively easy to implement. There are other benefits that will also accrue from taking training online. It would be possible to provide post-training support to officers/staff in a far more sustained and systematic manner than has hitherto been possible. Most importantly, it would be available online and thus improve efficiency and effectiveness at the workplace. The creation of a resource base, ideally in common, could help serve the purpose of a virtual reference library for online consulting and scanning. Thus, taking training online for the government sector opens the way to a whole new methodology for developing human resources.

It is not my intention to substitute or marginalize the conventional classroom method of training that is presently followed. In fact, the use of online training will enrich the quality of the conventional method, as also allow for concentration on quality programmes aimed at specific topics and groups. It will also help training institutes to upgrade their own skill levels and achieve a higher degree of specialization that is possible in the present scheme. Training institutes will no longer be mere 'training shops' that desperately accommodate larger and larger candidates in the ever-increasing number of stereotyped courses, straining resources both physical and financial. There is an opportunity here that we cannot afford to miss, if we do not take the lead now circumstances will compel us to do so in the future.

24 E-Learning

The Key to Future Training

Neeraj Gupta

In the rapidly changing and globalized environment, continuous learning has become a necessity for all organizational members of corporate sector as well as government system. Effective learning plus effective resources equal effective outcomes and training is the means by which a systematic process is directed at improving performance, through organized training, to produce effective outcomes.[1] Training is an investment necessary for long-term success of the organization. However, in the coming era of competitive global environment, training has to be more focused and a joint responsibility of organizations as well as individuals. Not only the responsibility and scope of training has to be widened, the whole approach to training must change if it has to cover all the employees in government system.

Advancements in information and communication technology (ICT) present immense opportunities to restructure training system and use innovative and more effective learning methods. Traditional face-to-face training has its own limitations in terms of physical infrastructure, willingness of organization to spare efficient and sincere workers for training and resources – financial as well as human. If "training for all" mandate of the National Training Policy is to be achieved, e-learning is the key. The rapid changes taking place in workplace will require training to be delivered quickly. Such training must be high-speed, low-cost and capable of reaching small and big groups. Traditional ways of delivering training are time-consuming, require intensive human resources, and costly. E-learning, especially online courses, offers a solution.

E-learning is training that takes place through a network, usually over the Internet or organization's Intranet. The term 'e-learning' may sound trendy but the concept itself has been around for many years. It has its roots in computer-based training, which used CD-ROMs to train/teach people.

This paper attempts to explain the term 'e-learning' and highlight its advantages for training in government systems and thus shows that the key to future training is e-learning.

What is E-learning?

Electronic learning or e-learning has its roots in computer-based training used since 1980s mostly to train technical persons, using CD-ROMs. With the phenomenal advancements in ICT, it is now possible to deliver instructional material through a network of computers in a manner that learners anywhere in the world can access information without any restrictions of time, space and number of persons accessing the material. Colloquially speaking, the term 'e-learning' can be used for learning made available through use of any electronic media, including computer-based instructional material using CD-ROMs. In the present context and for the purposes of this paper, by the term 'e-learning' we mean training which takes place through a network of computers using Internet or Intranet. E-learning has now become almost synonymous with online learning where instructions are passed from a computer system at a distinct venue, away from learner's personal computer. This distinct venue may be across the institute's campus or can be across the world.

Online course can be defined as a course or unit of study in which some or all of its parts are presented wholly or partially to learners through computer-based environment, especially www. There are many courses which utilize computer networking to deliver information about courses and the registration procedures etc. Institutes may have tendency to claim delivery of courses online.

Online courses are distinguished in terms of use of computer-based environment for delivery of most of the course components. These components include course information and registration, course material, supplementary reading, tutorial, assignments, examinations, and evaluation of the course.[2]

Synchronous and Asynchronous Learning

E-learning can be synchronous or asynchronous. Synchronous learning imitates the real classroom in electronic medium where learners and the instructor or trainer may be sitting miles away connected through computer network. Classes take place in real time and connect the users through streaming audio, video or through chat room.

Asynchronous learning involves similar process as synchronous learning but in this case, instructor/trainer and the learner may not be sitting on their respective terminals at the same time. Learners often receive a pre-packaged instructional material, which they access at their own time and pace and get in touch with the instructor through e-mail. Instructor may then respond to learner's queries either collectively grouping various questions or individually, depending upon the nature of programme.

In both cases, i.e., synchronous as well as asynchronous learning discussion forums can be set up which allow learner and subject experts sitting at different places to interact and share knowledge. Thus, it allows great flexibility to the learner and higher accessibility to subject specialists who may otherwise be not available in far off places.

E-learning packages normally require basic a computer with Internet connectivity. In case of in-house training programmes, internal network of the organization is also used. An effective e-learning programme requires a continuum of technologies and methodologies.

The need to focus on e-learning for enrichment of human capital was well spelt out at a seminar on "E-learning: Transforming Corporate Workplaces", organized by FICCI in May 2002. Delivering his address, Prof. Ashok Chandra, Special Secretary, Ministry of Human Resource Development, Government of India, said that the technological capability of a nation is a dominating factor in its economic development and e-learning would go a long way in doing so. He further said that e-learning systems had consistent pedagogy unlike traditional learning programmes that were prone to heterogeneity of approaches to impart training.[3]

Why Use E-learning?

"As India continues to move towards a knowledge-based economy and society, it will, like others in similar circumstances find citizens continuously demanding more learning while in workforce."[4]

Traditionally, education and training have been restricted to face-to-face classroom situations. In spite of increasing advancements in ICT, the personalized exchange of knowledge continues to command premium in the training market, especially in government systems. This situation, as it seems, is likely to continue as long as training programmes continue to attract learners not because of course content but for travel and tourism opportunities.

E-learning cannot replace the charms of personally meeting and interacting with a celebrity resource person or a senior cabinet minister. Aura of a learned person felt in the classroom cannot yet be transmitted through learners' computer terminal. E-learning can also not replace some tangible and wonderful advantages of face-to-face training like air travel to far off places, allowances in foreign currency, interaction with resources persons during gala pool side dinners, fancy bags and training kits, personal interaction with fellow participants both in formal and informal settings or opportunity for tourism and shopping sprees with spouse or friends.

However, what e-learning can offer is value for money in terms of fulfilling objectives of training. It can deliver highly effective and interactive learning experience even to the most introvert persons who may otherwise feel shy of asking questions in the classroom settings. Let us look at some of the key advantages of e-learning in following paragraphs.

Advantages of E-learning

Costs

Face-to-face training has many cost implications in terms of capital investment, operation and maintenance costs and recurring expenses. Face-to-face training can be an expensive proposition when we add all the costs like air travel, boarding and lodging of participants, resource persons and training managers, cost of operations and maintenance of physical facilities, audio-visual and other equipment, support services, and expenses on support personnel. Further, if we add the indirect cost of huge capital invested in physical facilities, the opportunity cost of people away from work and social cost to their families, it may be seem that face-to-face training is not a very cost-effective proposition.

Preparing e-learning packages is also not a cheap option. A good package requires a large amount of investment. However, the initial cost can be off set as we enrol more and more users for the programme. Similarly, the infrastructure costs of providing computer systems, networking, costs of communication lines and operations and maintenance may be quite high. Here also, we must realize that government is in any case going ahead with massive programmes for computerization and efforts are on way for e-governance. A large amount of this infrastructure can be successfully put to use for e-learning. Even if some systems have to be augmented, the overall per capita cost of training through e-learning packages is very low as compared to face-to-face training.

Flexibility of Learning

E-learning offers flexibility to learners in terms of time and place and pace of learning. Many people are excluded from learning, as they might be unable to attend face-to-face training for a variety of personal, social or official commitments, which restrict their movement from place of work. Quite often people who contribute most to the organization's work are not spared by their superiors for training. Many people in senior positions or on strategic postings may find it difficult to leave their headquarters for training in the state capital or other institutions.

For such persons e-learning may come as a boon. People can learn at the time most suitable for them that does not impose any time compulsion upon them. In addition, the pace of learning can be suited to individual's capacities.

Personalized Training

A face-to-face training programme is attended by a group of participants from different educational and experiential backgrounds, and they may have different learning capacities. In such a situation, the instructor has some difficulty in choosing the level at which a particular programme should be pitched. Often one finds few people struggling to catch up with the pace of instructions and yet few people may find the pace of instructions to be too slow for them. Such situations can be easily avoided in e-learning where individuals can maintain their own pace of learning. The instructor/trainer can individually respond to queries through e-mail thus making the learning experience close to one-on-one coaching. E-learning packages have potential to deliver personalized programmes to suit each individual's pace and ease of learning. It can be more effective for certain types of learners who may be shy, reflective, language challenged or those who need more time to learn.

Learner-centred Approach

One of the major mindset shifts in training and education is the learner-centred approach. Formerly, trainers were at the centre of learning universe and they often steered the learning. Now, it has been well established that a trainer must help facilitate the learning process and not try to control it. Many trainers in traditional training also adopt learner-focused framework. This is, however, not true for all classroom sessions. Quite often sessions in training programmes are focused on the instructor. Information tends to flow from trainers to learners and the result is a passive learner. Since most of the instructors are taught in instructor-focused classrooms, it is very hard for them to break away from this mould. The online classroom technologies (and student tendencies in that environment) are much more suited to a learner-focused environment.[5]

E-learning allows learners to play an active role in choosing their path along the course and selecting their own learning opportunities. An adult learner in training situation feels more satisfied in actively participating in the learning experience. E-learning offers adults a joyful learning experience where they are able to make best out of online resources and supporting materials in an easy-to-use, self-directed format while getting support from the distant facilitator as and when required. Technologies have helped bring distant learners and trainers closer where they can share common pool of knowledge and experience and apply them to personal work situations. Given the nature of course delivery, e-learning ensures learner-centred approach.

However, because much of e-learning is self-paced, it requires motivation and personal tenacity to succeed through a training programme. A learner must organize his own training schedule. Effective time management is necessary for e-learners. E-learning offers learners a side benefit of learning new technologies and technical skills.

Access

E-learning offers great advantage in terms of accessibility. Best of the resource persons sitting in different parts of the world can be made available in virtual classrooms. Normal face-to-face training takes place through centralized training institutes located in state capitals or selected cities. Efforts towards developing decentralized training programmes have met with little success largely due to constraints of financial and human resources. Except for national and state level apex institutions and few selected departmental training centres, training is often conducted by average quality trainers in ill-equipped physical facilities with little or no well-designed packages. In spite of best of the efforts of the central and state governments, there continues to be a dearth of 'trained trainers'. There are hundreds of faculty members in various local training institutions who have not received any formal training either in direct training skills or training design. In such a situation, what happens in the training classroom can be anybody's guess.

E-learning is very useful in terms of making available good quality training programmes developed by experts accessible to the remote corners of the country – something which is quite difficult to achieve by face-to-face training methods. Thus, e-learning has a unique advantage of access at comparatively low costs.

One major constraint for access to e-learning is the availability of support infrastructure of computers and network connectivity.

However, this situation is fast improving. It is estimated that penetration of Internet in India is about 5 per cent (5.5 million users on January 2001), but the situation is likely to change very quickly. As per the National Association of Software and Service Companies (NASSCOM) survey, by 2000, India is expected to have 50 million net subscribers. It is expected that the real growth of the Internet in India will take place through cable TV. The number of cable TV subscribers will increase from 37 million as on August 2000 to 70 million in 2008. The survey also showed that 81 per cent of stand alone PCs sold during 1999–2000 were driven by the need to access Internet.[6] An interesting feature is that 48 per cent Internet users in the country accessed the Internet daily, which is higher than international average of 43 per cent.[7]

Further, if we take into account the accessibility of Internet to government employees, the figures would be high enough to support launch of e-learning campaign. The level of teledensity is fast improving in the country and with the progress of cable network supporting computer networking, PC users will have easy access to the Internet.

E-learning Supports Physically Challenged

Physically challenged persons would appreciate that they can participate in e-learning programmes with greater ease as compared to face-to-face training, given the difficulties of travel and preparedness of our infrastructure to facilitate the physically challenged. E-learning obviates the need for travel and physical access. It can open doors of learning for those with restricted mobility or difficulty in accessing buildings.

However, there is a need to design e-learning packages for certain disabilities. For those unable to use mouse or keyboard, speech commands can be provided. Designers of e-learning packages need to be sensitive to the needs of those physically challenged. These challenges may vary from colour blindness to total blindness or hearing impairment. E-learning material can be easily modified to cater to special demands of the physically challenged. The courses can also be run for such population taking into account their pace of progress through the courses.

Gender and E-learning

E-learning can also help reduce the gender inequity in delivery of training. Women many times have to forego face-to-face training opportunities, as they may be required to nurse the children or take care of other family commitments. E-learning can come as a good boon for such women. Similarly, some women may feel restrained or be hesitant to actively participate in a face-to-face discussion. Discussion using electronic chat rooms can be very useful in such situations. Some authorities believe that women's way of communicating and working lends themselves particularly happily to computer-mediated conferences.[8] With the increasing access of women to networked computers, the prospects of e-learning are very bright.

Pedagogy

The quality of training and learning in our institutes has often been a cause of concern for all of us. The ICT environment-enabled e-learning can make significant contribution to the improvement of pedagogy. E-learning helps the adult to actively engage in learning by using information and materials to construct their own understanding and knowledge. Learners can enjoy the self-paced interactive environment that e-learning offers. For adults, learning is more related to their life situation. E-learning offers an environment wherein the officers with substantial experience could learn more effectively through sharing of experience, collaborating with others across the country and solving problems.

In terms of learning theories, the humanistic approach close to constructivism and social learning orientation would be most effective for most of the training courses. This can be easily provided by online courses. E-learning provides new sets of tools that can add value to all the traditional learning modes, viz., classrooms, textbooks, CDROMs and traditional computer-based learning. E-learning has capacity to enhance classroom learning.

Does it mean that traditional training will be replaced by e-learning? It has been argued that class cohorts, campuses and face-to-face teaching will not disappear. There will always be place for real-time face-to-face training which requires apprentice-based training, where the human cost of error is unacceptable but the reliance on e-learning courses will increase manifold as supply of these courses expands.[9]

Speed of Delivery and Modification in Course Contents

Rapid changes taking place in the workplace require training to be delivered quickly. Changes in rules, regulations, policies and official procedures demand that these changes be rapidly incorporated in the course contents of various types of training. Many projects and programmes require quick assemblage of instructions/procedures and large number of employees to be deputed in remote blocks or villages who are to be trained at very short notice. Traditional ways of training cannot cater to such demands. They can be very time-consuming, labour-intensive and costly. Online courses offer a solution. E-learning can be high speed, easily modifiable, low cost and capable of reaching large and small groups without any limitation of distance and very few limitations of location. The biggest advantage offered by the electronic medium is the speed of delivery, ease of modifications and updating.

Convergence of E-learning and E-governance

As more and more government organizations embrace e-governance and employees become familiar with e-mail and Internet, their comfort level with web-based learning will increase massively and quickly. As more and more educational institutions combine e-learning with other educational innovations, the barriers to participation in e-learning course will diminish.

The flexibility and ease of getting day-to-day work done using Internet applications will draw and attract larger population base to e-learning. It is inevitable that e-governance and e-learning will converge and the advantages of e-learning will surpass other learning methods.

Conclusion

Rapid changes in our external and internal environment demand continuous learning by all organizational members. It requires training to be delivered quickly at a low cost that can reach small and large groups in distant locations. Traditional ways of training, which are time-consuming, labour-intensive and costly cannot cope up with demands of continuous learning and accelerating pace of change. All those who are living in remote areas are unable to leave their workplace for personal or other reasons or are physically challenged can be easily served by e-learning.

E-learning can be used either independently or in configuration with other traditional training methods to impart effective training at a low cost. E-learning has an advantage of providing flexibility in terms of time, place and pace of learning to the participants. It gives opportunity to the adult learner to share knowledge and delve into problem-based learning experiences in an interactive and interesting environment.

E-learning can effectively support e-governance. The two are complementary to each other. With the increasing emphasis on e-governance, e-learning is going to be the key to future training.

To reach 50 million users, the telephone took 74 years, the radio 38 years, the PC 16 years, the television 13 years, and the www only four years. In India, places that did not have telephone now have Internet kiosks where families can e-mail their relatives abroad. Reduced costs, simplification of technologies and efficiency encourage us to believe that countries and communities can leap frog from technology stages (e.g., the absence of telephone lines) to state-of-art strategies.[10]

Notes

1. Jill Brookes, *Training and Development Competence: A Practical Guide*, Kogan Page Limited, 1995, p. 36.
2. Olugbemiro Jegede, The Meaning of Online Delivery of Instruction in Open and Distance Learning, Global Institute of Open, Flexible and Distance Education, 1(1), 2001, p. 19.
3. Http:/www.netvarsity/nr000/printer,asp? Nun - 19 & Mode= 1.
4. Prof. Gajaraj Dhanarajan, President and Chief Executive Officer of the Commonwealth of Learning, in his inaugural remarks at the 76th Annual Meeting of the Association of India Universities at Chandigarh, 5–8 December, 2001.
5. Http:/www.justcolleges.com/elearn/index.phtml?el=difference.htm.
6. Udain Lal Rai, September 27, 2000; NASSCOM: India to have 50 million net subscribers by 2008; http:/asia.internet.com/asia-news/article.
7. Udain Lal Rai, February 8, 2001; India has 5.5 million new users: Nasscom; http:/asia.internet.com/asia-news/article.
8. C. Lapham, (1989), A mindset for the new millennium, CMC magazine, 5 (10); http:www.December.com/cmc/mag/1998/Oct/lapnp.html.
9. Paul J.Edelson and Von V. Pittman, "E-Learning in United States: New Directions and Opportunities for University Continuing Education," *Global E-journal of Open, Flexible and Distance Education,* 1 (1), 2001 pp. 71–83.
10. Wadi D. Haddad, Technologies for All: A Dream or a Nightmare, *Technowlogia,* July-September, 2002; www.technowlogia.org.

25 Publishing a House Journal in a Training Institution

K.K. Parnami

A journal, published with a fixed periodicity, by an institution or organization, and mainly aiming at fulfilling the objectives of the institution or organization that brings it out, is called a house journal. The salient components of a good house journal are articles, book reviews, book notes, research notes, latest developments in the area of the functioning of the institution or organization, etc. In the present world scenario, the importance of publishing a house journal in a training institution cannot be overemphasized because a journal not only disseminates knowledge but also plays an important role in the development of a discipline or profession. By publishing a journal, a major requirement of a profession, i.e., possession of a body of knowledge, can be met. A journal serves to preserve and document the past, disseminate ideas of contemporary scholars, and aids the development of a profession's knowledge base by identifying appropriate contributions and preserving them in an archival source (Lindsey and Kirk, 1992, cited in Desai, 2004). For example, *Prashasnika,* a journal published by the HCM Rajasthan State Institute of Public Administration, Jaipur, through literature devoted to the study of administrative processes in developing countries, realizes one of its objectives of developing training material, which enables training with minimal effort.

Those who invest money on subscribing to journals also expect them to be readable, interesting, theme-based, aesthetically produced and reasonably free from errors. To make them so is the responsibility of not only the publisher but also the editor.

Days are gone when journal publishing was a simple and artless task. Today, it has become an important function, particularly in an institution of civil service training, which is regarded as the place of not only preparing future administrators, but also reorienting the present ones towards new innovations in their respective fields. The publication department in a training institution is normally structured into various sub-departments, viz., editing, production, sales, etc. Since the goods to be produced here is a journal, which is entirely different from any factory-made consumables like TV or refrigerator, publishing a house journal ought to be one of the most important activities. Besides, publication of a journal is the major system for knowledge dissemination. As, generally, in comparison to books, subscribing to journals is not very difficult and financially burdensome for both libraries and individuals, it becomes easier to utilize the literature contained and thus make further spread of knowledge possible.

In this backdrop, it would be pertinent to describe various phases in the publication of a house journal in a training institution.

Editing

In simpler terms, to edit a document means to improve it, usually for publication either in a journal, book or any other form. Or, in other words, it is a process by which a manuscript is turned into a final published product (e.g., book, journal, newsletter, etc.). Editing helps the author to communicate effectively by making his/her piece more appropriate and accurate for the readers (Samson, Jr., 1993).

For a house journal, an editorial board is normally constituted, and if a training establishment is publishing the journal, as far as possible, both the editor and members of the editorial board should be drawn mainly from amongst the training field, especially trainers, who would be familiar with the training knowledge. However, some academics, preferably with training background, may also be included. The editorial board should adopt a standardized editorial style, which may include, among other things, typescript, language, presentation, referencing, etc. Apart from the articles of training utility, articles having academic inputs may also be included.

The criteria used for judging the suitability of an article received for publication include contemporary relevance, contribution to knowledge, conceptual clarity and logic in analysis, readable language, sound methodology, implications for intervention, appropriateness of references and, above all, originality (Desai, 2004). If possible, before taking final decision regarding its publication, it may be referred to one or two subject experts. The journals publishing 'refereed' articles enjoy greater reputation than those having 'non-refereed' articles.

Relationship between Editing (Editor) and Writing (Writer)

Here, it would be pertinent to understand the difference between writing and editing, While writing produces the words in a document, editing changes them. Many scholars distinguish between the writing activities that produce a first draft of a document – invention and composing – and editing activities, viz., revising, rewriting and proof-reading. However, these activities often overlap. For example, both the writer and the editor must consider the audience's familiarity with the material and interest in it (Samson Jr., 1993).

At the same time, the relationship between writer and editor often links their activities. For example, editors are sometimes asked to help writers develop their abilities and also provide with guidelines for better writing. A truly cultured author should always understand an editor's efforts. There are many authors who think that their writing is unimprovable, unchangeable and untouchable (Sharda Prasad, 1993). Sometimes they even create their own vocabulary. There are several authors, who, in order to cover their 'mistakes', label these as part of "their own style". The authors should shun this mentality. An author is, of course, an expert on the subject of his/her article, but an editor can notice errors and inconsistencies that are generally ignored by the author. The author's focus is normally on the contents and exposition of the subject. Matters regarding language, presentation and organization might take a back seat. Many authors are not aware of the nuances of writing skills or do not want to get distracted by attention to language or style, and indeed want to focus on the presentation of thoughts. The editor, on the other hand, acts as the author's second pair of eyes for the purpose of identifying the 'slips', if any. There is no manuscript that cannot be improved. At the same time, the editors should not have an obsessive and adamant attitude. Such editors are generally not satisfied unless they chop and change an author's contents to the extent of redesigning these into their own. The editors should also keep in mind that they are not rewriters.

In a nutshell, an editor's principal tasks can be enumerated as under (Einsohn, 2000):

Copy Editing

Copy editing, which sometimes is also referred to as mechanical editing, consists of making the papers selected for publication conform to an editorial style which includes spelling, hyphenation, capitalization, punctuation, treatment of numbers and numerals, treatment of quotations, use of abbreviations and acronyms, use of italics and bold type, treatment of special elements like headings, lists, tables, charts, graphs, etc., and format of footnotes or endnotes. In fact, there is nothing mechanical – it just requires a sharp eye, a solid grasp of a wide range of conventions, and good judgement.

Language Editing

Then comes the language editing, which involves correcting errors or lapses in grammar, syntax, usage and diction. Ideally, an editor sets right whatever is incorrect, unidiomatic, confusing, ambiguous, or inappropriate without attempting to impose his/her stylistic preferences or prejudices upon the author. For example, academic authors treat 'data' as a plural noun whereas corporate editors treat it as a singular noun. The editor, in this case, should not change it and retain it in its original form.

Thus, in all the matters pertaining to language editing, editors must strive to make a balance between being overly permissive and overly pedantic. They are expected to correct author's style of writing which is likely to confuse, distract or disturb readers, but not impose their own taste and sense of style on the author.

Content Editing

In case of any internal inconsistencies or discrepancies in contents as well as any structural and organizational problems, the editor must bring it to the notice of the author. An editor alone cannot be held responsible for factual errors in an article, but can offer a query regarding this to the author. For example, if in a manuscript 'February 29, 1985' is written, this should be brought to the author's notice as 1985 was not a leap year. Even if an editor has some knowledge on the subject matter, and is able to catch an error that would go unquestioned, it should also be brought to the notice of the author who should gratefully appreciate it.

Proofreading

The importance of proofreading is often underrated. Careful proofreading can ensure that an article is not only correct but it also creates a good impression about the journal and the institution that published it. It is, therefore, necessary that the task of proofreading should be not be assigned to new or inexperienced staff, as is done in most of the cases. Proofreading is, in fact, much more than tallying the proofs with the original manuscript. A proofreader should play the role of a 'second-line' editor and while doing so he/she should also identify mistakes in spellings, grammar, punctuation, sentence structure and format, and in contents, if possible.

Production

During the last one decade, journal publishing has become an automated process, using advanced technology. The emergence of desktop publishing system has proved to be another significant advancement, which is able to format text and graphics on a computer screen with the aid of relevant softwares. Once a page is formatted, it is transferred to a plate-making device and then the plates so prepared are printed on offset printing machine. Today, one can get a large number of printed copies of any material in a few hours' time.

To conclude, it can be said that the task of publishing a house journal, particularly in a training institution, should be performed seriously with all the above aspects taken into consideration.

References

Desai, Murli (2004), *Methodology of Progressive Social Work Education,* Jaipur, Rawat Publications.

Einsohn, Amy, *The Copyeditor's Handbook,* Berkeley, University of California Press. Lindsey, D. and S.A. Kirk (1992), The Role of Social Work Journals in the Development of a Knowledge Base for the Profession, *Social Science Review, pp.* 295–310.

Samson, Donald C. Jr. (1993), *Editing Technical Writing,* Oxford, Oxford University Press.

Sharda Prasad, H.Y. et al. (2004), *Editors on Editing,* New Delhi, National Book Trust.

Section VI
Appendices

Appendix I

Rajasthan State Training Policy

Preamble

Globalization has resulted in tremendous pressure on governments and the individuals who constitute them. Governmental and government servants need to be able to take benefit of the opportunities being offered by globalization (and by technological developments) as also to take steps to mitigate or to prevent its negative impacts. One of the important means of ensuring faith of the people, particularly the weaker sections of the society, in the fairness and capacity of the functioning of state administration in the changing environment, is to have a responsible and responsive workforce. However, making the government machinery responsive and responsible largely depends upon the attitudes as well as the knowledge and skills of its employees at various levels. It has long been accepted that training can do much to improve the administrative effectiveness. A conscious policy for the development of the human resources available to the state government would, therefore, require to be fostered for harvesting technological, economical, political and social change.

Training is a useful tool for performance enhancement of the people. It aims at upgrading knowledge and skills of the personnel. The role of training in improving performance of the government is most crucial and important. This calls for a sound and conscious training policy in the state, especially since the National Training Policy already stands formulated by the Government of India in 1996.

This draft was prepared by HCM Rajasthan State Institute of Public Administration in September 2006, following a meeting with select senior officers of Government of Rajasthan who commented upon on earlier draft. It was approved by State Governmenment in 2008.

Major Challenges

The main problems and concerns relating to the training function are as follows:

- Low priority accorded to training and education, and the low level and uneven nature of provision for training;
- Lack of funding and effective management of training budgets;
- Lack of coordination and communication;
- Number and quality of trainers;
- Barriers to access and entitlement;
- Overly prescriptive, supply-driven and outdated nature of training and education;
- Lack of effective systems of accreditation and quality assurance;
- Poor linkages between higher education institutions and training;
- Training through distance education for government servants is not available;
- Lack of effective systems for training related strategic planning and review;
- There is no induction training for many of the civil servants and there is lack of a comprehensive scheme of systematic and regular subsequent in-service training after their induction;
- Lack of adequate cadre and training plan for career progression of civil servants; and
- People who matter more in various categories of government service (age group 45 to 60 years) need updating of knowledge and reorientation to face the challenges of rapid change and need to be able to use newer technologies, procedures, systems, approaches for good governance.

Accordingly, the core problems that this policy seeks to address comprise three related elements:

- Fragmented and uncoordinated approach to training and education across public service, resulting in problems of resources and accountability for ensuring that public servants are empowered and developed to take on the challenges they face;
- Lack of a strategic, need-based, outcome-based and competency-based approach to training, directly related to the developmental needs of the public service; and
- Inappropriate nature of the training and education that is provided by internal as well as external providers.

Vision

Public service training and development will be founded on the following vision:

> Assisting government departments and agencies to adopt practices geared at better governance and improved service delivery by empowering public officials to act as prime catalysts for holistic and equity based transformation.

This vision is based on the belief that any organization is only as strong as the people who work for it, and in particular on the conviction that training should and must play an integral and strategic part in the processes of building a new public service ready to deliver what is being expected from it in the contemporary world. While acknowledging the danger of seeing training as the sole solution to all organizational problems, the government nevertheless recognizes the significant contribution that training can make, as part of a broader strategy for human resources development, to the efficiency, effectiveness, accountability, responsiveness and citizen friendliness of the public service. In particular, training and education, if properly conceived and structured, can:

(a) help to equip all public servants, whether support staff or officers, with the necessary knowledge, skills and competence as well as appropriate attitude and values to carry out their jobs effectively in pursuit of the vision and mission for the public service,

(b) enable public servants to deal effectively and proactively with change and the challenges of a dynamic work and external environment;

(c) enable public servants to acquire a new development-oriented professionalism and the appropriate attitude, skills and knowledge;

(d) help to address issues of diversity, besides promoting a common organizational culture to support unity at the workplace and the ethos of a single public service;

(e) become a powerful instrument for anticipating as well as facilitating the introduction of institutional changes within the public service; and

(f) assist public servants in developing a better understanding of the needs of the communities that they are serving as well as a capacity to respond to these needs.

Mission

In pursuit of the above vision, the government sees its mission as:

To create an institutional framework for optimum productivity of public servants in organizations, in a team or as individuals in their current as well as future roles.

Goals

Through the creation of such a policy framework for training, the government will seek in particular:

- to enable all public servants to develop their knowledge, skills and attitudes in ways which would optimize performance in their current roles;
- to inculcate values among trainees that would strengthen their sense of commitment;
- to encourage them to regularly review their training needs and requirements, and to provide ways of meeting these;
- to provide opportunities for them to prepare themselves for changing roles, duties and responsibilities within and without public service;
- to increase job satisfaction and facilitate career progression;
- to motivate and enable all public servants to contribute positively to the transformation of the society, economy and polity;
- to provide distance education capsules to the government employees to enable them to continuously update their competency; and
- to prepare category-wise development plans.

Category-wise Development Plans

While eventually a personal development plan focusing on the specific personal training needs of each individual public employee should be prepared and implemented, this would need to be preceded by categorization of employees for conducting training needs assessment for each category of employee as a means to the preparation of category-wise development plans. The category-wise development plans would encompass all the attributes of personal development plans being described in the succeeding section.

Personal Development Plans

In order to ensure a needs-based approach to training and education, personal development plans will be drawn up for all categories and for all members of the public services. These will be designed to identify the training needs of public servants and measures to fulfil them within the context of the individual's overall career progression as well as within the context of organizational objectives and priorities of the respective organization and the state.

The introduction of a personal development plan system in all departments will help to ensure that the principle of access and entitlement of all staff to meaningful training and education opportunities becomes a practical reality.

Personal development plan will be based upon category-wise employee development plans and will seek to identify in particular:

- the current competence of staff (which will help to form the basis for an effective skills audit);
- work values of staff (e.g., career progression, helping others, creativity, being skilled and respected in one's work, honesty, etc.);
- work and career targets of staff;
- the competence (skills, knowledge and attitudes) that will need to be developed to enable the staff to successfully meet their work and career targets;
- an individually tailored programme of staff development, training, education and support designed to enable staff to acquire the relevant competence and meet their work targets and personal and career objectives;
- enhancement of capabilities and status of trainers (faculty, resource persons and experts) by providing them regular and repeated opportunities for training in India and abroad, repeated and sustained training and other benefits like trainer's allowance and rent-free accommodation which are presently available in the Government of India and in many states, allowance to purchase books/journals, etc.;
- link to be established between training and future postings and promotions;
- opportunities for higher education inputs in career progression;
- cadre and training plan in service career of a civil servant; and
- opportunities to extract benefits of experienced people as resource persons in training by re-employing them for some period after retirement.

Personal development plans will be drawn up in a negotiated way between the supervisory officer and the individual staff member. They will be regularly reviewed, and will be formally appraised and updated on an annual basis. The Department of Personnel (Training), Government of Rajasthan, will provide technical assistance in the form standards of checklists and "how to ..." instructions and guidelines, etc., to the departments and agencies in developing personal development plans.

Adding Values through Positive Learning Outcomes

A major shift in the process through which public service training and education programmes are designed and delivered is clearly required. In the past such programmes were essentially supply-driven and input-based. They reflected the views of the various training providers (internal or external) about what should be learned and the ways in which it should be learned, i.e., what they thought would be good for the trainees. Public, servants either volunteered or were required to attend what were essentially pre-determined training programmes.

In future, training providers will be required to move towards a demand-driven and outcomes-based approach to their work. Such an approach will be designed to promote access to competence and accreditation by recognizing that there are many different routes to obtaining knowledge and skills, and that the choice of the best route for an individual will depend on a variety of circumstances, including the experience and learning that have occurred to date (popularly known as entry behaviour).

A key assumption of this approach is that transfer of learning will be more effective when it is trainee-centred in delivery and context.

Competency-based Approach to Training and Education

Training institutes will ensure that learning outcomes are expressed in terms of specific, measurable, achievable and realistic performance goals. A competency-based approach to training and education will, therefore, be integral to a move towards broader need-based and outcome-based approach to public service training and education. Competence can be defined as the application of skills, knowledge and attitudes to the performance of tasks or combination of tasks at appropriate high standards under operational conditions. As such competence does not refer to the unique characteristics of an individual worker but rather serves as a measure against which individuals may be judged for the purposes of formal or informal evaluation and accreditation.

All public service institutions will define tasks and responsibilities of each employee and set prescribed standards of performance. Physical and financial targets for different categories of personnel will be prescribed clearly at the beginning of a financial year.

All public service institutions will be required to conduct job evaluations or re-evaluations of all posts, with the purpose of ensuring that they are expressed in terms of the essential competence required for effective job performance. This will involve both sector-specific competence and core transversal competence.

In the case of core transversal competence, the definition of competence will encompass a broad range of skills, knowledge and attitudes, including:

- ability to carry out effectively the routine tasks of the job;
- ability to transfer skills, knowledge and attitudes to new situations within the same occupational area;
- ability to innovate and cope with non-routine activities; and
- personal effectiveness to deal effectively with co-workers, managers and customers.

The introduction of a competency-based approach will assist the development of an outcomes-led model of training and education in a number of important ways.

These will include forming an effective and measurable basis:

- for the objective evaluation of current performance, and the effective assessment of current and future needs;
- for the design and delivery of training programmes and courses as well as other staff development interventions targeted at the achievement of specific and meaningful competence;
- for the standardization and accreditation of such programmes and courses; and
- for the subsequent evaluation of the effectiveness of such programmes and courses.

The introduction of a competency-based approach will also form the basis for improvement in the current systems of performance appraisal, recruitment, selection and promotion of personnel.

Strategic Planning at the Government Level

At the level of individual departments, a number of related elements will be involved in this process:

- In the *first place,* training and education will need to be systematically linked to broader processes of human resources development.
- In the *second place,* plans and programmes for human resources development and training must be strategically linked to broader plans for service delivery, institution building, transformation, and in particular to the budget planning process. This will be an essential step in ensuring that the training plans and programmes identified as a result of the training needs assessment are effectively prioritized, equipped with the appropriate levels of budgetary support, and provided with the

necessary commitment and support from top management to ensure their success.

- In the *third place,* the status of training and trainers as well as human resources specialists, more generally, will need to be significantly enhanced. The concept of once a trainer always a trainer will be honoured under which expertise developed as a trainer will be used even after he returns to his line department and is placed on regular departmental postings.
- In the *fourth place,* training and education programmes will themselves need to be systematically and strategically planned, monitored and evaluated. The planning and review process should be fully consultative, involving management and staff, and plans for training and education will need to be effectively communicated at all levels within the institution. Steps involved in the planning and review process will include:
  - Both individual and organizational training needs assessment;
  - Consideration of possible solutions (including training and other non-training interventions); and
  - To review some of the key implications of this new approach with respect to such issues as performance appraisal, accreditation, and the relation of training to policies on recruitment, promotion, grading, and remuneration; and to make appropriate recommendations for changes in existing regulations and prescripts governing public service training and education.
- In the *fifth place,* a unit for training function will have to be created within the departments and agencies and linked with training imparting organizations in the state more effectively.
- In the *sixth place,* some thrust areas will have to be identified in training institutes and the civil servants and government employees should be trained in those areas to cope up with the challenges facing the government.
- Greater synergy would be ensured between all the state level training institutions in the government. As a first step towards that a coordination committee of state level training institutes has been constituted by the government in August 2005.

Strategic Planning for State Level Institutes

Each state level training institute would be based on detailed reviews undertaking the following:

- Prepare or redefine its vision and mission statements;
- Design a ten-year vision document;
- Formulate five-yearly action plans for institute incorporating physical infrastructure needs as well as the development of faculty and preparation of training modules and training material, etc.;
- Develop annual action plan and programme calendars; and
- Ensure optimal implementation of the annual and five-yearly action plans.

Core Principles for Training in the State

The formulation, implementation and evaluation of programmes of public service training and education will be carried out in accordance with the following broad principles:

(a) *Improving work procedure:* Using training to help departments/organizations improve their work procedures, supervision and monitoring practices, etc.

(b *Access and entitlement:* All public servants in government and public sector undertakings will be entitled to ongoing and meaningful opportunities for foundation, induction, institutional, refresher and in-service training at the time of entry into service and at suitable intervals in their career. The points at which training requires more focus are at the time of entry, after about eight years of service, after 15 years of service and most importantly after the public servant has crossed the age of 45 and is moving into senior positions where he/she has greater influence over how the department functions. Even persons nearing retirement should receive training to ensure that they do not become a drag of the system. Every public servant should undergo at least two core trainings to develop generic skills as a public servant. Such trainings should augment basic knowledge about working of government and the expectations from all government servants and these training should be different from, and in addition to, other professional trainings which aim at improving knowledge, skills and attitudes for performance of specific jobs or specific types of jobs. Recently, a State Level Advisory Committee for Foundational, Institutional and Compulsory In-Service Training of officers of Rajasthan State Services along with a sub-committee on the same subject have been created the by state government and this would facilitate planning of systematic training at various stages in an officer's career.

(c) *Training for all:* Training would be imparted to all rungs of the civil services in the state from the lowest and cutting-edge to the highest levels in policy making.
(d) *Training concerns:* Training programmes for the civil services would necessarily focus on strengthening of responsiveness, commitment, and accountability towards citizens.
(e) *Training needs analysis:* Programmes of training and education will be based on a detailed assessment of the needs of individual organizations or departments and employees, and will be designed in particular to secure an optimal fit between these two sets of needs.
(f) *Elevating the status of training and trainers:* To ensure that training, education and human resources development more generally play an increasingly strategic and integral part in building a vibrant public service in Rajasthan, the position, role and status of trainers as human resource specialists will need to be significantly redefined and enhanced. For enhancing the status and capacity of trainers (faculty, resource persons and experts) they would be provided special opportunities for regular and repeated training and study tours both within India and abroad, other benefits like a monthly trainer's allowance as is available in Government of India, rent-free accommodation while working at a training institute, personal allowances to purchase books, journals, CDs, etc., and special opportunities for higher education.
(g) A *competency-based approach to learning outcome:* The new approach to public service training and education will focus on outputs and outcomes rather than inputs, with particular reference to the competence required at different levels to build individual and organizational capacity.
(h) *Integration between policy formulation, strategic planning and transformation:* Far from being marginalized, training and education will be systematically and integrally linked to the broader processes of policy formulation, strategic planning and transformation, particularly in relation to service delivery, institution-building and management, human resources development.
(i) *Adequate resourcing:* It will be vital for the success of the training and education system, and will be ensured in particular by integrating plans and priorities for training and education as a central element in the budget planning process.
(j) *Flexibility and decentralization:* To ensure that programmes of training and education are designed flexibly to meet the individual

and changing needs of particular departments, responsibility will be decentralized as much as possible, within agreed norms and standards.

(k) *Career pathing:* Programmes of training and education will be targeted in particular at facilitating career paths for the entire staff that promote progression (vertical and lateral) and productivity, and for this reason such programmes will need to be positively related to policies on recruitment, promotion, grading, remuneration and performance appraisal.

(l) *Life-long learning:* Public service training and education will promote life-long learning and develop portable skills and competence.

(m) *Learning organizations:* Training, education and development will be promoted in ways that enable public service training institutions to become learning organizations, capable of continuous development and adaptation through the creative integration of learning with work at all levels.

(n) *Quality and cost-effectiveness:* It will be promoted through the effective utilization of available resources; the avoidance of duplication; the establishment of effective structures and mechanisms for the coordination of training and education at national and provincial levels; the introduction of improved forms of standard setting and accreditation; and the targeting of training and education activities that add value by developing skills, knowledge and attitudes that can be readily transferred to the job. External service providers, their capabilities and their areas of excellence and relevance will be identified so that public servants may take advantage of their excellence.

(o) *Equity and empowerment:* Training and education will be linked to broader plans and programmes for promoting employment and occupational equity.

(p) *Consultation and participation*: To ensure broad commitment and support at all levels within the public service plans and programmes for training and education will be formulated, implemented and evaluated with the full participation and involvement of all relevant stakeholders.

(q) *Information and communication:* Information about training and education opportunities will be collected and collated, and effectively disseminated at all levels throughout the public service.

(r) Coordination of classroom and field as well as on-the-job training with distance education, e-learning and regular higher education.

(s) *Effective design and delivery:* To enhance the relevance, quality and cost-effectiveness of training and education, programmes will be designed and delivered in accordance with guidelines issued by the Department of Training, Government of Rajasthan. While issuing such guidelines effective use of IT and other relevant technologies and existing training infrastructure will be taken into account.

(t) *Monitoring and evaluation:* In order to ensure that plans and programmes of training and education are carried out throughout the public service in accordance with the above principles, effective mechanisms for ongoing monitoring and evaluation of all training related activities will be put into place.

Roles and Responsibilities

Roles and responsibilities of government departments/training institutes and heads of departments would be as under:

Department of Training, Government of Rajasthan

To take overall responsibility for the effective formulation, implementation, monitoring and review of State Training Policy;

- To create required institutional framework;
- To translate the broad policy framework into specific and achievable policy objectives, norms and standards, performance measures and time-frames;
- To ensure that these processes are based on effective consultation and liaison with all major stakeholders;
- To ensure that the training policy is strategically linked to key transformation goals and processes;
- To ensure that the policy is effectively coordinated;
- To anticipate training needs of future,
- To review existing courses of internal training providers to bring them in line with the policy;
- To accredit internal and external training providers in domain-specific training and education both for sending government servants to the training providers as also for their being called to conduct specific training programmes;
- To prepare guidelines for selecting and calling, by various departments, of personnel from prominent and suitable institutes to come and deliver specific short courses;
- To prepare domain-specific resource persons in public service;

- To lay down standards for preparation of a training module;
- To lay down norms for honorarium payable to guest faculty at state level training institutes;
- To review the draft vision document and the draft five-yearly action Plans of each state level training institute before they are finalized;
- To lay down minimum standards of infrastructure for each public sector training institute;
- To prepare policies and strategies for Training of Trainers (ToT) and arrange for common standards for ToT strategies;
- To allocate resources to training organizations for strengthening and upgrading infrastructure, special programmes, creating new training modules, organizing ToT programmes, etc.;
- To liaise with all government departments and public sector enterprises on matters related to training, capacity building and governance;
- To follow-up training received by officers through HCM RIPA after their training;
- To formulate policy for the State Government as a whole to obtain benefits of experienced persons as resource persons in training by re-employing them after retirement; and
- To work out strategies for enhancement of capabilities of trainers (training faculties) including a system of incentives for persons dealing with training function and those acting as faculty at various state level training institutes;
- To coordinate a committee to screen government servants to send for training outside Rajasthan, but within India where a course fee is involved.

Department of Personnel, Government of Rajasthan

- To set and periodically review standard of competence for each category of post in public service with an emphasis on multi-skilling;
- To design incentives for receiving and imparting training;
- To insert a column in Annual Performance Appraisal Report to compulsorily identify training needs of an individual for his professional growth and also for organizational growth;
- To ensure that senior public servants invest time and effort in Human Resource Development; and
- To amend service rules to link training with future postings and promotions and to provide for compulsory trainings as per Annexure-IV and additional training needs.

Finance and Planning Departments, Government of Rajasthan

- To earmark budget for training and education for each department as a percentage of personnel costs for that department. It may vary for each category of department (for example, category of departments having an extremely large budget could have a lower percentage fixed for training, category of departments where government wants to push new initiatives or feels that the department should give higher priority to training or where training needs analysis so justifies could have a higher percentage fixed for training);
- To place a corpus at the disposal of Department of Training, and to replenish funds in the corpus on an annual basis, for allocating resources to training organizations for strengthening and upgrading common/specific infrastructure, special programmes, creating new training modules, organizing ToT programmes, etc., providing special incentives for enhancing capabilities of all trainers and for taking steps to synergise the efforts of all State Level Training Institutes; and
- To help HCM RIPA and its centres to obtain technical assistance from foreign agencies to develop the institute further and jointly with the Department of Training, to help other state level training institutes to access such technical assistance.

All Administrative Departments

- To ensure that a departmental training and education strategy is formulated in consultation with stakeholders and implanted in partnership with providers;
- To translate such strategies into five-year training plans for each category of public officials;
- To ensure that based on category-wise training development plans for employees, the concerned Heads of Departments initiate exercises to develop personal development plans catering to the individual training and related capacity building of each specific officer/official in the department;
- To ensure that such strategic plans are prepared within a definite time-frame not exceeding nine months from the date of adoption of this State Training Policy, and that they are based on a detailed assessment of individual and organizational training related needs, and skills audit;

- To ensure that strategic plans for training and education are effectively integrated into broader plans for HR and organizational development as well as into the budgetary process;
- To ensure that the plans are strategically linked to the achievement of key transformation goals of the department; and
- To review the mission statements and five-yearly action plan of state level training institute attached to the departments before they are finalized.

Various Heads of Departments and CEOs of State Public Sector Bodies

- To take overall responsibility for operational decision-making, planning and implementation related to the department's training needs;
- To ensure that category-wise and personal development plans are prepared and that persons are sponsored for training accordingly;
- To set up appropriate and effective arrangements including use of appropriate computer software for coordination and monitoring of training in their department;
- To ensure an integrated approach to training, designating an officer as "Training Manager", who will be actively involved in various activities leading to organization of training programmes/courses such as the analysis of training requirements, the design of training programme, the selection of appropriate training institutions and persons to be trained and the evaluation of training;
- Police, Education, and Medical and Health Departments should gradually further develop their in-house training delivery system, while continuing to make use of apex training institution – HCM RIPA. All medical and education department personnel should, before they are permitted to assume administrative responsibilities at district level, be compulsorily made to undergo a general administration, rules and office procedures course for district level officers;
- A system of training of Secretariat staff should be developed so that each Secretariat employee goes through repeated training through various training courses. A separate Secretariat Training and Management Institute could be set up for this purpose.

HCM Rajasthan State Institute of Public Administration

- To function as the primary training institution in the state and to act as an example for other training institutes in the state;

- To work as the State Administrative Training Institute (ATI) for various DoPT, Government of India sponsored programmes;
- To conduct foundation courses for all state services and subordinate services as well as institutional professional courses of Rajasthan Administrative Service, Rajasthan Accounts Service and other state services which do not have their own specialized training institute for this purpose;
- To arrange for Training of Trainers and Management of Training Courses (DTS, DoT, TNA, MoT, EoT) for faculty in various state level training institutes and enable preparation of common training modules;
- To liaise with all government departments and public sector enterprises regarding training and capacity building matters;
- To provide training advice and material, etc., to other training institutes;
- To conduct various departmental examinations on behalf of state government; and
- Through trainings, workshops, preparation of policy papers, etc., directly or through its centres like Centre for Good Governance, enable government departments to adopt practices and procedures aimed at better governance, better administration and performance and better service delivery.

Other Training Institutes

- To ensure appropriate standard setting, accreditation and quality assurance with respect to training and education within their institute;
- To prepare mission and vision statements, ten-year vision document, five-yearly action plans and annual action plans and programme calendars for the institute and ensure their implementation in an optimal manner;
- To promote a strategic approach to human resources development within the public service;
- To market and promote the value of training and education throughout the public service;
- To design and recommend appropriate learnerships for the service or services that the institute provides;
- To promote effective partnerships between public, and private interests with respect to training and education; and
- To ensure minimum infrastructure facilities for training at the state level training institute.

Operationalizing the State Training Policy

Once the State Training Policy is approved in principle by the government, the Department of Training, Government of Rajasthan, shall get a department by department, agency by agency five-year operationalization training plan prepared in consultation with concerned stakeholders to ensure that the State Training Policy is implemented in an optimal manner.

Appendix II

Report of Impact Assessment of Trainer Development Programmes and Faculty Development Scheme of Government of India: Executive Summary

At the instance of the Committee on Plan Training Scheme (CPTS), the Department of Personnel and Training (Training Division) has undertaken an 'impact assessment study' of the efforts under the Trainer Development Programmes (TDP) and Faculty Development Scheme (FDS) through the agency of HCM Rajasthan State Institute of Public Administration (HCM RIPA), Jaipur. A core group consisting of Dr A.N. Chakravarty, former Joint Director, Institute of Secretariat Training and Management (ISTM), New Delhi; Shri S.C. Sen, Consultant; Shri R.K. Choubisa, Associate Professor, HCM RIPA, Jaipur; and Ms Manisha Bhatnagar, Desk Officer, Training Division, New Delhi, has accordingly been constituted by HCM RIPA, Jaipur, vide its Office Order No. F.2()(B)RIPA/PLAN/2006/13551–61 dated 23 November, 2006, to work for a review study of TDP and FDS by assessing the feedback, relevance and sustainability of these schemes. Dr Rakesh Hooja, Director, HCM RIPA, Jaipur, facilitated and oversaw the study.

Objectives

Precisely, this exercise is aimed at helping CPTS to take view in the matter of continuance of the TDP and FDS in its present form or otherwise. Accordingly, the main objectives set for completion of the task assigned were:

- To consult as many stakeholders as possible to elicit information on their experience of TDP and FDS courses; and
- To draw inferences from the responses of stakeholders.

Methodology

Soon after formation of the core group, its first meeting was held on 6 December, 2006, with the Joint Secretary (Training) and other officers of the DoPT, Government of India, had agreed upon the objective strategy and scope of the study, the constraints, and the time frame within which an interim report, followed by the final report, is to be submitted by the core group.

In order to proceed with the task the core group had preliminary discussions/correspondence with eminent trainers (Master Trainers) and heads of training institutions who had been directly associated with the two schemes. As a result of the aforesaid interaction, the following issues emerged.

Issues

1. The DTS and DoT courses have helped subject trainers, who are required to conduct training at the cutting-edge level of the government, to function systematically while designing and delivering their training sessions. How would you justify that the TS and DoT courses indeed helped you or any such trainer you know in functioning systematically? In particular, please indicate how DTS and DoT courses have made any impact in the areas of educational or social development etc. in increasing the effectiveness of teachers, primary health educators, the aanganwadi or agriculture extensions functionaries?
2. Generally, it is to conclude that
    - MoT has helped Training Managers to manage training functions efficiently;
    - EoT has encouraged meaningful evaluation of training; and
    - TNA has prompted comparatively higher emphasis on identification of training needs before deployment of functionaries on training.

According to your perception, to what extent each of these conclusions are actually the outcome of implementation of these courses in various training institutions in the country, particularly the ones with which you or the members of your sub-group have been associated? In case of any apprehensions, please feel free to spell them out with instances.

3. TDP has developed trainers in the area of public services including training of teachers of SCERT/DIETs in the states. Please consider:

- Will it be desirable and feasible to extend the scope of coverage of DTS/DoT to even the higher education in universities/colleges in increasing effectiveness of professors, lecturers, etc.?
- If so, please list out different inputs from these course packages which can, in a condensed form, be put on the web as an online package for the benefit of all who need it but are not in a position to attend these courses due to some legitimate constraints.

4. TDP has all along been striving to fulfil the need for 'training' as part of individual development of a trainer. As a result, a number of varied training courses have been included in its fold. Yet, it was noticed that a number of useful training courses were available outside TDP. Hence, to provide for a comprehensive approach, the FDS was taken up by the Training Division. To what extent do you think the FDS has been able to meet this need? Please qualify with specific instances and suggest ways and means to bring in further improvements.

With a view to elicit reactions on the above broad issues, the trainers under TDP fold were provoked through (1) questionnaires, and (2) workshops of trainers at certain identified training institutions. Separate questionnaires were devised on TDP and FDS courses for the trainers and another questionnaire for the head of training institutions.

Constraints

The biggest constraint for carrying out a systematic study based on accurate data was the limitation of time. The core group was given a time-frame of only seven weeks for submission of an interim report and to complete the study in just eleven weeks.

Summary of Findings and Recommendations

1. The Direct Training Skills (DTS) and Design of Training (DoT) courses may be continued and implemented in increased numbers.
2. Management of Training (MoT), Training Needs Analysis and Evaluation of Training (EoT) courses may be continued.
3. Government departments/organizations, particularly those who are heading them, may be sensitized about the role of training and development in an integrated human resource system in the organization.
4. It may be ensured that Training Managers are in a position in every organization/unit to play well-defined roles and responsibilities.

5. External validation may be carried out in selected organizations by EoT trained trainers and Training Managers of the concerned organizations. Such evaluation projects may be funded by DoPT (Training Division), Government of India, while the projects would be designed and monitored by respective ATIs etc.
6. Courses under TDP may be made available to the trainers in NGOs as well. Modalities for nominating such trainers may be worked out by the state ATIs.
7. Centralized effort for publishing the reading material for all TDP courses in Hindi and other regional languages may be coordinated by the Training Division for the benefit of different language groups of trainees.
8. Implementation of DTS-II course may be taken up by the Training Division in a time-bound project mode. A target for number of DTS-II courses may be fixed for implementation within the next one year or so and be conducted at ATIs. This will produce a good number of Potential Recognized Users (PRUs) for implementation of DTS-11, who may then be developed as Recognized Users (RUs).
9. Coverage of DTS/DoT may be adapted for the faculty of higher education in universities/colleges. The Ministry of Personnel may interact with the HRD ministry and University Grants Commission (UGC) with a view to establishing acceptability and feasibility of such adaptation.
10. FDS may be made broad based to cover all trainers irrespective of their being in ATIs or outside.

Some Supplementary Suggestions by Director, HCM RIPA

1. The TDP should be expanded by including new short courses for (i) training of course coordinators including do's and don'ts for them; (ii) preparation, revision and validation of training modules; (iii) design and delivery of a cascade or series of interrelated training programmes aimed at a common objective, (iv) designing and implementation of 12-week or longer foundation and professional courses for fresh inductees to government service; (v) a self-study orientation programme for personnel joining state ATIs or central training institutions either on deputation, or on regular appointments, or on contract basis about the expectations from training faculty and about systematic approach to training. Such an orientation programme should also be developed for those newly appointed as heads of training institutes; and (vi) design and conduct of training-related action research and studies and

training workshops and seminars. In addition, Distance Learning Methodology (DLM) courses should receive greater emphasis.

2. FDS should not only include opportunities for faculty to attend existing training courses at training or related institutions, but also for (i) faculty of state ATIs for visiting other ATIs or central training institutions for, say, a week or two to observe how they conduct their training and capacity building activities and to pick up lessons from the same; and (ii) for Training Division of DoPT to commission specific faculty development courses at appropriate institutions if it is felt that sufficient trainers spread across the country may require such a course.
3. The five regional training centres and two link institutions already identified for DTS and DoT courses should be developed as apex centres for the purpose of all TDP and FDS activities. They should be involved in review and development of TDP courses, in conducting such courses as well as in developing documentation and library facilities on TDP and on training of trainers' activities.
4. Both the TDP and FDS activities should be reviewed once a year in a meeting of heads of state ATIs to be convened in the second or third quarter of every financial year by Training Division of DoPT, Government of India.

Areas for Further Study

- Review of content and structure of DTS and DoT.
- Sensitizing the heads of organizations on need for placement of a trained training manager, and utility of TNA of their employees.
- Designing of comprehensive training programmes for training manager development.
- Master trainers/recognized users' development and certification.
- Creating a separate TDP unit as a centre of excellence for research, development and consultancy in DoPT.
- Expansion of TDP.

Contributors

Anita Karwal, IAS, former Director General, Sardar Patel Institute of Public Administration, Ahmedabad, is presently Chief Electoral Officer, Gujarat.

C. Lobo, Senior Manager, IL&FS Education Technology Services Ltd., Jaipur

G.S. Narwani, IAS (retired), former Special Secretary, Rural Development, Government of Rajasthan, Jaipur.

Gireesh Pradhan, IAS, former Director General, YASHDA, Pune, is presently Additional Secretary, Ministry of Power, Government of India.

Girish K. Srivastava, former Professor of Management, HCM Rajasthan State Institute of Public Administration, Jaipur.

Gitika Kapoor, Dean, R.A. Podar Institute of Management, University of Rajasthan, Jaipur.

K.K. Parnami, Publication Officer, HCM Rajasthan State Institute of Public Administration, Jaipur

Kiran Lekha Walia, Financial Advisor, Haryana Bureau of Public Enterprises, Chandigarh.

Neeraj Gupta, Visiting Faculty, IIT-Rajasthan, Jodhpur.

P.K. Jain, former Faculty, Centre for Good Governance, HCM Rajasthan State Institute of Public Administration, Jaipur, now senior executive at RSMM Ltd., Udaipur.

R.K. Mishra, Professor and Dean (Research), Institute of Public Enterprises, Hyderabad.

R.N. Gupta, IAS (retired), former Director, Mahatma Gandhi State Institute of Public Administration, Chandigarh.

Rakesh Hooja, IAS (retired), Director, Indian Institute of Public Administration, New Delhi. He was Director, HCM Rajasthan State Institute of Public Administration from 2005 to 2009.

Ramesh K. Arora, Visiting Professor, HCM Rajasthan State Institute of Public Administration, Jaipur.

Sanjay Kothari, IAS, is Additional Secretary, Ministry of Tourism, Government of India.

Siran Mukerji, Assistant Professor of Management, Jaipur Institute for Integrated Learning in Management, Jaipur.

T.K. Jain, former Associate Professor, Department of Public Administration, University of Rajasthan, Jaipur, presently Director, Shankar Institute of Management, Jaipur.

Tanjul Saxena is Assistant Professor, Indian Institute of Health Management and Research, Jaipur.

Udai Pareek (late), former Visiting Professor, Indian Institute of Health Management and Research, Jaipur, had earlier worked in Indian Institute of Management, Ahmedabad.

V. Srinivas, IAS, Joint Secretary, Ministry of Textiles, Government of India.

V.P. Mathur, Senior Manager, Videocon, 25, Twin Building, Pratap Nagar, Aurangabad, Maharasthra.